HISTORY AND TRADITIONS OF EARLY ISRAEL

SUPPLEMENTS

TO

VETUS TESTAMENTUM

VOLUME L

Eduard Nielsen

HISTORY AND TRADITIONS OF EARLY ISRAEL

STUDIES PRESENTED TO EDUARD NIELSEN

May 8th 1993

EDITED BY

ANDRÉ LEMAIRE AND BENEDIKT OTZEN

E.J. BRILL
LEIDEN · NEW YORK · KÖLN
1993

Some of the English articles in this volume have been translated or revised by Fred Cryer. This was made possible through a generous grant from G.E.C. Gads Fond, Copenhagen

The paper in this book meets the guidelines for permanence and durability of the Committee on Production Guidelines for Book Longevity of the Council on Library Resources.

Library of Congress Cataloging-in-Publication Data

History and traditions of early Israel / edited by B. Otzen.
p. cm. — (Supplements to Vetus testamentum; v. 50)
ISBN 9004098518
1. Bible. O.T.—History of Biblical events. 2. Bible. O.T.—History of contemporary events. 3. Jews—History—To 70 A.D. 4. Middle East—Civilization—To 622. 5. Bible. O.T.—Criticism. interpretation, etc. I. Otzen, Benedikt. II. Series
BS410.V452 vol. 50
221 s—dc20
[221.6'7] 93-1636
CIP

Die Deutsche Bibliothek - CIP-Einheitsaufnahme

History and traditions of early Israel / ed. by B. Otzen. -
Leiden ; New York ; Köln : Brill, 1993
(Supplements to Vetus testamentum : Vol. 50)
ISBN 90-04-09851-8
NE: Otzen, Benedikt [Hrsg.]; Vetus testamentum / Supplements

ISSN 0083-5889
ISBN 90 04 09851 8

PRINTED IN THE NETHERLANDS

CONTENTS

PREFACE

For many years Eduard Nielsen has been an outstanding representative of Scandinavian Old Testament scholarship. He was Professor of Old Testament Exegesis at the University of Copenhagen in the years 1956-1991, but his influence has not been restricted to Denmark or to Scandinavia. Through his rich scholarly productions he has become a highly respected figure in the international guild of Old Testament scholars. In his young days he wrote two books that came out in several impressions: *Oral Tradition* (1954), and his dissertation *Shechem. A Traditio-Historical Investigation* (1955). Here he stood out as a most independent and inventive scholar, continuing some of the best elements in Scandinavian scholarship in his own way. In the years since then he has been the inspiring teacher of a generation of theologians, and he has written several textbooks and commentaries in Danish, numerous articles (a selection of which were issued in the volume *Law, History and Tradition* in 1983), a book *The Ten Commandments* that came out both in Danish, English, and German (1965-68), and a great commentary on *Deuteronomy* which will appear in the near future in the German *Handbuch zum Alten Testament*.

Among many other responsibilities Eduard Nielsen was member of the Editorial Board of *Vetus Testamentum* from 1971 to 1989. In this capacity he was editor of the *Supplements* series, and so it is natural that a *Festschrift* to him on the occasion of his 70th birthday, 8th May 1993, should be published as a volume of the *Supplements*.

With his now classical book on *Shechem* Eduard Nielsen demonstrated his special interest in the history and traditions of early Israel—and precisely in the complicated relationship between history and tradition. Hence we have tried to make a collection of articles that in various ways throw light upon such problems. The contributors are some of Eduard Nielsen's colleagues from the Editorial Board of *Vetus Testamentum*, and a group of Scandinavian scholars. To all of us he has been a good friend during the years, and we are happy to have the possibility of honouring and thanking him in this way.

John Emerton André Lemaire Benedikt Otzen

PHARAOH SHOSHENQ'S CAMPAIGN TO PALESTINE

by

GÖSTA W. AHLSTRÖM*

The Libyan chieftain Shoshenq (biblical Shishaq or Shushaq), founder of the 22nd Dynasty (the Bubastite Dynasty), was determined to rebuild Egypt's power in former domains, including Palestine. He began his political plan by regaining control over Upper Egypt. He did this by ending the independent Theban dynasty of army commanders who had served as hereditary priests of Amon, substituting family members in their place and appointing loyal northerners in the Theban administration.[1] He then turned his attention further afield. He renewed ties with Byblos[2] and tried to reconquer Nubia after it had experienced one and a half centuries of independence.[3] After these goals were met he was in a position to turn his attention to the former Egyptian dominion of Palestine. The dissolution of the union between Israel and Judah left this territory divided into a number of small political units, providing Shoshenq with a good opportunity to renew Egypt's power in southwestern Asia. An inscription from the temple of Amon at Karnak

* G.W. Ahlström died on January 17, 1992. He had completed a first draft of the present article before his death, which was edited and revised slightly for posthumous publication by his former student, Diana Edelman. To orient the reader unfamiliar with the subject, she has added a fuller description of the location and layout of the actual inscription from Karnak, as well as the section summarizing past reconstructions of Shoshenq's campaign route. She has also expanded the bibliography in a few of the notes, knowing that Prof. Ahlström would have supplemented his initial citations himself before final publication.

[1] J.A. Breasted, *Ancient Records of Egypt IV* (Chicago, [1906] 1927), p. 344, sec. 699; K.A. Kitchen, *The Third Intermediate Period in Egypt (1100–650 B.C.)* (Warminster, 1973), pp. 288–90, secs. 243–45.

[2] There is an inscription of Abiba'al of Byblos on the socle of a statue of Shoshenq I. For the text, see H. Donner and W. Röllig, *Kanaanäische und aramäische Inschriften II* (Wiesbaden, [1964] 1973), p. 7, text I.5.

[3] Kitchen thinks it probable that Shoshenq campaigned in Nubia ([n.1], p. 293).

indicates that he undertook a military campaign to accomplish this goal in the twenty-first year of his reign. This paper will explore his specific objectives in that campaign and try to reconstruct the route he undertook.

The biblical testimony

The Bible provides a brief mention of Shoshenq's campaign to Palestine in 1 Kgs. xiv 25–28. It reports that in the fifth year of Rehoboam, Shishaq of Egypt went up against Jerusalem and took away the treasures of the king's house and the shields of gold that Solomon had made—everything. From the biblical perspective, Shishaq's main objective seems to have been Jerusalem. However, we must remember that this account reflects the limited interests of the Judahite historiographer and so may not accurately represent the Egyptian objectives.

The Chronicler's statement about the campaign in 2 Chr. xii 1–12 can be seen to be an exaggerated expansion of the account in 1 Kgs. xiv 25–28. The report that Shishaq's troops included 1,200 chariots, 60,000 horsemen[4] and allies without number from the Libyans, Sukkiyim (Libyan Tjukten) and Ethiopians (Nubians) is done for rhetorical effect to emphasize the large size of God's punishing enemy force. The reference to Shishaq's capture of fortified cities in addition to Jerusalem, a detail not found in Kings, is the invention of the Chronicler, who wanted to have Shishaq inflict an even greater punishment on the sinful king. The Chronicler provides as the specific reason for Shishaq's success Rehoboam's abandonment of Yahweh (vv. 1, 5, 8). His account is merely a pious embellishment of the information about Shishaq's campaign found in 1 Kgs. xiv 25.

The Egyptian testimony

An inscription detailing Shoshenq's campaign was engraved in the Amon temple complex at Karnak, on the SW hypostyle wall near

[4] Kitchen suggests that the 60,000 horsemen may have been six divisions ([n.1], p. 295, n. 289). S. Herrmann argues that Shoshenq's army could not have been greater than the one fielded by Ramses II ("Operation Pharao Schoschenks I, im östlichen Ephraim", *ZDPV* 80 [1964], p. 72). The truth is that we cannot be certain.

the south exit of a new court that this pharaoh built before pylon II of the great temple of Amon. The wall is immediately east the so-called Bubastite Gate and was built by the pharaoh as a westward extension from pylon II. It features a huge scene of the king smiting his Palestinian foes before Amon, who gives the king the sword of victory. The figure of the king is unfinished. Below the relief scene are ten rows of name rings of subjugated towns and cities, headed by captive figures. The higher five rows are led to the king by Amon while all but the final row in the lower part are led by the goddess Wast. Above the smiting scene is a long rhetorical text praising the king's prowess in traditional, stereotypical terms found in similar New Kingdom victory texts.[5]

The date of Shoshenq's campaign to Palestine is disputed, but probably can be placed shortly before 926 BC. The inscription is dated to the twenty-first year of Shoshenq's reign, i.e. 926 BC.[6] We cannot be certain how long it took to engrave the list of cities and towns conquered during the campaign, but it seems likely that the campaign took place shortly before—within a few years of the inscription.[7] While Shoshenq is commonly assigned a reign of twenty-two years, E.F. Wente has assigned him a reign of thirty-three years, pointing out that the Egyptian Book of Sothis reports that Shoshenq ruled thirty-four years. The longer regnal figure would mean that the campaign did not necessarily take place in the closing year of his reign, as commonly assumed.[8].

Shoshenq's goals for his Palestinian campaign must be deduced from the approximately 180 place names listed in the inscription at Karnak. The lower inscription is too badly damaged to make an accurate count of names. The list is divided into two parts. The upper part, consisting of five columns of thirteen name rings each, lists the names of the conventional enemies of Egypt, the nine peoples of the

---

[5] See J. Simons, *Handbook to the Study of Egyptian Topographical Lists Relating to Western Asia* (Leiden, 1937), p. 91, plan XXI.

[6] See Breasted (n. 1), p. 347, sec. 706; Simons (n. 5), p. 89.

[7] "Studies in Relations between Palestine and Egypt in the First Millenium BC: The Twenty-Second Dynasty", *JAOS* 93 (1973), pp. 10–12 contra i.e. W. Helck, *Die Beziehungen Ägyptens zu Vorderasien im 3. und 2. Jahrtausend v. Chr.*, Ägyptologische Abhandlungen 5 (Wiesbaden, 1971), p. 238; Kitchen (n. 1), pp. 293–4.

[8] E.F. Wente, review of K.A. Kitchen's *Third Intermediate Period in Egypt*, in *JNES* 35 (1976), p. 278. Breasted places Shoshenq's accession to the throne in 945 BC (*Ancient Records* I [n. 1], p. 71).

bow (#1 – 9), before proceeding to the official list of conquered towns and cities (#11 – 65). The Palestinian locales are set off from the nine bows by the scribal subheading "list" or "copy" (#10). The lower part consists of five columns of place names (#66 – 180). The first four columns contain seventeen name rings each. The final column seems to have contained some fifty name rings. At present only the first twenty names and final five are fully or partially legible. Parts of the inscription have been destroyed, especially in the lower half and in the fourth and fifth column of the upper half, so all the site names cannot be read. In addition, the list appears to contain a number of compound names requiring the linking of two rings to form a single name, so the total number of sites listed is unknown, but closer to eighty. About twenty of the names in both parts have been identified with sites mentioned in the Bible.[9]

Past reconstructions

On the basis of the proposed site identifications, scholars have had trouble understanding how Shoshenq's list was ordered. The few clusters of identifiable sites do not seem to fall into a logical campaign sequence as they stand. For example, #11 – 13, Gaza (?), Gezer, and *rbt*, Rubute (?), suggest a march along the main coastal road, yet Aijalon, a nearby site that one would expect to appear within this cluster, is found later as entry #26 in another cluster of sites. These include Gibeon (#23), Beth-Horon (#24) and *qaḏtam* (#25),[10] which are located east-northeast of Aijalon. The order of the numbering of the latter group suggest that a detachment traveled west from Gibeon via Beth-Horon and *qaḏtam* to Aijalon.

The confusing geographical sequences have led B. Mazar, working in cooperation with B. Grdseloff, to suggest that the first four

---

[9] G. Hughes et. al., *Reliefs and Inscriptions at Karnak, Vol. III: The Bubastite Portal*, Oriental Institute Publications 74 (Chicago, 1954). See also M. Noth, "Die Wege der Pharaonenheere in Palästina und Syrien. IV. Die Schoschenkliste", *ZDPV* 61 (1938), pp. 277 – 304. Cf. Simons (n. 5), p. 89.

[10] R. Giveon thinks this is a misspelling of *qrṯm*, Qirythaim, i.e. Kiriath Jearim ("Remarks on Some Egyptian Toponym Lists Concerning Canaan", in M. Görg and E. Pusch [eds.], *Festschrift Elmar Edel 12. März 1979*, Ägypten und Altes Testament 1 [Bamberg, 1979], p. 136). As S. Aḥituv correctly points out, the reading could equally be *qarṯam* since an *ʾaleph* can be associated with *r* (*Canaanite Toponyms in Ancient Egyptian Documents* [Jerusalem/Leiden, 1984], p. 126).

columns of the upper part of the list are to be read "boustrophedron" style i.e. the first line left to right, the second line right to left, etc.[11] However, the failure of other such campaign lists to be written in this style makes their hypothesis less probable.[12]

Whether read boustrophedron style or not, two current reconstructions of Shoshenq's campaign agree in large part as to the main route taken by the pharaoh. They disagree in their understandings of how much of the route was traversed by the pharaoh directly and how much was covered by flying columns and lesser task force operations dispatched by pharaoh from a headquarters position. Both K.A. Kitchen and B. Mazar have Shoshenq heading north to Gaza and then going north through the Shephelah to Aijalon. There, he was to have taken the main east-west route into the hill country, via the Beth-Horons, to Gibeon, where he would have received Rehoboam's tribute of submission as described in 1 Kgs. xiv 25–28. He then was to have moved northward into Israel along the main watershed road, to Zemaraim. At this point, the route reconstructions diverge.

Kitchen thinks Shoshenq continued north, via Shechem, to Tirzah, the capital of Jeroboam. Discovering that Jeroboam had fled to Transjordan, he believes the pharaoh dispatched a task force in pursuit of the Israelite king while he moved onward through the Valley of Jezreel, to Megiddo, where he set up headquarters. The task force would have gone down the Wadi Farah, across the Jordan at Adam, past Sukkoth, to Penuel and Mahanaim, the king's other fortified palace. This group then would have returned to the Jordan and headed north, passing Rehob and Hapharaim, turning west to Beth She'an, and proceeding onward to the rendezvous point at Megiddo. A second task force would have been dispatched from Megiddo to take Ta'anach and Shunem, while other contingents would have been sent on missions to the plain of Acco and Galilee. After the various task forces returned to Megiddo, the main force was to have returned home to Egypt, meeting up at Gaza with task forces that had been sent out from there at the beginning of the campaign to subdue the Negeb.[13]

---

11 "The Campaign of Pharaoh Shishak to Palestine", *VTS* 4 (1957), pp. 57–66.

12 See Kitchen (n. 1), p. 444, sec. 412.

13 Kitchen (n. 1), pp. 294–99, secs. 253–57.

Mazar, on the other hand, thinks that Shoshenq himself led his main force eastward from Zemaraim to the vale of Sukkoth in the Jordan Valley. He then was to have crossed the river to Penuel and Mahanaim and returned again to the ghor, travelling up the eastern side to Tell es-Sa'idiyeh. There he would have forded the river and ascended the Wadi Farah to Tirzah. From Tirzah, he was to have led his army into the Beth She'an Valley, taking Rehob, Beth She'an, Shunem, Ta'anach, and Megiddo. He agrees with Kitchen concerning the final march home via the coastal trunk road. While he discusses the Negeb portion of the campaign, Mazar does not clearly locate this leg of the campaign within his larger reconstruction of the route.[14]

A third reconstruction by S. Herrmann suggests a much different route for the first five columns of name rings. He proposes that Shoshenq followed the campaign strategy of pharaohs in Palestine since Thutmosis III, which was to have two main theatres of operation, one in the Jezreel-Beth She'an Valley and the other in the central hill country between Gibeon and Aijalon. In his reconstruction, Shoshenq marched north to Megiddo, where he assembled his main force and established a headquarters. From there he sent out a contingent to Mahanaim, via the Jezreel-Beth She'an Valley and the ghor. He sent another contingent into the Samarian hills, whose main objective was to capture Shechem. He apparently dispatched a third southern force to deal with the traditional theatre of operations around Gibeon. The Mahanaim force then ascended into the hill-country, perhaps to join forces with the Samarian hills contingent and together, reinforce the troops around Gibeon to create the traditional press from the south and north. The actions of these three contingents after they captured their primary targets can only be guessed, however. Herrmann suggests that the names that have been destroyed in column 5 detailed the operations that were carried out by the Mahanaim contingent after it ascended into the hill country, probably along one of three routes between the Wadi Farah in the north and et-Taiyibe and Betin in the south.[15]

Neither of the first two reconstructions is consistent with the present sequence of site names. Each either reverses the order of a string of recognizable sites along a known road, or groups together

---

[14] Mazar (n. 11), pp. 61–64.
[15] Herrmann (n. 4), pp. 73–76.

sites that lay close geographically, but which appear dispersed in the inscription's list. The third reconstruction does not adequately explain how the present sequence of names reflects the operations of the contingents assigned to the Samarian hills or to Gibeon. It does not provide a logical route taken by the Gibeon force from Megiddo to their target area that can be deduced from the order of the names, nor does it explain how the Samarian hills contingent, column 3, had as its main objective Shechem, which is not named in the list according to Herrmann's own reconstruction of site names. It should also be noted that the majority of the sites in column 3 lie outside the Samarian hills, in the Sharon Plain. If we are to take seriously the present order of the site names and understand them to reflect segments of the historical campaign, another solution must be sought for Shoshenq's campaign route.

The campaign reconsidered

A quick review of the list of sites from the Amon temple at Karnak reveals a few identifiable places in Judah proper and in the Negev, but most of the names, especially in the upper part, seem to refer to places in Israel. A few sites are located in Transjordan. We cannot be certain that Shoshenq conquered all of the sites named in the list. Smaller towns or villages might have surrendered without armed resistance when faced with the superior Egyptian force, and some of the places named may simply have been bypassed. If Shoshenq followed the custom of pharaohs of the 18th and 19th dynasties who named the main stations of the campaign and most of the fortified cities that had been taken but not very many of the smaller settlements, we cannot even be certain that we have a complete list of all the sites that were officially conquered. These same pharaohs customarily did not penetrate the hills of Judah because of the sparse settlement and lack of large cities.

If any of the information on the fragmentary stela found in Hall K at Karnak can be trusted,[16] the campaign apparently began at the Bitter Lakes in the eastern Delta (*km wr*) and went north along the coast to Gaza (#11). The reading of Gaza for entry #11 is not cer-

---

16 For the text, see Breasted (n. 1), p. 358, sec. 724A. Kitchen suggests that the stela indicates that Shoshenq used a border dispute as an excuse to invade southern Palestine ([n. 1], p. 294, sec. 253).

tain,[17] but if it is correct, we may surmise either that the town was captured or that it opened its gates to the Egyptian army. Gaza had been an old Egyptian administrative base in Canaan in preceding years when Palestine had been an Egyptian domain. For this reason, Shoshenq may have been able to enter the city with little or no resistance.

Continuing north, the pharaoh proceeded to Gezer (#12) and took that city. Since no other pharaoh of the 21st Dynasty is known to have campaigned in Palestine, the report in 1 Kgs. ix 16 mentioning the destruction of Gezer by Pharaoh as a dowry for the marriage of his daughter to Solomon would appear to be most plausibly linked to Shishaq's campaign in 926 BC, when Rehoboam had already succeeded Solomon and had been ruling for five years (1 Kgs. xiv 25). Shoshenq's destruction of Gezer may have been remembered and misused by the biblical writer in his zeal to make Solomon one of the greatest kings of Israel.[18]

The route after Gezer becomes more problematic. The best way to solve the apparent lack of geographical coherence in the list seems to me to be to assume that Shoshenq followed an old Egyptian strategy of dividing his army into two or more columns.[19] He probably continued to march north with one column up the trunk road past *rbt* (#13-Rubute?) to Megiddo (#27), where he apparently established his headquarters.[20] A fragment of a commemorative stela prepared in his honor (his name is written *ššnq*) has been found at Megiddo in excavations.[21] The destruction of buildings 6000 and

---

[17] Compare, for example, the reconstructions by W.M. Müller (*Egyptological Researches I* [Washington, 1906], pl. 76) and by Aḥituv ([n. 10], p. 98, n. 197).

[18] This would mean that Solomon did not fortify Gezer. It must have been done by a later king of Israel. For the reconstruction of name ring #12 as Gezer, see i.e. Aḥituv (n. 10), p. 102, n. 220, contra, i.e., Kitchen (n. 1), p. 435 and n. 57, who proposes the reading *m-[q]3-[d]*, Makkeda. For the linking of excavated destruction levels with Shoshenq, see W.G. Dever, H.D. Lance, and G.E. Wright, *Gezer I: Preliminary Report of the 1964–66 Seasons*, Annual of the HUCBASJ 1 (Jerusalem, 1970), p. 6.

[19] W.J. Murnane, *The Road to Kadesh. A Historical Interpretation of the Battle Reliefs of King Sety I at Karnak*, Studies in Ancient Oriental Civilizations 42 (Chicago, 1985), p. 68; Kitchen (n. 1), p. 296; Herrmann (n. 4), p. 72.

[20] See Herrmann (n. 40), pp. 58–9.

[21] C.S. Fischer, *The Excavation of Armageddon*, Oriental Institute Communications 4 (Chicago, 1929), pp. 22–24. According to Kitchen, the "rough carving of the surviving fragment suggests a job done locally and quite rapidly" ([n. 1], p. 299, n. 202).

1723 of stratum V/IVB has been associated with Shoshenq's capture of the city.[22]

A detachment from this main column would then seem to have been dispatched *from* Megiddo eastward to capture the Esdraelon-Jezreel Valley, as indicated by entries #14–17: Ta'anach, Shunem, Beth-She'an, and *rḥb* (Rehob).[23] It apparently continued southward down the northern end of the ghor, taking *ḥaparam* (#18),[24] *adruma* (#19), an illegible (#20),[25] *šawadi* (*šwt*) (#21),[26] to Mahanaim, (#22). It then turned westward into the central hills and captured Gibeon (#23), Beth-Horon (#24), *qadṯam* (#25), and Aijalon (#26),[27] before rejoining the main part of the army returning to Egypt along the coastal trunk road. While the specific route from the ghor into the hills is not specified, a plausible route would have been via the Wadi Qelt,[28] which would have led conveniently to Gibeon. This route would have bypassed Jerusalem, which is conspicuously absent from the list of captured cities.

Entries #27–39 seem to represent the efforts of either the main

---

22 Thus D. Saltz, "Greek Geometric Pottery in the East. The Chronological Implications" (Ph. D. dissertation, Harvard University, 1978), pp. 371–73. For the stratigraphy, see also Y. Yadin, "Megiddo of the Kings of Israel", *BA* 33 (1970), pp. 69–75. The seal of Shema', an official of Jeroboam, that was found at Megiddo, may date on both archaeological and epigraphic grounds to the later part of the 10th century B.C. For details, see G.W. Ahlström, "The Seal of Shema'", *SJOT*, forthcoming, 1992.

23 Cf. Noth (n. 9), p. 283; Herrmann (n. 4), pp. 57–8.

24 Aḥituv thinks this is probably not Hapharaim of Josh 19:19 (n. 10), p. 114).

25 Mazar reads this entry as Zaphon ([n. 11], p. 62). However, according to Helck, the hieroglyphs are not legible ([n. 7], p. 239). W.F. Albright identified Tell es-Sa'idiyeh with biblical Zaphon ("The Jordan Valley in the Bronze Age", *AASOR* 6 [1926], p. 108). J.N. Tubb found a continuous settlement on the tell from the middle or late half of the 10th century to the mid 9th century BC ("Tell es-Sa'idiyeh 1986: Interim Report of the Second Season of Excavations", *ADAJ* 30 [1986], pp. 115–17).

26 F.M. Abel identifies this with Beth-Shittah of Judg 7:22, a place located close to Abel-Meholah (*Géographie de la Palestine* II [Paris, 1938, 1967], p. 273). However, *šwt* is mentioned in Shoshenq's list just before Mahanaim (#22) and therefore, ought to be east of the Jordan River. It might have been Tell es-Sa'idiyeh, which was an important industrial site.

27 It is noteworthy that this is the only one of the fifteen cities that are reported in 2 Chr. xi 5–12 to have been fortified by Rehoboam that appears in Shoshenq's list. This suggests either that Rehoboam fortified these cities in the wake of the Egyptian campaign, as suggested for instance by Kitchen ([n. 1], p. 300), or that the list derives from another king and has been secondarily associated with Rehoboam.

28 Noth (n. 9), p. 284.

column under Shoshenq's personal command at Megiddo or another detachment dispatched by him from his headquarters at Megiddo. It took Adar ("threshing floor") (#28), Yad-hammelek (#29) on Mt. Carmel (?),[29] *habiruta*$_2$ (#30) (Abu Hawam?),[30] and Henam (#31) (Acco?).[31] The troops either went around Carmel[32] or marched back to Megiddo and then continued down through the 'Aruna Pass to Henam (#31) and 'Aruna (#32) and on to Borim (#33), *s̱/ḏdptar* (#34),[32a] Yaḥam (#35), Beth 'Olam (#36), *kqrw* (#37), Socoh (#38),[33] and *bitatipu(ḥ)* (#39).[34] In the latter case,

---

[29] So i.e. D. Edelman, "Saul's Battle Against Amaleq (1 Sam. 15)", *JSOT* 35 (1986), pp. 77–8. Compare Mazar, who suggests it was a royal monument that stood at the entrance to the Wadi 'Arah as a landmark and possibly as a holy place ("The Aramean Empire and Its Relations with Israel," *BA* 25 [1962], p. 113, n. 26).

[30] This cannot be the same Mahaleb in Josh. xix 29 that has been identified with modern Kh. el-Mahalib ca 6.5 km. north of Tyre. On the basis of a topographical list of Seti I, Tell Abu Hawam might be equated with Libnath. Cf. Shihor-Libnath in Josh. xix 26, which is a name for the Kishon River. See also Aḥituv, (n. 10), p. 132. Tell Abu Hawam seems to have been destroyed in the late 10th cent. BC. It would have been a likely target for Shoshenq because it served as the port for Megiddo and the Jezreel Valley: see Saltz (n. 21), pp. 147–49. For a revision of the stratification and for new excavations, see J. Balensi, "Revisiting Tell Abu Hawam", *BASOR* 257 (1985), pp. 65–74 and J. Balensi and M.-D. Herrera, "Tell Abu Hawam 1983–1984. Rapport préliminaire", *RB* 92 (1985), pp. 82–128.

[31] Mazar derives the name Henam from *ḥānāh* and sees it as a "resting place" located in the Wadi 'Arah, north of 'Aruna ([n. 11], p. 62). The Iron IIa town of Shiqmona was also one of the sites destroyed in the late 10th cent. BC. See J. Elgavish, "Shiqmona, Tel", in M. Avi-Yonah and E. Stern (eds.), *Encyclopedia of Archaeological Excavations in the Holy Land* IV (Englewood Cliffs, NJ, 1978), p. 1101.

[32] Cf. S. Yeivin, "Topographic and Ethnic Notes. III", *JEA* 48 (1962), pp. 75–80.

[32a] This site is usually identified with biblical Gath-padalla that is mentioned in Amarna letter EA 250:13, but the identification is philogically uncertain. See E. Ebeling in J.A. Knudtzon (ed.), *Die Amarna Tafeln* II (Leipzig, 1915), p. 1311.

[33] Yaḥam and Socoh also occur in Tutmosis III's list of conquered cities, but in reverse order. So i.e. Helck (n. 7), p. 121. They could have been copied from this earlier list.

[34] *bitatipu[ḥ]* has been identified with biblical Tappuah, which is no more than a guess. Abel locates Tappuah at Tell Seḥ 'Abu Zarad ("Tappouah", *RB* 45 [1936], pp. 103–12). Biblical Tappuah appears between Bethel and Hepher in the list of conquered territories in Josh. xii 17. According to Josh. xvii 8, the "land of Tappuah" was located in Manasseh, but the city proper was located "on the border of Manasseh," i.e. the Brook of Qana, which belonged to Ephraim. Cf. Josh. xvi 8 and N. Na'aman, *Borders and Districts in Biblical Historiography*, Jerusalem Biblical Studies 4 (Jerusalem, 1986), pp. 148–51. The land of Hepher, which is mentioned in the list of Solomon's districts in 1 Kgs. iv 7–19, was located south of the Jezreel Valley and included, among other places, the cities of Arubboth and Socoh. Like Tappuah, Socoh also lay close to the border of Ephraim. As suggested by Aḥituv,

entries #31 – 39 would have been listed as though they were taken on the return march south to Egypt.

Entries #40 – 52 in column IV cannot be identified. Most of the names have been erased and the few that can be read cannot be identified with any known places in Palestine. Helck reads #40 as *'a-bí-rú-'ê*, a possible site named 'Ubal after its location near a watercourse or canal.[35] Kitchen proposes that #45, *bt-ḏbi[ ]*, might be an otherwise unknown Beth-ṣaba/ṣoba.[36]

A detachment from the Mahanaim troops seems to have been sent to subjugate entries #53 – 65. Leaving *n.pu-a-ru* (*pnw-3r*), Penuel (?) (#53),[37] it seems to have marched to *ḥadašata* (#54),[38] Sukkoth (?), "the huts," (#55),[39] *'adame* (#56), Adamah in the Valley of Sukkoth,[40] Zemaraim (#57),[41] (*mg/k*)*dr* (#58), Migdal (?),[42] and on to

Tappuah could perhaps be sought south of Socoh, #38 in Shoshenq's list ([n. 10], p. 80).

35 Helck (n. 7), p. 241 and Kitchen (n. 1), p. 437.

36 Kitchen (n. 1), p. 437.

37 For the probable reading of this name ring as Penuel, see Kitchen (n. 1), p. 438, sec. 402.

38 Following the reading of Müller, Mazar restores this damaged ring as Qodesh, "the sacred site near Penuel with an important place in Israelite tradition" (n. 11), pp. 61 – 62. Herrmann also prefers this reading (n. 4), p. 61.

39 The name *pa-?-k-t-ta*$_2$ (thus Helck) or *p3-k-t-t* (thus Simons) is enigmatic. Its identification with Sukkoth is hypothetical. Because it precedes Adam but follows Penuel (if that is the right reading), a location in the Jordan Valley is probable. Since *sukkôt* means "huts," the site name probably does not designate a town. It may refer to the territory in which traders temporarily stayed in huts. H.J. Franken believes that the Arab name Deir 'Alla is a corruption of *tar'ēlāh*, "staggering," which occurs in Ps. lx:5 (3). In verse 8 (6) of the same psalm the "Valley of Sukkoth" is mentioned ("Deir 'Alla Re-visited", in J. Hoftijzer and G. van der Kooij [eds.], *The Balaam Text from Deir 'Alla Re-evaluated* [Leiden, 1991], pp. 13 – 4).

40 Modern Tell ed-Damiye.

41 Zemaraim is thought to be located close to the mountain of Zemaraim in the vicinity of Bethel and Ramallah. Cf. Z. Kallai, *Historical Geography of the Bible. The Tribal Territories of Israel* (Jerusalem and Leiden, 1986), p. 401. G. Dalman located Zemaraim at Ras Et-Taḫune in the Ramallah area ("Einige geschichtliche Stätten im norden Jerusalems", *JBL* 48 [1929], p. 360).

42 The frequent suggestion that *mg/kdr* refers to Migdal Shechem is very hypothetical. Both *m* and *g/k* are missing in the inscription. However, the *[-]dr* has the determinative for "wall." Thus, it might refer to a fort or fortified city anywhere in the hill country. Herrmann, following Noth, identifies the place with Khirbet beni Fadil (165 – 187) close to the Wadi Bershe ([n. 4], pp. 62 – 67). However, this site is far away from any main road. Migdal Shechem, even if an insignificant village at this time (cf. 1 Kgs. xii 25), was at least located close to the main north-south road through the hills and so would have been passed by any Egyptian forces in the area. According to G.E. Wright, stratum X was a hastily rebuilt city after the destruction of the previous layer by Shoshenq ("Shechem," in *EAEHL* IV (n. 30), p. 1093.

Tirzah (#59). From there it went via #60–64, the names of which are erased on the inscription, to *pa ʿemeq* (#65), "the valley," perhaps the Beth-She'an-Jezreel Valleys.[43] A logical route from Tirzah to "the valley" would have been to move northwest from Tirzah to Marj Sanur and then down into the Dothan Valley. Given the uncertain readings in #53–58, this portion of the campaign must remain very hypothetical.[44]

A second column would seem to have been left behind at Gaza, with detachments dispatched from there into the Negev.[45] Entries #66–150 seem to list localities in the Negev.[46] Because of the poor condition of this part of the inscription, very few names are legible and among those that are, many are obscure. Identifiable names include *ʿḏm* (#66), probably Eṣem in Josh 15:29 and mod. Umm el ʿAzam;[47] *ḥqr 3brm* (#71–72), usually rendered "the fortress of Abram;"[48] and *ʿrd rbt* (#110), "Great Arad." Entry #112, *ʿrd yrḥm*, has been associated with an Arad belonging either to Jerahmeel or the Calebite clan of Raham,[49] while entry #125, *šrḥm*, is commonly equated with Sharuhen.[50] With so few identifiable names and sites, we cannot get a clear understanding of the route of the Egyptian troops in the Negeb, nor the extent of penetration. Nevertheless, Shoshenq's objectives in this region are easily deduced: he wanted to gain control over the trade routes to Aqaba and Arabia.

---

[43] Thus Kitchen (n. 1), p. 299.

[44] Herrmann (n. 4), p. 62.

[45] Thus Kitchen (n. 1), p. 296, sec. 254.

[46] Herrmann (n. 4), p. 56.

[47] Abel, *Géographie* II (n. 25), p. 254; Noth (n. 9), p. 295; Helck (n. 7), p. 242. For dissenting views about Eṣem's equation with Umm el-ʿAzam, see Aḥituv (n. 10), p. 93 and Kallai (n. 39), p. 352.

[48] Y. Aharoni would like to identify this with modern Tell es-Seba, but does not present arguments why (*The Land of the Bible* [Philadelphia, (1962) 1979], p. 329). Aḥituv, on the other hand, reads the compound name ring as *ḥgr ʾblm*, "fortress of the stream/wadi" or "the canal fortress," opting to read the Egyptian *r* as a Semitic *l*, which is often represented in texts ([n. 10], p. 109).

[49] Mazar (n. 11), p. 64, who has been widely followed. However, Na'aman has disputed this reading of the three name rings (#110–112), *ʿrd nbyt yrḥm*, as a single entry, "Arad of the House of Yarḥam." He points out that in ring #111, which reads *nb3t*, the *b(3)t* portion is written differently from all other instances in the list where *bt* stands for "house of." In addition, he notes that when *bt* carries the latter meaning, it always is written in a single ring with the personal name it introduces, which is not the case here. He concludes that rings #110–111 form the compound entry Arad-*nb3t* and that ring #112 begins a new compound entry that continues with the destroyed #113 ("Arad in the Topographical List of Shishak", *Tel Aviv* 12 [1985], pp. 91–2).

[50] Helck (n. 7), p. 244.

According to the preceding reconstruction, Shoshenq set up his main campaign headquarters at Megiddo and had a possible second station further south, at Gaza. Detachments were then sent out from these two bases to gain control over the Esdraelon-Jezreel valleys, the eastern and western sides of the ghor, the main east-west road through the territory of Benjamin from the ghor to the coastal trunk road, the route from the ghor to the Dothan valley, and probably the trade routes running through the Negeb to Arabia and Aqaba. Some small mopping operations were also carried out, perhaps on the way home to Egypt.[51] My reconstruction reverses the assumed orders of the campaign by Kitchen and Mazar, but explains why towns that lay close geographically are not clustered together in the list of captured settlements. It presumes that segments of the campaign were recorded by various scribes attached to the different columns and detachments and that these records of limited operations within the larger campaign were set side by side by to create the text of the inscription detailing the Palestinian campaign on the Temple of Amon at Karnak.

Shoshenq's campaign goals

The above reconstruction suggests that Shoshenq's primary goal during the campaign was to gain control over key trade routes in Palestine. We may assume that trade in this area had been resumed by Saul and continued by David and Solomon. By immobilizing the trade system of the kingdom of Israel, Jeroboam's nation, Shoshenq would have been able to build his own trade network in Palestine. Since most trade routes bypassed the mountains of Judah, Rehoboam's Judah would not have been as big a concern as a campaign target. Nothing would really have been gained in conquering the hill country of Judah, with its sparse population. Archaeological

[51] On the return trip, Raphia (#177) and Laban (#175) could have been reinstituted as Egyptian garrisons in Palestine, if any sort of permanent Egyptian force was established in the land. According to A. Alt, this Laban is the same place that is mentioned in an inscription of Sargon II and is located at the Brook of Egypt ("Neue assyrische Nachrichten über Palästina", in *Kleine Schriften* II [Munich, 1953], pp. 230–1). Cf. Helck (n. 7), p. 244; Aharoni (n. 46), p. 152. It can also be noted that Albright thinks that Tell Beit Mirsim was destroyed at some point during Shoshenq's campaign (*Excavations at Tell Beit Mirsim III*, AASOR 21–22 [New Haven, 1943], p. 38).

surveys and excavations have yielded very few settlements datable to the 10th century BC in the Judean hills. A study of building remains and luxury items from the territory of Judah indicates an increase in settlements and quality of life only in the 8th century BC.[52]

Shoshenq may have been encouraged to undertake this task because of the political fragmentation within the territory, hoping to raise the Egyptian flag again in the old dominion. Alternatively, did he want to subdue Rehoboam or to punish Jeroboam for not being a faithful vassal (cf. 1 Kgs. xi 40)? He might have wanted to prevent Rehoboam from attempting to rebuild the union between Israel and Judah. If this were the case, Jeroboam would have been dangerously close to losing the struggle for Israelite independence. In light of the absence of any mention of Dor, Joppa, and the cities of the Philistine pentapolis, Shoshenq might have intended to lend his support to the Sea-Peoples along the coastal region who were experiencing welcome relief in the wake of the collapse of the Solomonic kingdom.[53] Whatever his specific political excuse,[54] his attack along the major trade arteries indicates that he intended to re-establish Egyptian economic dominion in the area, whether or not he set out with the deliberate intention of resubjugating Palestine politically and making it once more an Egyptian province.[55]

---

[52] See D.W. Jamieson-Drake, *Scribes and Schools in Monarchic Judah: A Socio-Archaeological Approach*, JSOTSup 109 (Sheffield, 1991), pp. 80–159.

[53] Thus, A. Strobel, *Der spätbronzezeitliche Seevölkersturm*, BZAW 145 (Berlin, 1976), p. 95. This could explain why we do not find any mention of Dor, Joppa, and the cities of the Philistine pentapolis. The reading for ring #11 as Gaza may be right, but is uncertain.

[54] See note 15.

[55] The site of Deir ʿAlla, located in the *ʿemeq sukkôt*, "the valley of the huts," (Ps. 1x 8; cviii 8) close to the Jabbok Rover (modern Nahr ez-Zerqa) was most probably a trading center from which the products of Gilead that arrived via Mahanaim were collected and sent to the Egyptian base at Beth She'an and to the cities of the Syro-Palestinian coast for exchange with Cyprus and the Aegean world. See for instance, Franken (n. 37), pp. 10–14. The sanctuary at the site would have afforded divine protection for the trade conducted in the market place. The occurrence of so-called Philistine pottery at the site does not in itself indicate that Philistines settled at the site, contra R. de Vaux, *Histoire ancienne d'Israël, des origines à l'installation en Canaan* (Paris, 1971), p. 479. Some "Sea-Peoples" groups were in the service of the Egyptians and could have been living for a time in the Valley of Sukkoth. An Egyptian faience vase with the name of Queen Tausert, who reigned from 1193–1188 BC as the final ruler of the 19th Dynasty, has been found at Deir ʿAlla. For the inscription, see J. Yoyotte, "Un souvenir du 'pharaon' Taousert en Jordanie", *VT* 12 (1962), pp. 464–69.

Although Shoshenq may have devastated some sites in Palestine, his campaign does not appear to have established a long term Egyptian political presence in the region. Judah may have temporarily lost control over the Negeb and other parts of the hill country proper, but these setbacks do not appear to have outlasted Shoshenq's reign. There is no known indication, textual or archaeological, that his son, Osorkon I, ruled over any part of Palestine. Thus, under Shoshenq, Egypt was only able to regain its former might during a brief interlude. In light of the absence of any long-term Egyptian control, we can suspect that the campaign was carried out hastily and that no garrison troops were stationed in the country to keep it firmly under Egyptian rule. Such an inability to maintain control of Palestine after the campaign may have been symptomatic of Shoshenq's failure to have established firmly his rule at home over Egypt.

Unless Jerusalem is one of the names that has been erased on the inscription, it appears that it was bypassed during the campaign and never besieged. Thus, Shoshenq's campaign list does not corroborate the report in 1 Kgs. xiv 25 that pharaoh Shishaq besieged Jerusalem in Rehoboam's fifth year. It only provides corroboration for a more general Egyptian campaign conducted by Shoshenq in Palestine at this time. On the other hand, it is perhaps important to realize that Shoshenq is the first pharaoh known by name to the biblical writers. This suggests in turn that the learned scribes of Judah had no knowledge of the Egyptian rule over Palestine in the Late Bronze and earliest Iron I periods and had almost no access to recollections of historical events before the emergence of the Israelite monarchy. If the claim that Rehoboam stripped the palace and temple of all its wealth in 1 Kgs. xiv 26–27 is historically reliable and not merely a recurring literary convention, it suggests that Rehoboam sent "gifts" to the Egyptian army at some place north of Jerusalem to save his throne and prevent devastation of the Judahite countryside.

Why are the kingdoms of Israel and Judah not named in Shoshenq's campaign list when the Bible claims they existed? Two answers to this question come readily to mind. The first is that there were no kingdoms of Israel and Judah at this time, which would mean that the biblical recreation of the early monarchy is not reliable chronologically nor perhaps, historically. The second is that the Egyptian scribes deliberately ignored the names of the contemporaneous political units in Palestine as part of their desire to further Shoshenq's ideological claims to the land. They may have deliberately depicted Shoshenq's campaign in a way that followed the earlier dynastic victory lists from late Bronze predecessors who had included Palestine within the Egyptian domain. In this regard one should note that the list deals with the country as if no nations existed there.

DAVID AND THE ARK IN 2 SAMUEL 6

by

R.A. CARLSON

Uppsala

The present arrangement of the traditions in 2 Sam. displays a special interest in the description of the attitudes and activities of David vis à vis the Ark of the Lord. What does the rather conspicuous role of the Ark in these traditions involve in the light of biblical historiography, and in relation to modern scholarly approaches? To what extent is it possible to evaluate the historicity in an often subtle and sophisticated biblical story, or to postulate grounds and motives of an historical nature behind the narrative description?

These questions are both justified and inevitable in trying to consider and evaluate the narrative presentation of David's actions and behaviour in the important account of David and the Ark in 2 Sam. 6:1-23.

In Pedersen's well-known analysis of the tradition in 1-2 Sam., the term "continuity" is conceived of as an appropriate and pertinent one to describe David's entrance into and role in the history of Israel. In addition, Pedersen drew attention to passages in the stories about David which pointed to a "definite conception of divinity" in his conduct and manner of behaving.[1]

Pedersen's portrayal of David may form a suitable starting-point for some reflections on the ideas of the "traditional" versus the "innovatory" and the "factual" versus the "fictional" with respect to the relationship between David and the Ark. The author wishes to pay homage with these lines to a scholar and friend who, in the most inspiring way, has himself "reflected" on both the history of the Ark and its two main cult-sites, Shiloh and Jerusalem.[2]

---

[1] J.Pedersen, *Israel. Its Life and Culture* III-IV (London-Copenhagen, 1959), p.526. For an interpretation of the much-debated Ps. 132 along "continuity" lines, see A.Laato, "Psalm 132 and the Development of the Jerusalemite/Israelite Royal Ideology", *CBQ* 54 (1992), pp.49-66.

[2] E.Nielsen, "Some Reflections on the History of the Ark", in *Congress Volume: Oxford 1959*, SVT 7(Leiden, 1960), pp.61-74, reprinted in idem, *Law, History and*

2 Sam. 6: The Transfer of the Ark from Kiriath-jearim to Jerusalem

Context

The separate elements in the passage 5:6-25 provide a distinctive setting for the narrative in ch.6. The opening lines announce the important "innovation", the conquest of Jerusalem. The renaming of the "fortress of Zion" to the "city of David" demonstrates that this "innovation" is of an essentially personal character.[3]

The personal note, however, informs the entire passage in order to describe David's growing prosperity and his role as actor under the guidance of the Lord. In this connexion the name "the Lord of Hosts" appears once (v. 10), a word-bridge between Jerusalem and Shiloh, which prepares the "continuity" for the story in ch.6.

This story is linked to the account of the two battles with the Philistines in 5:17-21 and 5:22-25. The integration of these elements in the surrounding materials may indicate their *ad hoc* origin in the context in question.[4]

Some threads which run counter to the traditions in Judg. 4-5 are of special interest for the Ark-theme. The enemies are swept away by "waters" (5:20–Judg. 4:7, 5:21), when "the Lord goes out before you" (5:24–Judg. 4:14), a linkage of qualifying character.[5] The latter expression returns in the archaic Ps. 68, where the opening line alludes to the "signal words" in Num. 10:35, cf. vv. 2 and 8. Is it by chance that the author has by this linkage connected the most crucial wars in Israel's early history, and thereby paved the way for the account of the Ark's triumphal return to the "thousands of Israel" and to the "city of David", 6:1,10,12,16?

Tradition (Copenhagen, 1983), pp.59-70. A substantial background of the actual topics is presented in idem, *Shechem*, (Copenhagen, 1955), pp.315-346.

3 On the private, Davidic status of Jerusalem, see J.A.Soggin, *A History of Ancient Israel* (Philadelphia, 1985), pp.59-63, and his discussion of Buccellati's criticisms of Alt. For an excellent re-examination of the narrative in 2 Sam. 5:6-25 as part of the complex in 2 Sam. 5:6-8:18, see J.P.Fokkelman, *Narrative Art and Poetry in the Books of Samuel III, Throne and City (II Sam 2-8 & 21-24)*, Studia Semitica Neerlandica 27 (Assen / Maastricht, 1990), pp.153-76. The lucid description of the personal aspects in the portrayal of David is of special value in this context.

4 So Fokkelman. His hermeneutics, however, leads to the controversial identification of "the fortress" in 5:17 with "the fortress of Zion".

5 See further R.A.Carlson, *David, the Chosen King* (Stockholm, 1964), pp.56-57. If the Ark was actually present in Deborah's battle (cf. Noth), this would surely have cast some light on the above-mentioned concatenation.

Another thread leads via word-bridges to the tragic account of Saul's death in 1 Sam. 31 and apparently to the Ark narrative in 1 Sam. 4-6. According to the description of the first encounter with the Philistines, David and his men took "their idols" as trophies of war, a victorious counterpart to Saul's fate vis à vis "their idols" 5:21–31:9.[6] This polarity is in itself an expected one in traditions formed by the "binary law", but the significance is fully revealed in the light of its background in the Ark narrative in 1 Sam. 4–6.

In contrast to Saul, David defeated the Philistines, and the battlefield is named Baal-perazim in honour of Yahweh, the real "lord" of the victory in this conflict. This clearly indicates that the man who gave his sons names like Ishbaal and Meribbaal (cf. Jonathan), and who at the same time could be characterised as an almost meticulous worshipper of Yahweh, is succeeded on the throne by the true devotee of Yahweh, David. Moreover, the intention behind this memorialising name is to make evident the fact that Baal has been dethroned, and that Yahweh has virtually replaced him in exercising divine authority and functions. The description of the second and decisive encounter in 5:22-25 is in line with these aspects, since the victory is granted by virtue of an oracle of "atmospheric" character. The final demonstration of the "lordship" of Yahweh is the Ark's removal from its "Baal-place" (*sic*!)—an allusive choice of name for Kiriath-jearim—to Jerusalem in ch. 6.[7]

This exposition of the ideas in the introduction to the following Ark-story splendidly establishes the connexion with the traditions in 1 Sam. 4-6. The three stations of the Ark during its sojourn in Philistia were Ashdod, Gath and Ekron. The number of towns may have been intended to accord with the norms of epic literature, but is ultimately dependent on principles of ideological character. The choice of stations seeks to include the Philistine pantheon in its totality, and perhaps even indicates its basic structure: God—consort—son, viz. Dagon—Asherah—Baal-zebul.[8] The main idea behind

---

[6] This association is supported by a supplementary contrast motif of strongly emphatic character; see Fokkelman (1990), p.174.

[7] The name has been changed to a Baal-Baalah compound in 6:1 from the former Kiriath-jearim in 1 Sam. 6:21-7:1-2 for ideological and literary reasons. On the text-critical features of 2 Sam. 6 see Carlson (1964), pp.62-63.

[8] The mention of the god Dagon alone in the Ark narrative in 1 Sam. 4-6 clearly shows that this god is considered the major deity in the Philistine pantheon. Ashdod, which is also the representative of Philistia in Am. 3:9, and Gaza (Judg. 16:23) were Dagon's cult-places, and his position of eminence here accords with

the story in question is in any case to demonstrate the hegemony of Yahweh over the gods of the Philistines, in whose hands the Ark has fallen.

The strong association of the tradition in 5:17-21 via 1 Sam. 31 to its reversal-narrative in 4-6 provides further evidence for the above-mentioned interpretation of the Baal-theme in this context.[9] The upholders of the old *banu Dagan*-traditions have to be "mastered" in a text which prepares for the transfer of the Ark to yet another Gittite way-station, namely the house of Obed-Edom in 6:11.

One unavoidable observation may be further offered. The original account in 1 Sam. 4-6 inspired the exilic Dtr to fulfil its intentions by inserting a claim for the denunciation of foreign gods, the Baalim and the Astharoth, into the story.[10] Similar dispositions are present in the passage in 5:17-25 where it is not least the link to the Deborah tradition that underlines the motif of loyalty to Yahweh contra the "new gods" (cf. Judg. 5:8). From the point of view of tradition, the actual passage has no affinities at all with the idiom or the stylistics of Dtr. A late exilic dating is impossible for both "fictional" and "historical" reasons. The solid integration of the passage in the "polar" description of the Saul-David relationship provides a strong argument for an early dating of the material. From an historical point of view, the passage provides a reliable and necessary presupposition ("from Gibeon to Gezer") for the following event, with its starting-point in Baalath-jehudah.

---

ancient Canaanite beliefs and traditions. Since Baal is regarded as Dagan's son (= Dagon), it is entirely in order to list Ekron, the city of Baal-zebul (cf. 2 Kings 1:2-16) as the third in the series of Philistine towns. In between, the narrative mentions Gath, the cult-place of a female deity who is to be identified with either Asherah, the consort of Dagon, or Ashtoret, the goddess related to Baal who was likewise worshipped in Ashkelon. For a general survey of the Canaanite-Ugaritic background, see P.D.Miller, Jr., "Aspects of the Religion of Ugarit", in P.D.Miller, Jr. – P.D.Hanson – S.D.McBride (eds.), *Ancient Israelite Religion. Essays in Honor of Frank Moore Cross* (Philadelphia, 1987), pp.53-66.

9 The Chronicler completes this association in a highly expressive way: Saul's skull is nailed up in the temple of Dagon, 1 Chron. 10:10. The connexion between 1 Sam 31 and chs. 4-6 is above all a matter of content, "Israel defeated by Philistia", but it is also supplied with formal links of specific character, such as "be heavy", "head", "cut off" (Saul-Dagon), "make sport of".

10 The embellishment of the story in 1 Sam. 4-6 with traits borrowed from an old-fashioned Exodus tradition, see D.Daube, *The Exodus Pattern in the Bible* (London, 1963), pp.73-88, emphasises the "denunciatory" quality of the Ark of Yahweh. See further below.

This introduction draws by the same token a clear line of demarcation between original historiography and the secondary transposition of themes in later actualisation.[11]

Tradition and History

The transfer of the Ark from Kiriath-jearim to Jerusalem is from an historical point of view a singular event (an *einmaliges Ereignis*), and, as such, it is of the utmost importance.[12] Understood as tradition, however, the account of the removal of the "Ark of God, which is called by the name of the Lord of Hosts, who is enthroned on the cherubim" (v. 2) from Baalath-jehudah to the City of David reveals features which connect the story with the annual succoth-festival. Among these are such traits as digits (three, six), instruments of music, dancing, sacrifices, blessings and the processional march.[13]

In continuation of the previously-mentioned allusions to the Philistine pantheon and to subsequent ideas in 5:17-25, 6:1, it might be justified to propose an understanding of the perplexing stops at the threshing-floor of Nacon and in the Gittite house in 6:6-11. The interruptions of the procession indicates a disguised denunciation of an old cult-place belonging to Asherah—cf. Keret's vows to Asherah and Elath on the third day of his march—and an authorisation of the site as the property of Yahweh.[14]

In any case, the Uzzah episode reveals the true agent of the enter-

---

[11] This is an objection in principle to the approach of J.Van Seters, *In Search of History. Historiography in the Ancient World and the Origins of Biblical History* (New Haven–London, 1983), pp.249-91, 346-53, although Van Seters enhances the understanding of Dtr's description of the Ark and its function. K.A.D.Smelik, "The Ark Narrative Reconsidered", in A.S.van der Woude (ed.), *New Avenues in the Study of the Old Testament*, OTS 25 (Leiden, 1989), pp. 128-44, attempts to interpret 1 Sam. 4-6 and 2 Sam. 6 in a sixth-century context. The actual "themes" in 2 Sam. 6 are, after all, better explained in a more authentic, Davidic-Solomonic setting. Note the general remarks by W.H.Schmidt, "A Theologian of the Solomonic Era? A Plea for the Yahwist", in T.Ishida (ed.), *Studies in the Period of David and Solomon and other Essays* (Tokyo, 1982), pp.55-73.

[12] D.G.Schley, *Shiloh: A Biblical City in Tradition and History*, JSOT SS 63 (Sheffield, 1989)(available to me only as a review in *VT* 42 (1992), pp. 143) seems once again to question the historical reliability of the statement that Kiriath-jearim was the Ark's point of departure. However, it is difficult to avoid accepting the witness of the tradition in this case; the notice in 1 Sam. 14:18 does not refer to the Ark.

[13] See Carlson (1964), pp.62-96; the Uzzah episode, pp.77-85.

[14] One notes, as a curiosity, that both Manasseh and Amon, apostates to Asherah, are buried in the garden of Uzza, 2 Kings 21.

prise described in ch. 6, namely *Yahweh*. The incompetent custodians of the Ark are eliminated, the house of Obed-edom is blessed, after which the sacred vehicle is called the "Ark of Yahweh" in sevenfold repetition in 6:9-17. This is introduced by David's query, "How can the Ark of Yahweh come to me?", and reflects the intimate relationship between the divine and human actor, as well as the continuing personal note in the entire drama.[15]

The vivid picture of David as a personage explains his joyful behaviour "before Yahweh", i.e., the Ark. His performance in connexion with the bringing of the Ark into the "City of David" has been interpreted as being dependent on Shilonite or Canaanite / Jebusite traditions. Such efforts would seem to ignore the signals in the narrative itself. A more accurate conclusion would be to characterise David's dance before the Ark as his own choreographic innovation. In joy, as in sorrow, David's behaviour is utterly distinctive; cf. his penitential conduct in 2 Sam. 12.[16]

In this respect the portrait of David in 2 Sam. 6 also betrays "a definite conception of divinity", which is reflected in the artistic description of his "anger" (v. 8), "fear" (v. 9), and "joy" (v. 12). Needless to say, the "fictional" delineation of David is best understood as having originated in impressions of authentic "facts". The same applies to the last episode in the story, the conflict between David, as king, and Michal, the daughter of Saul.[17] It would be hard to explain this scene as pure invention. David's devoted and chivalrous dance provokes indignation because it is an innovation. The result is the final outcome of the rejection-election theme in conjunction with Saul and David in the whole of 1-2 Sam.. Moreover, this theme is ultimately connected with the ideological thinking of the Yahwist, who assigns to the *theologoumenon* "the repentence of

---

[15] On these aspects, see Fokkelman (1990), pp.184-205. Fokkelman's remarks are noteworthy, that Perez-uzzah finally destroyed the Philistine mode of transport, and that the picture of Uzzah employs "elohistic" terms.

[16] The *hapax legomenon mkrkr* in 2 Sam. 6 indicates the originality of the dance. The corresponding verb in Ugaritic is strictly speaking no dance-term, but might be illustrative of the nature of the dance in 2 Sam. 6, cf. G.W. Ahlström, "*KRKR* and *TPD*", *VT* 28 (1978), pp. 100-102.—The sukkoth-dance at Shiloh, however, represents a female dancing and the supposed Jebusite origins of David's dance remain hypothetical.

[17] Fokkelman (1990), pp.185 n.70 and 196, emphasizes the motif of contrast in the episode by pointing to the single mention of the title "king" (v. 12) in this chapter. Michal's reaction is interpreted along psychological lines.

Yahweh'' a prominent place in his linkage of the material (Gen. 6 and 1 Sam. 15).[18]

All this surely means that the tradition had dynastic overtones from its very beginning, and emphasized the overwhelming significance of David's care for the Ark of the Lord. An original element of this kind is apparently the summoning of ''all the chosen men of Israel'' in 6:1, namely 30,000 men, a figure which highlights both the national glory of David and the Ichabod-catastrophe at Eben-ezer, where 30,000 men perished (1 Sam. 4:10).[19]

The above-cited solemn title of the Ark in 6:2 is, however, more difficult to evaluate. Its function is, of course, to relate the Ark to both the *hekal* in Jerusalem (the proclamation) and in Shiloh (1 Sam. 4:4). Its provenience would seem to be Dtr's conception of the Ark as the *arca foederis* and footstool in the Holy of Holies. The divine name Yahweh Sebaoth, in which David blesses the people in 6:18, is also under suspicion of Dtr affiliation, as it first occurs in a rather deuteronomised context in 1 Sam. 1:3,11. This complication does not nullify the otherwise firm connexion of the Ark with Shiloh. The growth of the tradition indicates the importance of the ''factual'', i.e., the historical basis. In building up his empire, David consolidates his tribal-national foundation by bringing the old sacred symbol of the leading Northern tribes, Ephraim-Manasseh-Benjamin, to his new political and religious centre, Jerusalem.[20]

Innovation is made in continuation.

---

[18] This has been pointed out by J.Jeremias, *Die Reue Gottes. Aspekte alttestamentlicher Gottesvorstellung*, Biblische Studien 65 (Neukirchen, 1975), pp.19-38.

[19] The magnifying expression in 2 Sam. 6:1 evidently had a real background in the king's position and capacity as feudal lord during the early Davidic-Solomonic monarchy; see G.Widengren, *Military Organization and Traces of Feudalism in Ancient Israel* (forthcoming).

[20] The Ark-event described in 2 Sam. 6 took place in a decisive period in David's empire-building; see A.Malamat, ''A Political Look at the Kingdom of David and Solomon and Its Relations with Egypt'', in Ishida (ed.) (1982), pp.189-204, esp. pp.191-97. Beyond doubt, David planned to build a temple for the Ark, as both textual evidence and general considerations indicate; see C.Meyers, ''David as Temple Builder'', in Miller, Jr.-Hanson-McBride (eds.) (1987), pp.357-76. On Shiloh as an old Canaanite-Israelite cult-place, see I.Finkelstein, *The Archaeology of the Israelite Settlement* (Jerusalem, 1988), pp. 228-34, whose analysis has brought about a new appraisal of the validity of the allotment traditions in Josh. 13-22. See M.Weinfeld, ''Historical Facts behind the Israelite Settlement Pattern'', *VT* 38 (1988), pp. 324-32, and, more hesitantly, M.Ottoson, *Josuaboken—en programskrift för davidisk restauration*, Acta Universitatis Upsaliensis, Studia Biblica Upsaliensia 1 (Uppsala, 1991), pp.127-46. For an evaluation of the Shiloh traditions in 1 Sam. 1-3, see the author's review of T.N.D.Mettinger, ''YHWH SABAOTH—The Heavenly King on the Cherubim Throne'', in Ishida (ed.) (1982), pp.109-38, in *SEÅ* 59 (1994).

THE "MOUNTAIN OF GOD" IN PSALM 68:16[1]

by

J.A. EMERTON
Cambridge

The text and interpretation of Psalm 68 are notoriously problematical, but it is widely believed to reflect a relatively early stage of Israelite religion. I shall not discuss the general question of the psalm as a whole or the particular difficulties of most of its verses, but it is necessary to say something about its unity, which has been questioned. Albright, for example, has argued that it is a collection of incipits, but his theory depends on Mesopotamian examples for which his alleged biblical analogies are not convincing.[2] His view is to be distinguished from that of Hans Schmidt, who held that we have here a collection of brief independent songs which have intentionally been brought together to form some kind of meaningful whole.[3] Certainly, a comparison of Ps. 108 with 57 and 60 shows that parts of psalms could be combined in a different poem, and it is likely that Ps. 19 consists of an older part in verses 2-7, to which verses 8-15 have been added later. Another possibility is that the original part of Ps. 68 has been supplemented at a later date; thus, de Moor argues that verses 2-25 are original, and that verses 26-36 are a later addition probably from the time of Solomon.[4] In any case, Ps. 68 has come down to us as a single psalm, and attempts have been made to interpret it as a whole.[5] That, at least, should be the exegete's

---

[1] I am grateful to Dr. William Horbury for reading a draft of the present article.

[2] W.F. Albright, "A Catalogue of Early Hebrew Lyric Poems (Psalm 68)", *HUCA* 23 (1950-51), Part 1, pp. 1-39. Cf. S. Mowinckel, *Der achtundsechzigste Psalm* (Oslo, 1953), pp. 6-9.

[3] Hans Schmidt, *Die Psalmen*, HAT I, 15 (Tübingen, 1934), pp. 125-131.

[4] J.C. de Moor, *The Rise of Yahwism* (Leuven, 1990), pp. 118, 212-213.

[5] See, for example, Mowinckel (1953), and J.P. Fokkelman, "The Structure of Psalm lxviii", in A.S. van der Woude (ed.), *In Quest of the Past*, OTS 26 (Leiden, 1990), pp. 72-83. I am grateful to Dr. Fokkelman for sending me a copy of his article before it was published and also a copy of another article to which I did not have access.

starting point, even though the unity may have been composed out of originally independent units. An attempt should be made to understand the individual parts in the light of the present whole.

Within the psalm as a whole I shall focus attention on the question of the translation of verse 16, which must be considered together with the verse that follows. The psalmist refers in verse 17 to the mountain chosen by God for his eternal dwelling. In the present form of the text the mountain must surely have been understood to be Zion, where the temple was situated to which verse 30 refers. That does not, however, exclude the possibility that some other mountain was originally meant. The mention of Bashan in verse 16 draws attention to the northern part of Israel, and some have supposed that the mountain chosen by God was a northern mountain, perhaps either Mount Hermon or Mount Tabor. Deut. 33:18-19 associates the tribes of Zebulun and Issachar with a mountain where sacrifice was offered, and Mount Tabor is the obvious candidate to be identified with it in that verse. There may well have been an Israelite sanctuary there (perhaps compare Hosea 5:1). Nevertheless, even if verse 16 may once have referred to a northern mountain, it is still desirable to find a translation of verse 16 that is compatible with a later understanding of verse 17 to refer to God's choice of Mount Zion.

16 *har-'ĕlōhîm har-bāšān*
har-gabnunnîm har-bāšān
17 *lāmmâ t^eraṣṣ^edûn hārîm gabnunnîm*
hāhār ḥāmad 'ĕlōhîm l^ešibtô
'ap-yhwh yiškōn lāneṣaḥ

These words have been translated in several ways. We begin with the *Revised Version*[6]:

16 A mountain of God is the mountain of Bashan
An high mountain is the mountain of Bashan.
17 Why look ye askance, ye high mountains,
At the mount which God hath desired for his abode?
Yea, the Lord will dwell *in it* for ever.

In this translation, "look ... askance" is probably intended to mean "look with envy"; and, as is usual in the *RV*, the italics indicate words supplied by the translators but not found in the Hebrew.

---

[6] The verse numbering of the MT is used throughout the present article.

The *RV* thus understands verse 16a to be a statement, and "A mountain of God" is a word-for word rendering. The *Revised Standard Version*, however, treats verse 16 as an exclamation addressed to the mountain, and understands "God" to be used as a superlative:

O mighty mountain, mountain of Bashan;
O many-peaked mountain,
mountain of Bashan!

The *Jerusalem Bible* regards verse 16a as a question, and 16b as a contrasting exclamation:

That peak of Bashan, a mountain of God?
Rather, a mountain of pride, that peak of Bashan!

The new translation of the Jewish Publication Society of America understands "God" in verse 16 to be a superlative ("O majestic mountain"), but has a semi-colon, not an exclamation mark, at the end of 16a and 16b. Mount Bashan is addressed, and the verse is presumably taken to be an introduction to the question in verse 17, where the mountains are asked why they are hostile to the mountain that God has chosen.

Yet another interpretation of verse 16 is found in the *Authorized Version* of 1611 in which, as in the later *RV*, italics indicate words supplied by the translators to bring out the sense:

The hill of God *is as* the hill of Bashan;
an high hill *as* the hill of Bashan.

Verse 16 has thus been interpreted in a variety of ways in English translations of the Bible. It is the purpose of the present article to enquire how best to understand the Hebrew.

II

Before discussing the different ways of construing verse 16, we must look at several questions concerning text and language in verses 16-17. First, Albright believes that these verses were written before the introduction of *matres lectionis*, and that it is possible to read *hr* as *hār(ē)*, the construct plural, in verse 16: "O mountains of God", etc.[7] His reason is that the plural is found in verse 17, and that

[7] Albright (1950-51), Part 1, pp. 13, 24, 37.

"This vocalization ... greatly aids the meter" (p. 24). It is not, however, self-evident that the mountains in verse 17 must be identified completely with the mountain in verse 16. The psalmist may have intended a difference. Further, questions of metre in the Hebrew Bible cannot yet be regarded as settled, and opinions differ. In addition, we do not know for certain when these verses were first written, or how long Hebrew (as distinct from Phoenician) was written in a purely consonantal script—if, indeed, it ever was (and it is uncertain whether the Gezer Calendar, which has played a large part in such discussions, is Israelite or Canaanite). The MT, which is the primary subject of our investigation, has the singular, and it is speculative to maintain that the words in question were once in the construct plural.

The word *har* can denote either a particular mountain or hill-country, and it is not always easy to say whether a particular mountainous area should be described as a mountain or whether the more general term is appropriate. An obvious identification of *har-bāšān* is with Mount Hermon, though the phrase may refer to the region of Bashan more generally.

I have nothing fresh to say about the meaning of *gabnunnîm*. It is plausible to connect it with *gibbēn*, which probably means "hunchback" in Lev. 21:20, and to accept the common view that it here refers to the humps or peaks of the mountain in the region of Bashan. It is unnecessary for the present purpose to consider other theories. The word is used in the plural after a singular noun in the construct state in verse 16, but after a plural noun in the absolute state in verse 17. That may be explained on the hypothesis that it is used as a noun in verse 16 and as an adjective in verse 17, or it may be a noun in apposition in the latter verse. More speculative is Albright's theory that the last letter of *hr(y)m* in verse 17 is an enclitic *mem* (p.24). One of the characteristics of Albright's article is an attempt to detect as many archaisms as he can in the psalm, but scholars should be careful lest they postulate unusual forms in Hebrew unnecessarily.

tᵉraṣṣᵉdûn in verse 17 remains a problem, but there is no need to emend it to *tᵉraqqᵉdûn* on the basis of the Targum, which may well have read the same Hebrew as the MT but interpreted the *hapax legomenon* in the light of Ps. 114:4,6; cp. Ps. 29:6. The verb also occurs in Ben Sira 14:22: *lṣ't 'ḥryh kḥqr wkl mbw'h yrṣd*. There the context concerns the man who seeks wisdom. It is possible that the verb has a meaning related to "lie in wait" (so the Greek; cf. Mishnaic Hebrew, Jewish Aramaic, and Arabic), though any idea of hostile intent must have been weakened to vanishing point. While the meaning "lie in wait" is uncertain in Ben Sira 14:22, it seems much less appropriate in Ps. 68:17. Albright translates the verb in Ps. 68 as "stand guard (?)" (p. 37), and says that his rendering "follows the usual Arabic meaning 'to watch'" (p.24). The translation "stand guard" does not have an obvious relevance to the context, even when Albright has turned the singular noun *hāhār* in verse 17 into a construct plural without the article, with the result that he understands the originally purely consonantal script *hār(ē) ḥmd 'lhm* to mean "Mountains chosen by God" (pp. 14, 24, 37).

A different view about *rṣd* is presented by Cassuto. While he believes that it means "to investigate" (*lḥqwr*) in Ben Sira 14:22, he ascribes a different meaning to the verb in Ps. 68:17. He thinks it may mean "Why do you query (*thrhrw 'ḥr*) the decree of the Lord...?" (though that is scarcely the same as "investigate"). But he prefers another meaning of the supposed Arabic cognate, namely, its use of someone who "waits yearningly" (*šmṣph bklywn ʿynym*) "for a favourable opportunity, or for the moment when his time will come". Verse 17 thus means "Why do you expect that after Mount Zion has become the Lord's dwelling-place your turn will come, and you, too, will be made His abode?"[8] It is questionable, however, whether we should explain the Hebrew on the basis of what may be a special development in Arabic. In any case, it is difficult to see how Cassuto can legitimately derive his paraphrase of the meaning when *hāhār* appears to be the direct object of the verb.

It is often suggested that a verb meaning "to watch" (one of the meanings in Arabic)[9] has acquired the nuance "to watch with envy". This theory too starts from Arabic but ascribes to the verb in the psalm a sense not attested in Arabic. Yet the meaning "to watch" fits Ben Sira 14:22, and the context of Ps. 68:17 suggests that there it has a hostile connotation. It seems to me best to accept as a working hypothesis the view that the verb in this verse means

---

[8] M.D. Cassuto, "Psalm lxviii" (Hebrew), *Tarbiz* 12 (1940-41), pp. 1-27; reprinted in *Studies on the Bible and Ancient Orient* (Hebrew) (Jerusalem, 1972), p. 167-199; E. tr. "Psalm lxviii", in *Biblical and Oriental Studies* I (Jerusalem, 1973), pp. 241-284. The quotation is from the first Hebrew version p. 15, and from the English version p. 264.

[9] F. Brown, S.R. Driver, C.A. Briggs, *A Hebrew and English Lexicon of the Old Testament* (Oxford, 1907), pp. 952f.

"to watch" or "look at with envy", but to recognize that the meaning is far from certain.

Finally, the last clause in verse 17 contains the tetragrammaton, although Elohim is normally used in this part of the Psalter. The name *yhwh* is also found in verses 21 and 27, although some manuscripts read *'dny* instead in the latter verse. It is possible that *'ĕlōhîm* earlier in verse 17 and in 16 has replaced *yhwh*, but it is also possible that *'ĕlōhîm* is original in either place or both. It would make a difference to the present discussion only if *'ĕlōhîm* in verse 16 were thought to have the plural meaning "gods". Then there would be a constrast with Yahweh. Otherwise, the psalmist probably understood *'ĕlōhîm* to have a singular sense and to refer to Yahweh.

III

An attempt must now be made to evaluate the various translations of verse 16. We begin with the view that the word "God" is here used to indicate a superlative, as in "mighty mountain" (*RSV*) or "majestic mountain" (NJPS). This is not the place to discuss again the whole question of the use of a word for God to indicate a superlative, and it is enough to refer to the careful examination of it by D.W. Thomas. He recognizes that there is a sense in which the word "God" is certainly used as a superlative. But, he says, "I do not find a single example which decisively supports" the view that the uses "have no religious significance at all and are merely intensifying epithets".[10] Not only is Thomas's judgement convincing in general; in this particular context, in which verse 17 speaks of God choosing a mountain on which to dwell, it is especially improbable that "God" in verse 16 has no religious significance but is merely an "intensifying epithet". Translations and interpretations that treat the first occurrence of Elohim merely as a superlative must be rejected.[11] So, for example, it is unlikely that Caquot is right in thinking that "mountain of God" could be used because the region of Bashan was famous for the richness of its pastures.[12] No doubt,

---

[10] D.W. Thomas, "A Consideration of Some Unusual Ways of Expressing the Superlative in Hebrew", *VT* 3 (1953), p. 215.

[11] So rightly J. Day, *God's Conflict with the Dragon and the Sea* (Cambridge, 1985), p. 116.

[12] A. Caquot, "Le psaume LXVIII", *RHR* 177 (1970), pp. 162f.

fertility was attributed to God's blessing, but it may be questioned whether that alone justifies the use of the phrase "mountain of God".

The word "God" in verse 16 must therefore be given a religious significance, and various interpretations that recognize the fact will now be examined. It does not, however, seem important for the present purpose to differentiate between those that regard the verse as a vocative, an exclamation, or a statement.

First, the interpretation implied by the *AV* must not be overlooked simply because it is old. What is implied by the addition of the words "is as" and "as" in the rendering "The hill of God *is as* the hill of Bashan; an high hill *as* the hill of Bashan"? Rosenmüller sets out such a view as follows: "Zionis mons etsi non sit altissimus, tamen quod Numinis sedes factus est, non inferior montanis Basaniticis regione fertilissima ac amoenissima".[13] But he rightly regards as unconvincing this attempt to make verse 16 say that God's mountain, namely, Zion, is the equal of the fertile mountain region of Bashan. It is scarcely likely that anyone would understand the Hebrew thus unless impelled by a strong desire to make sense of a difficult verse.

Secondly, is it possible to make sense of the verse if it says "A mountain of God is the mountain of Bashan" (*RV*), understanding "God" to denote Yahweh? If a particular mountain in the region of Bashan is to be considered, it is surely Mount Hermon, which is impressive in its size and whose name indicates a connexion with the sacred. Mount Tabor, which was mentioned earlier in the present article as the probable site of a sanctuary in early Israelite times, is too far to the west to be a likely candidate for a mountain in Bashan. Mowinckel considers the possibility that a mountain in Bashan was once the site of the chief sanctuary of the Israelites, but he recognizes that such a possibility does not fit the known early history of Israel, and he advances an alternative hypothesis. He suggests that "Bashan", like "Zaphon" in Ps. 43:3, had a mythological background and represented the mountain of the gods, the Near Eastern equivalent of Olympus (cp. the Ugaritic texts).[14]

Mowinckel adapts to Ps. 68:16 Albright's theory that "Bashan"

---

[13] E.F.C. Rosenmüller, *Scholia in Vetus Testamentum* 4/3 (2nd ed., Leipzig, 1823), pp. 1279f.

[14] Mowinckel (1953), p. 43.

in verse 23 denotes a snake. According to Mowinckel, verse 16 refers to a "Drachenberg", which was the principal sanctuary of the northern tribes, and he compares *'eben zōḥelet* in 1 Kings 1:9, *'ên tannîn* in Neh. 2:13, and *neḥuštān* in 2 Kings 18:4 as evidence for the place of snakes in the Israelite cult. He suggests that the "Drachenberg" was none other than Mount Tabor, and he compares the theory of Julius Lewy that the name of the mountain is related to *tabira/tabura*, a name of Tammuz, and he further suggests a connexion between Tammuz and an underworld serpent deity.[15] Even if the philological justification for regarding "snake" as a meaning of *bāšān* were well founded, it would remain a weakness of Mowinckel's theory that it involves too much correlation of comparative religious data. It would also involve the surprising view that Mount Tabor could be called "Bashan" in the sense of "snake" when there was a region called "Bashan" not far away. In any case, the philological basis of the theory, which will be examined in the following paragraphs, is questionable.

Albright finds a reference to a snake in verse 23 by emending the text to read "From smiting Serpent I return,/ I return from destroying Sea!": *mi⟨mḥōṣ⟩ bšn 'āšūb/'āšūb-m mṣ[m]t ym.*[16] It is a daring emendation, involving not only alteration of the vocalization, but also striking conjectural changes to the consonantal text as well as postulating the presence of an enclitic *mem*. Admittedly, the MT is not easy to understand, but so extensive a conjectural emendation is not a convincing solution to the problem. Moreover, whatever else may be obscure, a contrast between Bashan and the Sea is intelligible as a contrast between either height and depth or an eastern part of the land and the Mediterranean to the west.

Albright's emendation involves the explanation of *bāšān* with the help of Ugaritic *bṯn* (and its cognates), denoting some kind of a snake—Albright suggests a viper. This theory was first advanced by Cassuto.[17] The Ugaritic noun is convincingly supposed to be cognate with Hebrew *peṯen*. But Albright thinks that the same Semitic word also appeared in Hebrew as *bāšān* in a form not influenced by

---

[15] *idem*, p. 42, with reference to J. Lewy, "Tabor, Tibar, Atabyros", *HUCA* 23 (1950-51), Part 1, pp. 357-386.

[16] Albright (1950-51), pp. 14, 27f., 38.

[17] M.D. Cassuto, *Tarbiz* 12 (1940-41), p. 18 (E. tr. *Biblical and Oriental Studies I* (1973), p. 269). Cf. Day (1985), p. 114.

Aramaic. Against Albright, the geographical sense of "Bashan" is well attested in the Hebrew Bible, and it needs more than a conjecturally rewritten verse in Ps. 68:23 to establish another meaning for the word.

Albright's theory cannot gain support from his further comparison (p. 27) with Deut. 33:22, which he translates "Dan is a young lion/ Which attacks (*znq* = Accad. *sanāqu*) a viper". The second line of Albright's translation corresponds to the MT's *y^e^zannēq min-habbāšān*. He has somehow disposed of the first three letters of *mn hbšn*. Does he regard the first as an enclitic *mem* and simply delete the other two? Albright compares the treatment of this verse by Cross and Freedman, who take the relevant words to mean "Dan is a lion's whelp/ Who shies away from a viper".[18] They attribute the idea to Albright, but they delete only the definite article and keep the preposition meaning "from". What, however, is their justification for departing from the usual translation "from Bashan"? It appears to be their claim that "Contrary to the usual view there is no natural association between Dan and Bashan" (p. 208). Their statement is puzzling, since the site of the city of Dan is so close to the region of Bashan that it seems to make good sense to think of Bashan as the base of the Danites' movements. The reference by Cross and Freedman to Gen. 49:17, where Dan is compared to a snake, scarcely helps their explanation of Deut. 33:22 (or that of Albright). If the tribe of Dan is compared to a snake in Gen. 49:17, it is surprising that the tribe is said to shy away from (let alone attack) a snake in Deut. 33:22. The theory that *bāšān* sometimes means "a viper" must be rejected as lacking sufficient support in the contexts in which the word is used.

De Moor discusses Ps. 68 in detail and offers an interpretation of verses 16-17 that seeks to make sense of them in terms of the early history of the northern Israelite tribes.[19] He believes that verses 8, 18, 25 imply that the Israelites had been led "from Kadesh in the South through Transjordan to Mt. Bashan where they were living now" (pp. 122f.), and that Yahweh was identified with El (p. 124). De Moor maintains that in this region El had triumphed over Baal. He sees in the "so-called Job-stele from Sheikh Sa'd, dating from

---

[18] F.M. Cross and D.N. Freedman, "The Blessing of Moses", *JBL* 67 (1948), pp. 195, 208 (repr. in *Studies in Ancient Yahwistic Poetry* (Missoula 1975), pp. 97-122).

[19] J.C. de Moor (1990), pp. 122-126.

the reign of Ramses II (*c*. 1279-1212 B.C.)", evidence that El had taken over Baal's sacred mountain Zaphon. He interprets the inscription to read "*'il qny ṣpn* 'Ilū the Creator/Owner of the Zaphon' so that El had become the master of the mountain of Baal here" (pp. 125f.). Ps 68:17 shows that "It was Mt. Bashan on which he [i.e. Yahweh] wanted to dwell for ever" (p. 124). In his lecture at the Congress in Paris 1992 he developed further his theories about El, Zaphon, Bashan and Yahweh.[20]

It would be beyond the scope of the present article to discuss de Moor's theory in detail, though it may be noted that it is uncertain whether the Zaphon to which he believes the Job-stele to refer was necessarily in the region in which the stele was found, and that some Old Testament references to *ṣāpôn* which he mentions may be capable of interpretation in the sense of north rather than of the sacred mountain. What is relevant to the present discussion is that there may well have been a mountain sacred to Yahweh in the region of Bashan in the obscure early history of the Israelites. If that is so, then Ps. 68:16-17 must have been reinterpreted at a later stage in the light of belief in Yahweh's choice of Zion, and de Moor recognizes that such a reinterpretation took place. Whether or not the understanding of verses 16-17 in the days of Zion's supremacy involved a change in their interpretation, it is the purpose of the present article to discover how it may have been understood in later times.

Thirdly, some have understood Elohim in verse 16 to be a true plural and to refer, not to Yahweh, but to other gods. Thus, Cassuto sees in this passage a contrast between Mount Bashan and other high mountains on the one hand, and Mount Zion on the other. Mount Bashan, the mountain of gods, has temples of idols on it (verse 16), but it and the other high mountains of verse 17a must not expect that their turn will come for Yahweh to dwell on them. On the contrary, Elohim (understood in a singular sense) has chosen another mountain, namely, Zion (verse 17b).[21]

Day too sees in Mount Bashan and the other *hārîm gabnūnnîm* a

---

[20] J.C. de Moor, "Ugarit and Israelite Origins", forthcoming in J.A. Emerton (ed.), *Congress Volume: Paris 1992*, which is to appear in the series *Supplements to Vetus Testamentum*.

[21] M.D. Cassuto, *Tarbiz* 12 (1940-41), p. 15 (E. tr. *Biblical and Oriental Studies I* (1973), p. 264).

contrast with Yahweh's own mountain, and he argues that *har ʾĕlōhîm* in verse 16 should be rendered "mountain of the gods" (pp. 115-18). He also maintains that Mount Bashan "is probably to be equated with Mt Hermon" (p. 116). Further, he notes evidence adduced by E. Lipiński which, he claims, shows that Mount Hermon "actually was regarded as the mountain of the gods in Canaanite religion".[22] Similarly, de Moor allows the possibility that, when verses 26-36 were added to the psalm, *ʾĕlōhîm* in verse 16 was interpreted as a reference to a plurality of gods (unless it was regarded as a superlative).

At first sight, the understanding of *ʾĕlōhîm* in verse 16 to mean "gods" seems to be a satisfactory solution to the problem, especially in the scholarly and perceptive argument advanced by Day. Yet there is a difficulty. The theory involves understanding *ʾĕlōhîm* in verses 16 and 17 in different—indeed, contrary—senses. Is it likely that the word was used in such different senses in the same context? Verse 17 speaks of the mountain where Elohim has been pleased to dwell; and if verse 16 means "Mount Bashan is a mountain of Elohim", it is natural to suppose that Elohim in verse 17 is used in the same sense and that the mountain (in the singular) in the latter verse is the same mountain.[23] The contrast in verse 17 between the chosen mountain (in the singular) and the other mountains (in the plural) would be weakened by calling one of the latter a "mountain of Elohim". It may also be suspected that the phrase "mountain of Elohim" would have had Yahwistic associations in the minds of ancient Israelites, at least in the present context. It is true that the definite article is not used here as it is when the phrase *har hāʾĕlōhîm* refers to Sinai-Horeb in Exod. 3:1, 4:27, 18:5, 24:13; 1 Kings 19:8,[24] but Ps. 68 is poetry not prose, and the definite article is used more sparingly in Hebrew verse than in prose. Admittedly, *har ʾĕlōhîm*, without the article, is found in Ezek. 28:16 (cf. verse 14) with reference to a myth, perhaps originally a polytheistic myth, but Ezekiel uses it in a Yahwistic context.

---

22 Day (1985), pp. 115–118.

23 Mowinckel (1953), p. 42.

24 After I had written the first and second drafts of the present article, Professor de Moor sent me the typescript of his article for the *Congress Volume* (cf. note 20, above) and I saw that he uses the same references for a similar purpose.

The difficulty would be eased to some extent if it were held that *'ĕlōhîm* in verse 17 (but not in verse 16) has replaced an original *yhwh*. The difficulty would be eased, but it would not disappear: the contrast between Elohim and Yahweh would still be awkward. The theory that *'ĕlōhîm* in verse 16 means "gods" might perhaps be claimed as the best way of understanding the passage if no more satisfactory alternative could be found. But it is difficult, and we have not yet considered all the possibilities.

Fourthly, some have sought to solve the problem of verses 16-17 by emendation. It is unnecessary to consider the extensive conjectural reconstructions of these verses by Briggs and Buttenwieser, because their conjectures go too far to be plausible.[25] Weil is less radical, though scarcely more convincing. He explains *bāšān* by comparing *bošnâ*, "shame", in Hos. 10:6. Next, he supposes that a word for "shame" has been substituted for "Baal" (cf. the names Ishbosheth, Jerubbesheth and Mephibosheth). He translates verse 16a: "La montagne de Dieu est la montagne de *Baal*!"[26] He sees here a reference to Mount Zalmon (verse 15), which he identifies with the mountain of that name in Judg. 9:48, where he believes that the temple of El-berith was situated. Since El-berith (9:46) is to be identified with Baal-berith (9:4), Mount Zalmon was both a mountain of Baal and a mountain of El, and so he maintains that his translation of Ps. 68:16 makes sense. Weil's interpretation of Ps. 68:16-17 is part of a wider hypothesis that verses 7-11, 18-31 have as their background the events of 1 Sam. 6:10-7:1 and 2 Sam. 6:1-10. The whole hypothesis is open to question. Moreover, Judg. 9:48 does not say that the temple of El-berith was on Mount Zalmon. In any case, Weil's treatment of Ps. 68:16-17 is improbable. Bashan is a well-established geographical term for a region in the north-east of the land, and Weil sets against the natural meaning no more than a speculation. To suggest that the word in such an unattested sense is itself a substitute for "Baal" is to construct a second speculation on the insecure foundation of the first.

Aistleitner emends *bāšān* to *dešen* and translates Ps. 68:16a: "Ein Berg des Überflusses ist der Gottesberg"; and he compares the

---

[25] C.A. and E.G. Briggs, *A Critical and Exegetical Commentary on the Book of Psalms*, ICC (Edinburgh, 1907), vol. II, pp. 94-112; M. Buttenwieser, *The Psalms* (Chicago, 1938), pp. 29-47.

[26] H.M. Weil, "Exégèse du Psaume 68", *RHR* 117 (1938), p. 77; cp. p. 84.

LXX's *πῖον* (to which may be added Symmachus's *εὐτροφίας*) and Jerome's *mons pinguis* (carried over from the older translation) in the *Psalterium iuxta Hebraeos*.[27] The mountain is identified by Aistleitner with Mount Sinai, which is the object of the other mountains' envy in verse 17. The second *har-bāšān* in verse 16 is deleted on suspicion of being an intrusive gloss from the margin (Aistleitner does not make clear what the glossator's purpose was). It may be questioned, however, whether the LXX and the other relevant versions are based on a reading *dešen* (corrupted to *bāšān* because of the similarity of the letters in the old script). They may be merely an interpretation of *bāšān* in terms of *dešen*, which shares two of the same consonants. Before resorting to emendation, it is better to see whether the MT can be interpreted in an intelligible way.

There remains one further way of translating the MT of verse 16, and the next section of this article will examine it.

IV

Once, when I was puzzling about the translation and interpretation of verse 16, it occurred to me that it could be construed as a question. As so often happens, when one comes across an idea that is new to one, I later discovered that someone else had had the same idea previously. It was noted earlier in the present article that the *Jerusalem Bible* understands verse 16a as a question, and it is convenient to repeat its rendering of the whole verse here:

> That peak of Bashan, a mountian of God?
> Rather, a mountain of pride, that peak of Bashan!

It is interesting to note that the French translation of the psalm, which was the inspiration of the English version, does not see a question here:

> Montagne de Dieu, la montagne de Bashân!
> Montagne sourcilleuse, la montagne de Bashân!

Further, the question disappears in the *New Jerusalem Bible*:

> A mountain of God, the mountain of Bashan!
> a haughty mountain, the mountain of Bashan!

The translation as a question thus appears to be peculiar to the first edition in English.

The rendering of *har gabnunnîm* as "a mountain of pride" determines the way in which verse 16b is related to 16a in the *Jerusalem Bible*. That rendering goes back to Aquila (ὄρη ὠφρυωμένα), who perhaps knew a tradition about the second word's meaning. The understanding of verse 16a as a question does not, however, depend on it. It is also possible that verse 16b does not express a contrast to 16a, but is in apposition to it. It may perhaps be translated:

Is Mount Bashan a mountain of God,
Many-peaked mountain, Mount Bashan?

The advantage of understanding verse 16a as a question is that it gives full value to the expression "a mountain of God". Mount Bashan (Hermon?) is not the mountain which God has chosen, and to which verse 17 refers. In verse 17 various mountains, probably including Mount Bashan of verse 16, are told not to look with envy (if that is what the verb means) on the mountain on which God has been pleased to establish his dwelling. *hāhār ḥāmad 'ĕlōhîm lᵉšibtô* is the true *har 'ĕlōhîm*. It is scarcely necessary to make the point that questions are often expressed in Biblical Hebrew without the use of an interrogative particle (GK § 150*a*). Ps. 68:16a is best regarded as a question.

I am glad to dedicate this essay to Eduard Nielsen in gratitude for friendship, for years of co-operation on the Editorial Board of *Vetus Testamentum*, and for his many contributions to the understanding of the religion of early Israel and to the interpretation of the Old Testament in general.

DID JOAB CLIMB "WARREN'S SHAFT"?

by

SVEND HOLM-NIELSEN

Copenhagen

Although it has become fashionable to put a question-mark next to practically every tradition in the Old Testament which has to do with history prior to the Babylonian exile, there remains nevertheless what is at least a plausible tradition to the effect that in the time of David the Jebusite city of Jerusalem became an Israelite possession and the capital of a united Israel, although the latter phase may have taken place first under David's successor in Jerusalem, Solomon.

As is well known, there are two accounts in the Old Testament of this "seizure of power", namely in 2 Samuel 5:6-10 and 1 Chron 11:4-9.

2 Samuel 5:6-10

The king and his men went to Jerusalem against the Jebusites living in the land. And they said to David: "You shall not come in here unless you remove the blind and the lame", saying: "You shall not come in here". But David captured the stronghold of Zion, which is the city of David. And David said on that day: "Whoever smites a Jebusite *w^{e}jigga' baṣṣinnor*, and the lame and the blind are hated by David". That is why they say: "A blind and a lame shall not enter the house". And David settled in the stronghold, and he named it "City of David" ....

1 Chron 11:4-9

David and all Israel went to Jerusalem, which is Jebus, and there were the Jebusites living in the land. And the inhabitants of Jebus said to David: "You shall not come in here." But David captured the stronghold of Zion, which is the city of David. And David said: "Whoever smites a Jebusite first shall become chief and commander". And Joab son of Zeruiah went up first and he became chief. And David settled in the stronghold; that is why they called it "City of David".

Theories as to the course of events depend upon how one evaluates these texts in relation to one another. It is immediately apparent that we have to do with one and the same event. But there are notable differences, including the fact that 2 Sam contains the "special material" according to which the Jebusites, the inhabitants of the town, announce to David before the taking of the town that he cannot enter without removing the blind and the lame; we are also told that these blind and lame are hated by David, for which reason we are told that the blind and the lame may not come into the "house". Moreover, apparently as part of the plan of attack we also find the expression *wᵉyiggaʿ baṣṣinor*. It is specifically with the meaning of this expression that we shall be concerned in the following.

Unlike this account, 1 Chron 11:6 understands David's words *kål makkeh jᵉbusī*, which are attested in both versions, to be a challenge from David to perform an heroic deed. Thus, when Joab, the son of Zeruiah, was the first to go up he was rewarded by being made some sort of leader, a *rôʾš*. Now the Chronicler's version has often rather uncritically been regarded as a mere explanatory supplement to the book of Samuel, which has been understood to be the source of the Chronicler. It has been possible in this connexion to use the remark about Joab as an explanation of *wᵉyiggaʿ baṣṣinôr*. The absence of the expression itself in Chronicles has been explained as an omission by the author which was motivated by the fact that he did not understand it, "wie es uns ja auch geht", as Rudolph almost sorrowfully says in his commentary.[1]

However, it is not only unreasonable to attempt to create a single account from the two narratives; it is also unlikely that the author of Chronicles knew the Books of Samuel in their present form. A closer comparison of the two texts shows that there is an almost verbatim agreement in a number of phrases which, read in context, supply a brief notice as to David's conquest of the town: And David and his men[2] went to Jerusalem against the Jebusites, the inhabitants of the land.[3] And they said to David, "You cannot come in

[1] W. Rudolph, *Chronikbücher*, HAT I, 21 (Tübingen, 1955), p. 99.

[2] The reason why 2 Sam 5:6 says "the king and his men" is presumably that the immediately preceding context relates how David was made king. The more usual expression is "David and his men", which recurs repeatedly throughout the Books of Samuel. However, it does not occur in Chronicles, which tendentiously changes it to "all Israel".

[3] The difference between *jôšeb* (Sam.) and *jošbei* (Chron.) is insignificant, but the choice determines whether the following verb is in the singular (Sam.) or the plural (Chron.).

here." But David captured the stronghold of Zion, which is the city of David. And David said *kål makkeh y^ebusi*. The verbatim agreement continues a bit more, so as to include David's naming of the city, his construction work and progress, under the protection of Yahweh.

With respect to its lapidary form, this notice corresponds to comments elsewhere in the Old Testament,[4] and there is reason to believe that such a notice underlies both of the present conquest accounts, so that the "special material" is and will remain "special". However, something is missing from this narrative, as *kål makkeh y^ebusi*[5] requires a continuation. It is also present in both texts, but in different ways. As we have seen, in 1 Chron the expression is understood as a challenge from David, followed by a promise of reward. But it is uncertain whether this was the original meaning of the expression. Scholars like to refer by way of analogy to Josh 15:16 and the parallel in Judg 1:12, where it clearly is a challenge. In both cases, though, we read *'ašer makkeh*, "the one who strikes"[6]. A much better analogy is provided by Num 35:15, with a parallel in Josh 20:9, where *kål makkeh* means "whoever". In 2 Sam we find the continuation in the murky expression *w^eyigga' baṣṣinôr*. However, there is, in addition to doubt about the meaning of the expression also some uncertainty about the syntax. It is namely the case that *weyigga'* may be understood as a coordinated imperfect: "everyone who strikes.., and who . . ."; but it may also be taken as characterizing the resultant action: "everyone who strikes. . . and as a result of it. . .". Finally, it may be understood as a separate sentence: "everyone who strikes. . ., he shall. . ." In the first possibility, there is no concluding sentence; in the second, there is no object of *w^eyigga'*; and in the third the object is to be sought in the subsequent "the lame and the blind" if one refers the *w^e* back as a suffix to *ṣinnôr*. As we shall shortly see, all three possibilities are important for the understanding of the expression itself. In what follows, I do

---

4 See particularly Num 32:41f., which also has the verb *halak* and the topos of the naming of the town.

5 Being undetermined, the word ought properly to be translated "a Jebusite". Most scholars assume that a Hē has dropped out through haplography with the last letter in *makkeh*.

6 The verb *nakah* need not necessarily mean "to kill", although it certainly has this meaning when followed by the word *nefeš*. It can be used of taking a city, as, for example, in Judg 1:25.

not discuss the question of the "lame and the blind" in this context, as I do not feel that there is any connexion with the expression *w^e^yiggaʿ baṣṣinnôr*.

The majority of scholars who have concerned themselves with this passage have assumed that "the lame and the blind" in the mouths of the Jebusites (v.6) are a quasi-proverbial phrase intended to express the self-confidence of the inhabitants as to the impregnability of the town: even lame and blind people would be able to defend it against the assaults of David's conquerors. W.F.Albright[7] makes the more drastic assumption that the Jebusites actually assembled the lame and the blind on the wall of the town to scorn David. Then, of course, there is nothing remarkable in David's hatred of the lame and the blind in v.8!

The fact that the lame and the blind are not permitted to enter "the house" (v.8c) has generally been understood as a late gloss which has been determined by Lev 21:18, which forbids the lame, the blind and other types of invalids to enter the temple: a statement which has nothing whatever to do with the context in 2 Sam.

Only H.J.Stoebe goes completely his own way. One must agree with him that *hesīr* (v.6) is not the most characteristic verb to use to express "hostile removal from one's path", "to annihilate". He also broaches the moral question as to whether we may really ascribe hatred for the blind and the lame to David. It would in any event not have been politically wise, since David now had to acclamatise himself to life together with the Jebusites in Jerusalem. Stoebe assumes that the Jebusites' words to David do not merely reflect their self-confidence, but are also supposed to voice their contempt of David and his men. What the Jebusites mean is that the blind and the lame are to be sought in David's own ranks. If anyone should seek to take Jerusalem, he would have to have real men in his troop, unlike David's weaklings! David reacts to the insult; he may even have challenged his own "lame and blind", that is, the cowardly, among his people to return home, for he hates them. Moreover, Stoebe is able to retain v.8c as original, since he regards it as part of David's rejection of the "blind and the lame": he will not allow them in the "house", which is by no means the temple, but his own

---

7 "The Sinnor in the Story of David's Capture of Jerusalem", *JPOS* 2 (1922), pp.286ff. The very first to suggest this understanding was Josephus in his *Antiquities of the Jews*, Book 7, chapter 3.

house.[8] It seems to me that Stoebe's effort is one of the shots in the dark among the many which have been offered to solve the problems of 2 Sam 5:6-8. But I will not deal with the issue more closely here, and hence will leave the blind and the lame in peace![9]

Now what does *ṣinnôr* mean? And, in extension of this, how is *w^eyiggaʿ* to be understood and translated? For summaries and evaluations of all the efforts at interpretation the reader is referred to the detailed studies of G.Bressan[10] and H.J.Stoebe[11], and to the briefer account of J.Simons.[12] I have nothing new to add to these surveys. Here I will confine myself to arguing for the rightness of one of the above-mentioned viewpoints.

Ṣinnôr only occurs one other time in the Old Testament, in Ps 42:8 in the plural, where it occurs in conjunction with *t^ehôm*, continued by "waves and breakers". This suggests that the word has, one way or another, something to do with water. In addition to this, the same root appears in Zech 4:12 in fem. plural, *ṣanterôt*, where it seems to designate a pipeline conducting some sort of liquid. This leads to the commonest view of our passage in 2 Sam, namely that we have to do with a channel or conduit which has to do with running water. It is this understanding of the word that most scholars, though in widely different ways, have used as the basis for their interpretations of this expression in 2 Sam, and I hold this to be correct.

There are two interpretations which differ radically from this one. One of these still assumes the meaning to be "conduit, pipe", but does not require it to carry water. In this case one interprets the term as having to do with some part of the body, so that David's comment

[8] Which would have to have been termed *beiti*.

[9] Except that it ought to be mentioned that Y. Yadin has proposed a third explanation of the blind and the lame. He refers (*The Art of Warfare in Biblical Lands* (London, 1963), pp. 268ff) to a Hittite text from Boghazköy in which a blind woman and a deaf man act as symbols of such who will betray a treaty. Later G. Brunet has taken up this theory (*SVT* 30 (1979), p. 65ff., and 73 ff.). He takes it that an alliance existed between the Jebusites and David that he should keep out of Jerusalem. The blind and the lame were a token of this treaty. By way of *ṣinnor* David managed to capture Jerusalem without breaking his oath.—To this theory I have one main objection: That the Hittite treaty speaks of a blind woman and a deaf man, whereas 2 Samuel 5:6 speaks of blind and lame. Is that a difference without importance?

[10] "L'espugnazione di Sion in 2 Sam 5,6-8/1 Cron 11,4-6 e il problema del 'Sinnor'", *Biblica* 25 (1944), pp.346ff.

[11] "Die Einnahme Jerusalems und der Sinnôr", *ZDPV* 73 (1957), pp.73ff.

[12] *Jerusalem in the Old Testament* (Leiden, 1952), pp.157ff.

is understood to refer to the way the Jebusites are to be wounded. Whoever strikes the Jebusites is to hit them on the *ṣinnôr*, and in connexion with this the *w*^{e} of the following word is retracted so as to serve as a suffix. Then, dependent on the play of one's imagination, *ṣinnôr* may be taken to mean the windpipe, that is, the trachea, meaning that they are to be killed; or it may be taken to refer to the fibula of the leg, meaning that they are to be semi-crippled; alternatively, it may be taken to signify the *membrum virile*[13], meaning that they are to be made invalids for all time in a most efficient manner!

Of course, this way of understanding the context would indeed provide reason to wonder about David's ethical stance towards his fellowman. But perhaps the whole matter is made superfluous by the question as to whether the verb employed in this context actually fits the proposed interpretation. Admittedly, one might refer to Gen 32:26, where Yahweh strikes Jacob on the hip so that he, Jacob, limps, but the text does not seem to presuppose actual lameness, and, furthermore, might one not have expected a different verb than *naga'* for such a powerful touch?[14]

A different view which has been advanced by several scholars, is that *ṣinnôr* has nothing to do with any pipe-like structure; rather, it is explained on the basis of Arabic *ṣnr*, meaning "peg" or "hook". Albright[15] assumes this position and suggests that the task in question is to break part of the Jebusite backbone. One could not come any closer to an efficient paralysis! But other scholars use this understanding to interpret *ṣinnôr* as a type of weapon. Here, too, the *w*^{e} is retracted so as to form a suffix on *ṣinnôr*: "whoever wants to smite the Jebusites will strike with his *ṣinnôr*."[16]

---

[13] J.J.Glück, "The Conquest of Jerusalem in the Account of II Sam 5:6-8a", in *Biblical Essays* (Stellenbosch, 1966), pp.98ff., understands the word in this sense, but gets something quite different out of it. He reads *w*^{e}*jigga'* as a consecutive imperfect of which David is the subject, and takes the notion "he touched his penis" to signify a gesture which featured in conjunction with the swearing of oaths: ". . . and he swore an oath (that that man will be chief and captain)". Yet another false combination with 1 Chron 11!

[14] In addition to which, one might ask to what the blind could possibly have to do with such a context.

[15] (1922), pp.288f.

[16] In this event the *b*^{e} is to be understood instrumentally, and "the lame and the blind" are a compound direct object. But the object of the verb *naga'* is otherwise always introduced by a preposition, generally *b*^{e}.

Sukenik[17] also thinks he is able to define *ṣinnôr* more closely. He, too, proceeds on the basis of the Arabic sense of "flesh-hook", and proposes that it is a matter of a three-pronged instrument like a trident, specimens of which have been found in excavations in Gezer and Byblos. It is a hunting instrument which Sukenik compares with Poseidon's three-pronged instrument in Greek mythology; but in primitive cultures, hunting implements are frequently also weapons. And Sukenik goes even further. Most others who interpret *ṣinnôr* as a weapon are forced to surrender the parallel in Ps 42:8; Sukenik, however, imports the "weapon" sense into the psalm as well and holds that the idea is that of the trident of God, by means of which he whips the sea into a froth. Sukenik's theory strikes me as extremely far-fetched; one might be willing to forgive the Jebusites their scorn, if they had seen their attackers armed with "flesh-hooks".[18]

As was mentioned above, *ṣinnôr* is most often taken to signify "water-course", "conduit", and it is seen in relation to Jerusalem's water-supply from the spring of Gihon in the Kidron Valley. In 1867, Ch. Warren found on the east slope of the Ophel mound an underground passage which ended in a vertical shaft fourteen metres deep. Here it will have been possible to haul water up from the spring, if water was first led via a horizontal tunnel in the side of the cliff into a large basin directly beneath the vertical shaft. Warren himself did not connect his discovery with 2 Sam 5, but this was done shortly afterwards by an Anglican priest in Jerusalem, W.F.Birch, who was much interested in archaeology and Biblical history. In a number of short notes[19] he identified *ṣinnôr* with the underground passage and, uncritically employing 1 Chron 11 to illuminate the circumstances very imaginatively, he suggested that Joab had crawled up the shaft alone into the town, after which he managed to open the gates for David and his men. Birch went on to say that Joab was not entirely alone, as he happened to have an ally in the town to assist him. Moreover, Birch knew the identity of the latter: it was Araunah the Jebusite, whose threshing-floor was

---

17 "The Account of David's Capture of Jerusalem", *JPOS* 8 (1928), pp.12ff. Sukenik can support his argument in part by LXX "dagger"; however, LXX Ps 42:8 takes *ṣinnôr* to mean "waterfall".

18 Moreover, David and his men are equipped with swords; cf. e.g. 1 Sam 25:13.

19 *PEF, Quarterly Statements*, 1878-91.

later to be bought by David as the site for his projected temple construction. To Birch, this explains why Araunah was spared while the rest of the inhabitants were reduced to invalidism or simply killed.

If this theory was hyper-imaginative, it was nevertheless powerfully supported by L.-H.Vincent's detailed and very careful studies[20] in connexion with M.Parker's excavations in 1909-11. Furthermore, the objection that Joab's feat would have been physically impossible seemed to have been dealt with by the fact that one of Parker's team, equipped with some sort of crutches under both arms,—the shaft is two metres in diameter—and with the aid of one of his colleagues, managed to work his way up the shaft in the course of half an hour.[21] Since that time it has practically been accepted as fact that David's conquest of Jerusalem took place in this fashion, and the *y^ebusi* i v.6 has often been taken to signify a guard who will have been stationed either at the entrance to the shaft, at its exit, or, conceivably, in both places. Of course, as long as the so-called Macalister's Wall higher up the slope was regarded as the Jebusite city wall, there was always the objection that Joab's feat of derring-do would not have got him into the city. In this event the context had to be understood to imply that Joab managed to block the entrance to the passage or the opening of the shaft, and thus to deprive the inhabitants of the town of their water-supply.

This understanding of *w^eyigga' baṣṣinnôr* has made itself increasingly felt in recent times. However, one might be tempted to think that cutting the massive passage in the bedrock was an unnecessarily great piece of engineering, if in the end it could not even reach within the city wall. Fortunately, Kathleen Kenyon's discovery of the original, pre-Davidic city wall farther down the slope during her excavations on the Ophel mound in 1961-67 demonstrated that the entrance to the passage will have been inside the town, which rendered the theory about Joab's heroic act probable.

---

20 Extensively described in L.-H.Vincent, *Jérusalem sous terre* (London, 1911), pp.37ff., and again in "Le Sinnor dans la Prise de Jérusalem", *RB* 33 (1924), pp.357ff., where he defends his theory against Dalman and Albright. Vincent's studies have provided the basis for all subsequent discussions of the canal system from the Gihon Spring.

21 As depicted by Vincent in *RB* 33 (1924), p.365. Y.Shiloh relates in a preliminary report (*IEJ* 29 (1979), p.246) that some of the participants in his excavation crawled up through the shaft "aided by professional alpinists . . . and by means of climbing equipment. . .". Joab will hardly have had either such training or such assistants!

Nevertheless, it was possible to have one's doubts about the likelihood of the whole thing, and I can remember a day in April of 1962, when Kathleen Kenyon was taking her staff on a tour of the various excavational fields. We stood and regarded an exposed section of the city wall. There was a cut in an enormous boulder in the lowest course of the wall which served as an outlet for water. And then we heard K, as she was called by her friends and co-workers, mumble to herself: "I'd hate to think of Joab getting up that way!" And in her book *Digging Up Jerusalem* she also takes the traditional view of Joab's heroic feat as fact.[22]

Much of what has been written about the views I have related here almost sounds like a film scenario. And what marvellous drama! Blind and lame Jebusites are ranged along the walls of Jerusalem while the leaders of the town shout out their scorn of David and his men, a disorganized rabble armed with flesh-hooks. And then, in the thick of night the daredevil Joab works his way up the shaft and meets his accomplice, Araunah, and then creeps out to let David and his men into the town. One must acknowledge the fact that, if the Jebusites were so self-confident that they failed to protect their all-important water-supply effectively, then they deserved to have their town captured!

However, a shot across the bows of the theory has been fired by those who claim that the underground passage did not exist in David's time. Magnus Ottosson maintains[23] that engineering like that which produced Warren's Shaft could not have been carried out prior to Iron Age II. Likewise, Y.Shiloh claims that it is contemporaneous with other water systems known to date from Iron II, while still others hold that it was cut in the Late Bronze Age.[24] Now I do not know how you would go about dating cuts in bedrock. Unfortunately, no one has cut an inscription in the rock which might help date it, as is the case with Hezekiah's tunnel. If it really does

---

22 (London, 1974), pp.98f.

23 *Tidsskrift for Teologi og Kirke* 60 (1989), pp.263ff. Ottosson proposes instead to interpret *ṣinnôr* as the moat or fosse which seems to have been cut into the bedrock north of the Ophel mound as an extension of the natural depression which divided the southeastern prominence from the northeastern one. It was part of the defensive system in the northern section, which is by nature the weakest area, which is why the town has always been attacked from the north. I doubt whether it would be appropriate to term such a moat *ṣinnôr*, if the actual meaning of the term is "pipe". It had in any case nothing to do with water!

24 *IEJ* 29 (1979), p.246.

derive from Iron Age II, then I find it remarkable that someone chose shortly afterward to supplement such an extensive construction with one that was even more extensive. After all, more water does not flow from a spring just because one constructs more aqueducts for it!

Even if it were correct that the underground passage dates from the Late Bronze Age and is pre-Davidic, I still feel that the theory about Joab's heroic feat is a misunderstanding of the context. This is not because of unimaginative scepticism; rather, it is because I regard it as impossible that the verb *naga'* could be used to describe crawling up the bedrock walls of a shaft.[25] Others have also been aware of this fact, and they have claimed that "the town" was the original object of *w^e^yigga'*, but that it has dropped out of the present text, which must originally have read "...and reaches the town through *ṣinnôr*". However, as I mentioned previously, *b^e^* is the preposition usually employed to introduce the object of *naga'*. The basic meaning of the verb is to touch something, but it is used a number of times in the sense of a violent contact which may be translated as "to hit" or "to strike".[26]

I therefore agree with Stoebe and others who understand the context in question in such a way that David actually accepts the Jebusites' asssertion that he is not able to conquer the town. He accordingly gives orders as to how to get the town into his power, which is to be accomplished by cutting off the inhabitants of the town from their water-supply. It will therefore not be long before they have to surrender. It is hardly likely that we shall ever know how *sinnôr* looked or was constructed. It was not necessarily a channel that was cut in the bedrock under the town. It could easily be a question of a—presumably covered—channel which led the water from the source of the spring to a point so close to the town that it will always have been possible to get water during a siege, provided that the enemy had not cut the channel.

I have found no reference to 2 Chron 32:3f,30 in the discussions of 2 Sam 5:8. There is no question of a parallel here, and by no means a verbal one. Most importantly, the word *sinnôr* does not occur here. I nevertheless find it reasonable to regard the passage as

---

[25] Which is why scholars sometimes—quite arbitrarily—change the text to read *wayya'al*, in which case it is again 1 Chron 11:6 which interferes!

[26] E.g. 1 Sam 6:9; Ezek 17:10; Job 1:19.

a sort of analogy, as there is reference to the water-supply in connexion with the defense of Jerusalem. Admittedly, it is possible to read the text in such a way as to suggest that the idea is to prevent the enemy from finding water, so that thirst can force him to give up, that is, a parallel to 2 Sam 5, but with the signs reversed! However, I do not believe this reading, or rather, it could in any event have been, at best, only a side-motive. Although it may have been possible to make things difficult for him, a besieging enemy would always have been able to secure water from the surrounding areas. Nor do I know how it might be possible to "stop up" a spring, so that it stops running. The meaning of *satam* has something to do with the hidden or concealed, as, for example, in Ezek 28:3. The idea may actually be that Hezekiah covers up several water-courses and collects them into a single course through the tunnel which he had dug through the bedrock under Jerusalem.

Since the Gihon spring was of such decisive significance for Jerusalem, is it not reasonable to suppose that the attempt was made at a much earlier time to ensure the water-supply in case of emergency, even though this did not happen via extensive technical and engineering works? Thus, on the assumption that the Hebrew text in 2 Sam 5:8a is correct, I think the translation must be: "And David said on this day: 'Everyone who wants to smite the Jebusites must put his hand on *ṣinnôr*", however that aquaduct may have looked![27]

---

27 There are two problems which I have not touched on here, as they have no direct bearing on the question of the meaning of *sinnôr*. One has to do with the question as to how *m^{e}ṣudat ṣiyyôn* related to the town of Jerusalem. Like most scholars, I feel that these quantities are identical. However, it should be mentioned that already Vincent held that *ṣiyyôn* was originally only the name of a fortress complex in the southern part of the town, and that it was only this that David was trying to take. In recent times the same idea has been advocated by J.P.Floss, *David und Jerusalem. Ziele und Folgen des Stadteroberungsberichtes 2 Sam 5,6-9 literarwissenschaftlich betrachtet* (St. Ottilien, 1982). According to Floss there is only question of a fortress, as the Israelites had had contact with the city itself for quite some time, cf. Judg 1:21. This might remind us of the situation in Maccabaean times, with the Syrian fortress in Jerusalem. However, the town covered a much greater extent at that time than it did in David's day.

The second question has to do with how "on this day", 2 Sam 5:8, is to be understood. To be completely accurate, are we dealing with the day *before* the conquest? In this event it would be reasonable to suppose that the following words suggest how the conquest is to take place. However, if the phrase refers to—again, to be completely accurate—the day *after* the conquest, this would naturally support the theories about the *ṣinnôr* as some part or other of the Jebusite anatomy, or as some sort of weapon with which the Jebusites are to be grievously injured. If one insists on chronological connexion between the verses, then one inclines to the latter: in v.7 David takes the town, after which he announces what is to be done with the inhabitants. However, one cannot squeeze the text so as to produce such a logical chronology. If it is correct to assume that there was originally a "primary" lapidary narrative, then v. 8a served as a notice recounting how the conquest took place, and *bayyōm hahū'* was not chronologically part of the original account.

YOU SHALL SURELY NOT DIE

by

A.S. KAPELRUD

Oslo

In Christian theology, and even more so in popular opinion, the interpretation of the events narrated in Gen chs. 2-3 is usually based on Paul's understanding and use of the narrative in his letters. Sin came into the world through one man, the first man created by God. Only another man, Jesus Christ, could change this situation through his death on the cross and bring man back into fellowship with God, Rom 5:12-21, I Cor 15:21f.

In his view of sin as a corruption of man's ideal life with God, Paul is in harmony with a general way of thinking in the Old Testament. As a well educated rabbi he had learnt interpretation from his youth on, and it was part of his whole view of life. It is more astonishing that the O.T. writers and editors did not use the ancient narrative when they spoke about sin, in, for example, Ps 51:2-7, 69:6.[1] The origin of sin was not a question that interested them. Sin was always there and had to be defeated, Rom 5:13, but the question of how it originated was not relevant.[2] Paul obviously went further in his conclusions than the O.T. writers and editors did. He has drawn out one special aspect of the narrative in Gen 2-3 which he discusses and underlines as the most important trait, especially seen in its relation to the life and death of Christ.

In all its simplicity the brief narrative includes also other aspects of real importance. If one starts with its genre it is clearly an etiological myth. The author wants to explain why man must toil with an unwilling soil to earn his living. That was obviously not the original God's intention when he created man. He was intended to live in a garden whose fruits and vegetables would give him the necessary

---

[1] C. Westermann, *Genesis 1-11*, BKAT I/1 (2. Aufl.; Neukirchen, 1976), pp. 376-377.

[2] H. Gunkel, *Genesis übersetzt und erklärt*, GHAT I/1 (5. Aufl.; Göttingen, 1922), p. 33; Westermann (1976), pp. 378-380.

nourishment. His wife was intended to live a free life in God's garden, without fear and anxiety, without toil and tears. But because she broke the rules and disobeyed the orders of God everything went wrong. Therefore she is destined to be attracted to her husband so that she bears him children in toil and pain.

The third party in the event, the snake, was feared because of its secret life on and in the ground, and the danger it represents for men and women. Why was it so secret in its ways, why so dangerous? What had it done, since it was obviously damned by God?

The etiological intention of the author (or maybe better: the narrator) is so obvious that one cannot omit the question: is it his chief intention? Paul gives a firm answer: his intention is to depict how sin came into man's life through his disobedience to God's will, Rom 5:12ff.

The two chapters containing the narrative of God's garden are actually so packed with important traits pertaining to man's life and situation in the world that it may be characterized as impossible to decide which of them the narrator wanted to emphasize. The narrative runs so smoothly and one trait segues into another so easily that no one seems to be emphasized more than the other. Two aspects have been touched upon above: the idea of original sin, strongly underlined by Paul, and the etiological aspect, which is clearly present.

The point of departure, however, for both these aspects lies in the words of YHWH Elohim in 2:11f.: "You may eat freely from all trees in the garden, but you must not eat from the tree of the knowledge of good and evil. On the day you eat from that you shall surely die". These words start the action in the narrative, leading to enormous consequences.

All these consequences have been discussed and described for centuries, and probably always will be discussed. In the words of YHWH Elohim only one consequence is mentioned: You shall surely die. The idea of death is here brought into the world of man, without any definition of what it means. To the narrator the fact of death was well known—a threatening fact. That this fact might be unknown to the first man did not enter his mind.

In Gen 3 the snake immediately takes up the question of a possible death, also he as if this were a well known phenomenon. To him death seems to be the central point, and he uses God's own words, with a slight, but decisive change: You shall surely *not* die, Gen 3:4. After having decided this matter so authoritatively, the snake turns to the positive sides connected with the tree God has forbidden them to eat from. Its fruits would make them like God to know good and evil. Again the narrator speaks from his own experience: in human life both good and evil are found.

The woman to whom the words of the snake are directed has no possibility to determine what is good and what evil. She likes the fruit, and she and the man eat—and have their eyes opened for a new understanding of life. Here the narrator starts his etiological explanations. Human beings got their power to think and judge in this way, which also made them masters of all other living beings and nature.

In this matter the snake had indicated what would happen. The result was astonishing for the two human beings, who reacted in a way that in the narrative also has an etiological character: man and woman should not show themselves naked. They have to hide certain parts of their bodies . This was not God's intention, but a result of man's and woman's naive belief in the words of the snake.

Also in another respect the snake seems to have been right. The two did not fall dead on the ground. Instead, they continue to walk in the garden, now hiding from God, well knowing that they had acted contrary to his word and fearing his punishment. Their new insight gives them even more reason to fear God's response.

The snake, however, was not right, as the narrator and his audience (and readers) well knew. Death is every man's and woman's part, the only inevitable event for all. That death did not come immediately to those who broke God's orders, is not special for this narrative. It is a phenomenon which is found also in Sumerian and Babylonian myths. Adapa, who gives the wrong answer to the highest god Anu, does not lose his life, but is deprived of the possibility of obtaining everlasting life. Also illness and all kinds of misery follow in the wake of his loss. In the case of Gilgamesh death is already present, but the plant of life, which was to give him back his youth, is snatched by a snake, and Gilgamesh has to return to ordinary life, with death as its end.

In Adapa's and Gilgamesh's cases the narratives are centered on the question of everlasting life. That is the totally dominating theme. It mirrors the fear of man in the face of death as the end of his life on earth. Nothing else can be set against this fact: the threatening end.

The mighty Gilgamesh epos takes up important questions of life, the relationship between man and nature, the constant fight against evil forces. But it sums it all up in the great narrative of the Gilgamesh's struggle to attain everlasting life. There the decisive question of man's life is taken up, to show what it is all about. To be or not to be was always the final question.

But the Gilgamesh epos also has an additional tablet, no XII. It may not have been part of the Babylonian edition, but it propounds ideas which are found in other ancient myths from this part of the world, as, for example, the Adapa myth. Gilgamesh has his old friend and co-fighter Enkidu called forth from the underworld. Enkidu gives a dark picture of his existence in the world of shadows. Death is not simply the end. It is a constant pain which prolonged the pains of life: illness, loneliness, lack of helpers, hopelessness. All this is part of death and accompanies it, on earth as well as in the underworld.

In the myth of Adapa illness, poverty, and fatal events follow in the wake of Adapa's loss of everlasting life. Death and evil are interrelated. They are not seen as part of a god's creation, but rather spring out of evil forces which are not always expressly defined, as in the case of Adapa.

In three different narratives we find depicted apparently accidental events of an unimportant character, which nevertheless cause everlasting life to be lost, with death, pain and illness as the final result for man and woman. What forces were supposed to be active behind these events?

In the case of Adapa it seems to be easy to answer that question. His councillor Ea, the freshwater god, gave him the answers he ought to give to the questions of Anu, the god of heaven. Adapa followed his advice—and lost his chance. As the narrative runs Ea seems to have foreseen the questions which were going to be put by Anu. If that is the idea Ea must consciously have advised Adapa to answer in a way which necessarily would deprive him of the possibility of attaining everlasting life. Man should not be allowed to rise to the same height as the gods. There will always be a difference, according to the old Near Eastern myths.

The same view is found in the case of Utnapishtim and Gilgamesh. The former was taken up into the world of the gods, but he was not given full status; he never became a god. Gilgamesh was denied everlasting life directly, but with the help of Utnapishtim and his wife he got the chance through his own efforts. He really manages to find and get hold of the plant of life, but a snake steals it from him. In this way, which looks superficially like a pure accident, he loses his possibility to attain everlasting life.

But are these incidents really accidental? Did people in the ancient world really think that the fate of mankind was decided for all future through an accident? The question obliges us to take a closer look at the narratives. As already mentioned the Adapa myth was a pattern of its own. The structure lies in broad daylight, revealed by the narrator.

When Adapa is summoned to the chief god Anu, the god of heaven, he turns to his sponsor Ea, the freshwater god, to get advice. Ea tells him to decline the offers Anu may suggest to him. Adapa follows his advice, with the result that he also declines the offer which would have assured him everlasting life. Anu asks him: "Come now, Adapa! Why didst thou neither eat nor drink? Thou shalt not have (eternal) life! Ah, perverse mankind!" Adapa answers: "Ea, my master, commanded me: Thou shalt not eat, thou shalt not drink." Anu then gives the final verdict: "Take him away and return him to his earth."[3]

There must be certain ideas behind this myth. The main idea is mentioned above: the impression that the gods did not want man as their equal. And the only ones who could prevent man from attainimg a godlike status were the gods themselves. In the case of Ea there are two possibilities: either he knew the importance of Anu's questions, or he happened, by chance, to spoil Adapa's possibility to attain everlasting life. Naturally, there is no sure answer to this question, but the first possibility seems to be the more likely.

But why should it be Ea, the wise god, who causes man's tragedy? That it is Ea is probably not accidental. Ea, Sumerian Enki, is not only god of wisdom and magical craft, but also god of the earth and its fresh water. In this last capacity he was god of the underworld and what lives there. In ancient times he was considered to be the creator of the earth, until this act was transferred to his son Marduk, the chief god of Babylon. To Ea, Adapa is only an insignificant servant who has no claim to everlasting life. The god of the earth—and wisdom—closes man's door to eternity. The ancient narrator knew: that was no accident. The departing words of Anu have a double meaning: "Take him away and return him to his earth!"

---

[3] "Adapa", *ANET* (Princeton, 1969), p. 102.

The nature of the role-play between Anu and Ea is not evident in the fragment of the story from Tell Amarna which relates the main story. But in Fragment D from the library of Ashurbanipal more details are indicated. "Anu laughed aloud of the doing of Ea, (saying): "Of the gods of heaven and earth, as many as there be, whoever gave such a command? Who will make his own command exceed the command of Anu?"

However, Anu decrees release for the city of Ea and that his priesthood should glorify it in the future. But for "Adapa the human offspring, (who) lordlike, broke the south wind's wing, went up to heaven—and so forth—(and) what ill he has brought upon mankind, (and) the disease that he brought upon the bodies of men, these Ninkarrak will allay".[4]

One of the conclusions one may draw from this fragment is that Anu accepts Ea's action and even rewards him for it. Adapa, however, not only loses his possibility of everlasting life, but also brings ill upon mankind. The gods, in contrast, help man through the healing goddess.

What happened may be summarized thus: 1. Adapa acted rashly in breaking the south wind's wing. 2. The god of the freshwater, Ea, tricked him into giving the wrong answers to Anu. 3. Adapa, summoned to the chief god Anu, gave the wrong answers. 4. He was deprived of the possibility of obtaining everlasting life. 5. In the wake of this decision followed all kinds of toil and ill.

When we turn to the story of Gilgamesh we find a broader and more detailed narrative. 1. Gilgamesh toiled to find the plant of life. 2. When he had found it, he was inattentive and lost it. 3. The plant was snatched away by a snake. 4. The possibility of everlasting life was lost.

While the role of the gods is obvious in the Adapa myth, it is hidden in the Gilgamesh story. But Siduri, "who dwells by the deep sea", explains to Gilgamesh that the gods did not want man to attain the status they enjoy themselves.[5] The first step, then, must be to prevent man from getting everlasting life. This intention of the gods is clearly expressed in the Gilgamesh epos. But what about the snake, who really does the work? That takes us to a brief discussion

---

[4] *ANET* (1969), pp. 102-103.

[5] "The Epic of Gilgamesh" X:III, *ANET* (1969), p. 90.

of the figure and the role of the snake in ancient Near Eastern mythology.

The narrative in the Gilgamesh epos gives a picture of how the snake was apprehended: "A serpent snuffed the fragrance of the plant, and came up and carried off the plant. Going back it shed its slough".[6]

Three special features are mentioned: 1. It came up, either from the earth or from the water, both elements under the command of the mighty Ea. 2. It acted in a hurry, dangerously and unavoidably, before man could prevent it. 3. It shed its slough and became young again.

The snake thus has an ability not given to man and is supposed to have unusual powers. It was therefore worshipped as divine, and pictures of it were used as idols. Such idols have been found all over the ancient Near East. Archaeological excavations have shown that they were usual in Canaanite times and in the early Israelite periods. Places where they have been found are, for example, Hazor, Bet-Shan, Bet-Shemesh, Shechem and Gezer. The great number of them indicates that some kind of serpent cult must have been usual.

That this was so, can be seen in the Old Testament. The dramatic story in Num 21:6-9 tells us about an attack by poisonous snakes which killed Israelites in the desert. The people asked Moses to help them. He prayed for the people, and YHWH said to Moses: Make a fiery serpent and set it on a pole, and every one who is bitten, when he sees it, shall live. Then Moses made a bronze serpent and set it on a pole, and those who looked at it were saved.

The dangerous nature of snakes is underlined here, but also the healing power, indicating that a serpent was something more than an ordinary beast. What is further emphasized is the point that the cult of the bronze serpent is instituted by YHWH himself and established through the authority of Moses. That indicates that the cult was so widely spread that it could not be dismissed, but had to be accepted within the YHWH cult.

That it was regarded as a *foreign* cult is told in 2 Kings 18 about King Hezekiah of Judah: "He broke in pieces the bronze serpent that Moses had made, for until those days the people of Israel had burned incense to it, it was called Nehustan", 2 Kings 18:4.

---

6 "The Epic of Gilgamesh" XI:288f, *ANET* (1969), p. 96.

The fact that the people worshipped the bronze serpent shows that it was considered an idol, probably of a god who represented chtonic forces. Hezekiah had no doubt: it had no place in the YHWH religion. Not even the authority of Moses could save it.

The narrator in 2 Kings says directly that the people had burned incense to the bronze serpent for a long time. Also in their daily life they were used to seeing the serpent as a beast with special powers, both of a demonic and a healing kind, the latter probably connected with the knowledge that it could change its slough and thus be rejuvenated. The serpent was no usual animal, it possessed formidable abilities.

That was well known to both the hearers and readers of the Gilgamesh epos and even more so to those of the narrative in Gen 3. The Genesis narrative is so consciously built up that there can be no doubt that the narrator used the figure of the serpent in order to say something very important to the people. Actually, every word about the serpent has a special meaning, when seen against the background of the ancient view of the animal as it is painted in the Old Testament, as well as in the texts of the neighbouring peoples: the serpent as a divine force, representing the chtonic world.

Already the first word in the narrative in Gen 3, the word for snake, *naḥash*, may give some associations to another word of the same root, meaning magic curse, bewitchment, Num 23:23, 24:1. Such associations disappear in translations, but may have been easily discernible in Hebrew. The narrator has also used other puns. In the third word in v. 1 the snake is described as crafty, *'ārūm*, in contrast to the human beings, who found themselves naked, *'ērumim*, v. 7, cf. vv. 10-11. The snake was not only craftier than the other animals, it was also craftier than the naive man and woman, who were in any case "naked".

The way in which the serpent is introduced in Gen 3 is remarkable. The narrative says: "The serpent was more crafty than any wild creature that YHWH God had made", v. 1. As the construction runs the serpent is not necessarily among the creatures made by God. Nothing, however, prevents the interpretation that also the serpent was among these creatures. If the latter interpretation was intended by the author one might have expected another mode of expression. Nevertheless, two interpretations are possible. 1. The serpent is not part of God's creation. That means that ancient ideas of the snake as a creature representing chtonic powers of a divine character were present. The special fact that the serpent is able to talk and to have certain information supports this interpretation ? That the serpent is part of God's creation was a necessity for a monotheistic author. There existed no other divine forces, and the snake was only a creature among other creatures, as emphasized in the curse of it in vv. 14-15.

The second alternative covers the form the narrative is given in the text. The monotheistic tendency is distinct, but, as so often in Old Testament texts, ancient ideas shimmer through the present form of the narrative. No ordinary snake could talk, no ordinary snake could imagine what God intended to do. There is a discrepancy here that can only be explained if an original narrative has been monotheisized. The serpent in the story was originally a foreign (Canaanite) god, who tried to trick man and woman away from their god YHWH. As in the cases of Adapa and Gilgamesh, the human beings have no chance to stand up against the cunning of the chtonic powers; they are beaten.

The story in Gen 3 shows traces of ancient serpent cult, but the narrator tries to show that even if the serpent is really dangerous, it is nevertheless only a creature over whom man may rule. The temptation to which man and woman were exposed by it is real enough, but it was not compelling. That is why both the man and the woman have to take their respective punishments. But what happened was no rebellion from their side. Here is no Titan motive. They are tricked by a force whose power they do not apprehend. Like Adapa and Gilgamesh, they have no possiblity of resisting, and thus they lose their chance to attain everlasting life. The man will have to return to the earth from which he was taken, like Adapa, and the woman will be obliged to pass on life, hidden in her name *ḥawwāh*, to new generations.[7]

In discussions of the narrative emphasis is often laid on the etiological element in it. It is obviously present and has surely made a deep impression on hearers and readers of the story. But this element is only a part of the whole event. In a story such as this the climax usually comes at the end. And it is in the end that the decisive blow falls. Man and woman are definitely locked out from the last

---

[7] A.S. Kapelrud, "*ḥawwāh*", *Theologisches Wörterbuch zum Alten Testament*, hrsg. G.J. Botterweck und H. Ringgren, Band II (Stuttgart, 1977), pp. 794- 798; E. Nielsen, *Første Mosebog fortolket* (København, 1987), p. 71.

possibility to attain everlasting life. They are reduced to the status of beings who are doomed to toil, pain, sweat, and tears, and finally death. Everlasting life would have saved them from all this.

The punishments declared to man and woman must not be seen as isolated. Actually, they are not mere punishments. They are results which accompany the fact that man and woman had lost the possibility of everlasting life, which also included health and happiness. How this connection was seen, is told directly in the story of Adapa. After he had returned to the earth and had lost his chance to eternal life, disease, toil, and pain followed as a result of his new situation, not only for him, but also for coming generations.

The same connection is also found in Gen 3. The loss of eternal life brought all kinds of misery into the life of mankind. Eternal life was a quality, and when this quality was lost misery took its place. That was announced to the man and the woman at once. Their life on earth was going to be hard.

Also the words to the snake presage a hard life. But here the emphasis is laid on other elements than in the words to the man and the woman. First the responsibility is mentioned "Because you did this." Here it is said expressly that the serpent was the culprit. He had to take his punishment, but the words to the serpent have certain contents which have to be noticed. First, it is emphasized that the serpent had a special position among all cattle and all wild animals, being more cursed than any other animal. That very hard curse marks out the serpent as something different from other beasts. Even if the snake was feared because of its aggression and its apparently mysterious ways, it is striking that it is placed in this unique position, in a country where wolves, bears and lions were well known threats. Again ancient belief shimmers through: the serpent represented dangerous underground forces, whom man could not easily defeat. A talking serpent, who knew God's plans, could not possibly be an ordinary beast. The Christian interpretation that sees the Devil in the figure of the serpent is here close to the apprehension of the ancient narrator.[8]

But there is also another aspect in the curse upon the serpent. At the same time as the words emphasize the unique position of the serpent, they also underline that it is nevertheless only a beast, creeping

---

[8] Against Westermann (1976), pp. 323-325.

on the earth and eating dust. The monotheistic tendency takes over here: there existed no divine power apart from the one God. After all, the serpent was only the creature one could observe creeping on its belly in the dust of the earth, dangerous, but an enemy that could be crushed. However, no other animal was cursed in this way, no other animal had such a relationship to mankind.

Two different aspects are present in this view of the serpent. One of them is in accordance with the words to the man and the woman, the serpent being treated as a simple creature, the other one full of reminiscenses from a time and a world when the serpent was considered a representative of a divine underworld. It was in this latter capacity that it tricked the man and the woman and deprived them of their possibility of attaining everlasting life.

The last act in the story is the fulfilment of the sentence. The man and the woman are taken out of the protecting garden and left to live outside it for the rest of their lives, which were to be ended by death. There could be no return. There would be no everlasting life.

Even if the story is also an etiological myth the real climax of the story is here. The loss of everlasting life is the decisive event. Here is no talk of sin, but only of the greater knowledge which man had achieved.[9] Man had lost life, but won the necessary knowledge to master his situation. As the goddess Ninkarrak was placed to help man and woman in their trouble in the Adapa myth, so their new knowledge was going to help them when they were driven away from the Tree of Life. The monotheocizing narrator in Gen 3 could not allow any goddess to appear in a story that already includes a talking serpent. In his narrative, through their grasping of the fruit from the Tree of Knowledge man and woman had attained the resource which was supposed to help them in all kinds of trouble. Through his cunning, the serpent had opened a road for them to a knowledge, which could not compensate for the loss of eternal life, but which could help them to bear that loss.

Conclusions

For several centuries, especially in the 8th-6th B.C., but beginning long before that, there existed in Near Eastern countries ideas and traditions that man had once had the possibility of living eternally.

---

9 Westermann (1976), pp. 378-380; Gunkel (1922), p. 33.

However, this possibility was lost, not because man "sinned", but because chtonic forces, mostly in the form of a serpent, or in a direct encroachment by a god connected with such forces, deprived him of that possibility. The pattern has different forms, as shown above, but the main idea is the same: man is deprived of his possibility of attaining everlasting life by unexpected forces.

Scholars have long ago seen the parallels to Gen 3 in Near Eastern religions, but they have concentrated too much on the details instead of seeing the main issue in the narratives and have therefore disregarded the importance of the parallels.[10] This negative valuation had its root in a special attitude: only identical parallels were considered real parallels, while other ones were seen as accidental. In some kind of a protest attitude against the so-called "Religio-historical school" the importance of the context of the parallels was emphasized, but at the same time the *main* context: life—loss of life—death, was neglected.

Among "foreign" traits in Gen 3 are the serpent, the garden, the Tree of Life[11], the seduction, the future trouble, the helping hand of God, the returning to earth, the cherubim who watched the holy place.[12] All these traits reflect influence from the great cultures that dominated in the ancient Near Eastern world. Together they reflect a human wish and struggle to attain everlasting life and escape death. And they are features in stories that describe how strong forces of a non-human kind deprived man of his possibility to attain the life he wanted. Many details in the stories may be—and are—different, but the dominating idea is evident: everlasting life is lost, death is the fate of man, with all that that entails: illness, toil, and trouble. At the same time, there is a small note of hope: man will be helped in his trouble, either through his new insight, or through the helping hand of a god.[13]

---

10 E.g. Gunkel (1922), pp. 38f; Westermann (1977), p. 377.
11 Nielsen (1987), p. 53.
12 Nielsen (1987), p. 72.
13 Nielsen (1987), p. 73, p. 79.

CYCLE PRIMITIF D'ABRAHAM ET CONTEXTE GÉOGRAPHICO-HISTORIQUE

by

ANDRÉ LEMAIRE

Paris

Les traditions bibliques sur Abram/Abraham, contenues essentiellement dans Gn 12-25:18, restent très discutées. Les recherches sur l'histoire de leur rédaction et de leur interpretation historique ont été marquées par les livres de Th.L. Thompson[1] et de J. Van Seters[2] qui ont largement contribué à une remise en question de leur historicité et, pour le deuxième[3], à une datation tardive de la rédaction "yahviste" repoussée à l'époque exilique ou postexilique. Un certain nombre d'exégètes semblent s'être ralliés récemment à cette position, ainsi R. Kilian: "der theologisch orientierte und üblicherweise als Jahwist bezeichnete Autor ist in der exilisch-nachexilischen Zeit anzusetzen"[4], et A. de Pury: "Il s'avère donc difficile d'attribuer ne serait-ce qu'un seul élément de la substance narrative de Gen. 12-24 à une tradition indubitablement ancienne"[5]. D'une position majoritaire affirmant l'historicité des patriarches et leur datation à l'époque du Bronze Moyen[6], l'exégèse contemporaine semble être passée, en vingt ans, à une interprétation repoussant la rédaction des traditions patriarcales à l'époque

---

1 *The Historicity of the Patriarchal Narratives. The Quest for the Historical Abraham*, BZAW 133 (Berlin, 1974).

2 *Abraham in History and Tradition* (New Haven/London, 1975).

3 On notera les critiques du premier au deuxième: Th.L. Thompson, *The Origin Tradition of Ancient Israel I. The Literary Formation of Genesis and Exodus 1-23*, JSOT SS 55 (Sheffield, 1987).

4 "Nachtrag und Neuorientierung. Anmerkungen zum Jahwisten in der Abrahamserzählungen", dans M. Görg (éd.), *Die Väter Israels. Beiträge zur Theologie der Patriarchenüberlieferungen im Alten Testament. Festschrift J. Scharbert* (Stuttgart, 1989), pp. 155-167, spéc. p. 166.

5 "La tradition patriarcale en Genèse 12-35", dans A. de Pury (éd.), *Le Pentateuque en question* (Genève, 1989), pp. 259-270, spéc. p. 262.

6 Cf. encore R. de Vaux, *Histoire ancienne d'Israël I. Des origines à l'installation en Canaan* (Paris, 1971), pp. 250-252.

exilique ou postexilique, leur déniant pratiquement toute valeur historique.

Si le rejet de la datation d'une "époque patriarcale" au Bronze Moyen semble tout à fait fondée[7] car il paraît impossible de faire remonter la protohistoire de l'ancien Israël au-delà du XIIIe s. av. J.-C.[8], faut-il, pour autant, repousser la première mise par écrit des traditions patriarcales à l'époque exilique ou post-exilique?

Les différentes positions exégétiques actuelles manifestent la difficulté d'identifier et de dater les différents niveaux de rédaction et donc les plus anciens textes bibliques. On peut distinguer essentiellement trois approches:

1 – Une approche linguistique essayant d'identifier les textes présentant la morphologie, la syntaxe et le vocabulaire les plus anciens.

2 – Une approche de critique littéraire recherchant la couche rédactionnelle la plus ancienne et la datant d'après sa phraséologie et sa thématique, dans la mesure où on les retrouve dans d'autres textes bibliques considérés comme anciens.

3 – Une approche historique recherchant les références ou allusions à des évènements de l'histoire israélite ou proche-orientale connus par ailleurs; cette approche peut être directe ou indirecte; dans ce dernier cas, on recherche le contexte historique dans lequel ces textes semblent prendre la signification la plus riche et la plus concrète.

Les lacunes de la documentation extra-biblique limitent considérablement la probabilité des conclusions des deux premières approches risquant d'utiliser, en fait, un raisonnement circulaire. C'est pourquoi nous tenterons plutôt ici d'utiliser la troisième en essayant de resituer les traditions abrahamiques les plus anciennes dans leur contexte primitif.

L'approche historique directe semblant décevante puisqu'aucun des évènements évoqués en Gn 12-25:18 ne nous est connu par ailleurs, nous nous concentrerons sur l'approche historique in-

---

[7] Cf. A. Lemaire, "Recherches actuelles sur les origines de l'ancien Israël", *JA* 270 (1982), pp. 5-24.

[8] Id., "Aux origines d'Israël: La montagne d'Ephraïm et le territoire de Manassé (XIII-XIe siècle av. J.-C.)" et "La montagne de Juda (XIII-XIe siècle av. J.-C.)", dans E.M. Laperrousaz (éd.), *La Protohistoire d'Israël* (Paris, 1990), pp. 183-292 et 293-298.

directe: chercher le milieu dans lequel les détails du texte semblent prendre leur sens le plus riche et le plus concret.

Parmi ces détails du texte, on remarque particulièrement le rôle que semblent jouer certains toponymes. Depuis longtemps, les exégètes ont reconnu que chaque tradition patriarcale semble primitivement liée à un horizon géographique précis; "les attaches géographiques sont différentes: la tradition d'Abraham est surtout fixée à Hébron-Mambré et celle d'Isaac est très fortement ancrée à Bersabée et au puits voisin de Lahaï Roï"[9]. Cependant l'horizon géographique primitif des patriarches peut avoir été quelque peu obscurci par les rédactions postérieures unificatrices.

Ainsi, dans les traditions abrahamiques:

– "Harân" (Gn 11:31,32; 12:4,5) semble repris du cycle de Jacob (Gn 27:43; 28:10; 29:4), de même que "Sichem" (Gn 12:6; cf. 33:18,19; 34:2...)[10], "Béthel" (Gn 12:8; 13:3; cf. 28:19; 31:1...), "l'Egypte" (Gn 12:10-13:1; cf. 37:25,28,36...), "Aram-Naharayim" et "Nahor" (Gn 24:10).

– "Gérar" (Gn 20:1,2) vient probablement du cycle d'Isaac (Gn 26:1,6,17,20,26), de même que "Béérshéba" (Gn 21:14,31-33; 22:19; cf. 26:23,33; 28:10), "le puits de Lahaï Roï" (Gn 16:14; 24:62; 25:11) et "le pays des Philistins" (Gn 21:32,34; cf. 26:1,8...).

– Par ailleurs, la région de Sodome et des bords de la Mer Morte semble avoir été primitivement associée aux traditions particulières sur Loth (Gn 13:10,12,13; 14:2,8,10,12,17,21,22; 18:22,26; 19:1,28).

Si l'on tient compte de ce phénomène, la localisation d'Abraham à Mambré-Hébron[11] (Gn 13:18; 14:13,24; 18:1; 23:2,17,19; 25:9) ressort avec d'autant plus de clarté que c'est tout près de là, à Makpéla (Gn 23:9,17; 25:9), plus précisément dans "la caverne du champ de Makpéla, en face de Mambré, c'est à dire Hébron dans le pays de Canaan" (Gn 23:19), qu'est située la tombe de Sara et d'Abraham.

Si Mambré (cf. aussi Gn 35:27; 49:30; 50:13) et Makpéla (cf.

---

[9] R. de Vaux (1971), p. 163.

[10] Cf spécialement E. Nielsen, *Shechem* (Copenhagen, 1955), p. 215) auquel cette modeste recherche est dédiée.

[11] Cf., par ex., P. Weimar, "Abraham", dans M. Görg–B. Lang (éd.), *Neues Bibel-Lexikon* (Zürich, 1988), cols. 14-21, spéc. 19; K.A. Deurloo, "Narrative Geography in the Abraham Cycle", *OTS* 26 (1990), pp. 48-62, spéc. 62.

aussi Gn 49:30; 50:13) n'apparaissent que dans les légendes patriarcales, Hébron est attesté plus d'une cinquantaine de fois dans la Bible en dehors de la Genèse, cette ville s'appelant autrefois "Qiryat-Arba" (Jos 14:15; Jg 1:10; cf. Gn 23:2; 35:27; Jos 15:13,54; 20:7; 21:11; Ne 11:25). Si l'on met de côté la mention apparemment légendaire[12] de "Hohâm roi d'Hébron" en Jos 10:3 (cf. aussi 12:10), la tradition biblique ancienne nous précise surtout que la région d'Hébron était rattachée aux clans calébites (Jos 14:6-15; 15:13-14; 21:12; Jg 1:20; cf. Nb 13:6,22)[13] de la montagne de Juda (cf. Jos 15:54; 20:7).

Cette région d'Hébron et ces clans calébites jouent un rôle capital au début de l'histoire de David. C'est là que David se réfugie alors qu'il n'est encore qu'un chef de bande poursuivi par Saül dans la région de Ziph (1 S 23:14,15,19,24; 26:1,2 = Tell Zîf, 7 km au sud-est d'Hébron), de Maôn (1 S 23:24-25; 25:1-2 = Khirbet Ma'în, environ 14 km au sud d'Hébron) et de Carmel (1 S 25 = Khirbet Kirmil, environ 12 km au sud d'Hébron, 2 km au nord de Maôn), trois villes probablement calébites (cf. Jos 15:55; 1 Ch 2:42-45). Surtout, c'est là que David épouse Abigaïl, riche veuve de Nabal notable calébite (1 S 27:3; 30:5; 2 S 2:2; 3:3), propriétaire de 3000 moutons et de 1000 chèvres, habitant Maôn mais tondant son bétail à Carmel (1 S 25)[14]. Même si la conjecture de H. Winckler à propos de 2 S 3:8, où il propose d'interpréter *r'š klb*, "prince de Caleb", avec une allusion à David résidant à Hébron, reste très hasardeuse[15], ce marriage faisait pratiquement de David un (ou le) chef de Caleb[16]. Le lien de David avec la région d'Hébron fut probablement encore renforcé par son mariage avec Ahinoam de Yizréel (1 S 25:43; 27:3; 30:5; 2 S 2:2; 3:2; cf. Jos 15:56). Un peu plus tard, lorsque David offre ses services au philistin Akish de Gat, il se fait confier le fief de Ciqlag (1 S 26:6), vraisemblablement contigu au "Négeb de Caleb" (1 S 30:14; expression peut-être

---

[12] cf. déjà R. de Vaux (1971), pp. 505, 578.

[13] Cf., par ex., W. Beltz, *Die Kaleb-Traditionen im Alten Testament*, BWANT 18 (Stuttgart, 1974), p. 72.

[14] Cf. J.D. Levenson, "1 Samuel 25 as Literature and History", *CBQ* 40 (1978), pp. 11-28; J.D. Levenson–B. Halpern, "The Political Import of David's Marriages", *JBL* 99 (1980), pp. 507-518.

[15] Cf. R. de Vaux (1971), p. 510, n. 83.

[16] Sur l'importance de ce mariage dans la carrière politique de David, cf. déjà J.D. Levenson, *CBQ* 40 (1978), p. 25.

équivalente à "Négeb de Juda" en 1 S 27:10; 30:14). Bien plus, pendant son séjour de seize mois à Ciqlag (1 S 27:7), David veille à entretenir ses liens privilégiés avec Hébron (1 S 30:31) et c'est là qu'il s'installe bientôt avec ses deux femmes et ses mercenaires, se faisant reconnaître officiellement comme "roi sur la maison de Juda" (2 S 2:1-47)[17] et fondant, face à la "maison de Saül", la "maison de David"[18]. C'est aussi là qu'il enterre Abner assassiné lors d'une mission diplomatique (2 S 3:32) et dépose la tête d'Ishboshet/Ishbaal (2 S 4:12). C'est là, enfin, qu'il est sacré "roi d'Israël" (2 S 5:3), régnant au total à Hébron "sept ans et six mois" (2 S 5:5; cf. 1 R 2:11).

Le transfert par David de sa capitale à Jérusalem entraîna le déclin du rôle politique d'Hébron, spécialement après l'échec de la tentative de coup d'état d'Absalom, né à Hébron (2 S 3:3) et qui s'y était fait proclamer roi (2 S 15:7-10). Hébron ne joua plus, dès lors, que le rôle d'une ville lévitique (Jos 20:7; 21:11-13), mentionnée aussi dans la liste des villes fortifiées par Roboam en 2 Ch 11:5-12 dont la datation reste malheureusement discutée[19]. Quant à la mention de Qiryat-Arba dans Ne 11:25, elle semble assez clairement archaïsante car, à l'époque perse, la ville ne fait pas partie de la province de Judée mais se trouve sous le contrôle du royaume arabe de Qédar puis de la province d'Idumée[20]; Judas Maccabée ne la reconquiert que c. 163 av. J.-C. (1 Macc 5:65; AntJud XII § 353).

En dehors de la Bible, "Hébron" apparaît sur de nombreux exemplaires d'estampilles royales judéennes (c. 705-701 av. J.-C.)[21],

---

[17] La "maison de Juda" apparaît ici pour la première fois: le royaume de Juda entre dans l'histoire avec David; cf. déjà E. Lipinski (éd.), *The Land of Israel: Cross-Roads of Civilizations*, OLA 19 (Leuven, 1985), pp. 92-112.

[18] C'est probablement cette fondation du royaume de Juda et de sa capitale Hébron (c. 1010 av. J.-C.) qui est évoquée en Nb 13:22b. En effet, Tanis semble être devenue capitale et avoir été rebâtie comme telle sous Psousennès I (c. 1039-991 av. J.-C.); cf. N. Na'aman, "'Hébron was built seven years before Zoan in Egypt' (Numbers 13:22)", *VT* 31 (1981), pp. 488-492.

[19] Cf., par ex., V. Fritz, "The 'List of Rehoboam's Fortresses' in 2 Chr. 11:5-12—A Document from the Time of Josiah", dans *Y. Aharoni Memorial Volume*, ErIs 15 (Jérusalem, 1981), pp. 46*-53*; N. Na'aman, "Hezekiah's Fortified Cities and the LMLK Stamps", *BASOR* 261 (1986), pp. 5-21; S. Herrmann, "The So-Called 'Fortress System of Rehoboam', 2 Chron. 11:5-12: Theoretical Considerations", dans *Y. Yadin Memorial Volume*, ErIs 20 (Jérusalem, 1989), pp. 72*-78*.

[20] Cf. A. Lemaire, "Populations et territoires de la Palestine à l'époque perse", *Transeuphratène* 3 (1990), pp. 31-74, spéc. 40-41, 50, 52.

[21] Cf. N. Na'aman, "Sennacherib's campaign to Judah and the date of the *lmlk*

probablement liées à l'administration des biens de la couronne (soit poterie, soit produits stockés dans les magasins royaux). En dehors des sources paléo-hébraïques, on rappellera seulement la mention *ḥqr 'ibrm*, probablement "fort d'Abram"[22] dans la liste égyptienne de Shéshonq Ier, même si la localisation de ce site dans le sud judéen reste imprécise.

Les fouilles américaines (1964-1966)[23] puis israéliennes (à partir de 1984)[24] de Tell er-Rumeide ont révélé l'importance de la ville fortifiée au Bronze Moyen II (époque Hyksos) puis, surtout, vers l'an 1000 av. J.-C. Cependant, sauf au Bronze Récent et à l'époque perse où le site pourrait avoir été abandonné, les fouilles ont révélé une occupation quasi-continue du Bronze Ancien à l'époque ottomane. Même si, dans l'attente des rapports définitifs de fouille, il faut rester prudent quant à leur interprétation historique, les données archéologiques semblent concorder avec les indications textuelles concernant l'histoire d'Hébron à l'époque biblique.

Etant donné l'attache littéraire précise (Ortsgebundenheit) d'Abraham, il semble qu'on doive tenir compte de ce contexte géographico-historique éclairé par l'archéologie pour essayer de resituer les traditions abrahamiques les plus anciennes liées à la région d'Hébron.

On soulignera d'abord que l'exploitation, en vue de l'histoire des traditions, de l'attache géographique patriarcale suppose que celle-ci ne soit ni purement étiologique, ni artificielle, sinon les toponymes risqueraient de rester "a very uncertain criterion for deciding on a tradition's origin"[25]. Cependant, en distinguant, comme nous venons de le faire, les attaches locales primitives propres à Abraham de celles communes à d'autres patriarches, dérivant

---

stamps", *VT* 29 (1979), pp. 61-86; A. Lemaire, "Classification des estampilles royales judéennes", dans *Y. Aharoni Mem. Vol.*, ErIs 15 (1981), pp. 54*-60*; G. Barkay, "A Group of Stamped Handles from Judah", dans *A. Biran Volume*, ErIs 23 (1992), pp. 113-128.

22 Pour cette traduction "fort", cf. B. Mazar (1986), pp. 148-149; K.A. Kitchen, *The Third Intermediate Period in Egypt* (Warminster, 1986), p. 439. S. Aḥituv (*Canaanite Toponyms in Ancient Egyptian Documents*, Jérusalem/Leiden, 1984, p. 109) propose la lecture alternative "Ḥagar-Abelim".

23 Cf. P.C. Hammond, *RB* 72 (1965), pp. 267-270; 73 (1966), pp. 566-569; 75 (1968), pp. 253-258.

24 Cf. A. Ofer, "Excavations at Biblical Hebron", *Qadmoniot* 22 (1989), pp. 88-93.

25 J. Van Seters (1975), p. 148.

probablement de l'unification des traditions patriarcales, il nous semble possible d'éviter cet écueil.

La confrontation avec l'histoire d'Hébron, telle que nous venons de l'esquisser, semble assez clairement indiquer que les légendes abrahamiques primitives ont peu de chance d'être nées à l'époque exilique ou post-exilique. A cette époque, non seulement Hébron était-elle abandonnée ou très peu peuplée, mais encore et surtout elle ne faisait plus partie du territoire judéen à la suite de la chute de Jérusalem (587 av. J.-C.) et de l'expansion édomite. Il est, en effet, bien difficile de penser qu'on aurait alors créé de toutes pièces un ancêtre de Juda dans cette région et qu'on y aurait même situé précisément sa tombe. Il est aussi peu vraisemblable que ce soit à cette époque-là que l'on ait mis par écrit de telles légendes pour la première fois! En effet, les exilés représentaient surtout la classe dirigeante et lettrée dont une bonne partie venait de Jérusalem: on voit mal comment une légende patriarcale nationale avec des localisations aussi excentriques aurait pu intéresser ces exilés, à moins de supposer que ces traditions orales aient été alors mises par écrit par un scribe hébronite s'adressant à un cercle d'habitants de la région. Vue l'importance très relative d'Hébron à la fin de l'époque royale, cela paraît bien peu vraisemblable.

D'ailleurs, comme l'a bien noté A. de Pury, une première mise par écrit aussi tardive semble exclue par le fait que "les premières mentions d'Abraham se trouvent dans les textes exiliques d'Ez 33:24 et d'Es 51:1-2"[26], deux auteurs plus intéressés au sort de Jérusalem/Sion qu'au sort d'Hébron. Dans le premier texte, Abraham est apparemment mentionné par le peuple judéen resté au pays en ruine, ce qui laisse entendre qu'une légende présentant Abraham comme l'ancêtre des Judéens ayant reçu la promesse d'une nombreuse descendance possédant le pays existait en Judée avant la chute de Jérusalem et, probablement, avant le premier Exil de 597 av. J.-C. Is li 2 se réfère déjà explicitement à Sara, à une vocation et à une bénédiction[27]. Ces deux textes semblent donc impliquer l'existence d'un cycle d'Abraham pré-exilique.

En fait, si l'on cherche à préciser le contexte le plus vraisemblable d'un cycle abrahamique pré-exilique présentant Abraham comme l'ancêtre de Juda installé dans la région d'Hébron et non à Jérusalem, on est tout naturellement conduit à envisager l'époque pendant

---

[26] A. de Pury (1989), p. 261.
[27] Ibidem, p. 264.

laquelle Hébron fut capitale de Juda, c'est à dire la période de sept ans et demi du règne de David à Hébron (c. 1010-1003).

Peut-on remonter au-delà de la royauté de David à Hébron? Il est difficile de se prononcer: il est vraisemblable que le nom d'Abraham et l'emplacement de sa tombe à Makpéla, ainsi que l'existence d'un sanctuaire important à Mambré faisaient partie des traditions calébites[28]. Elles ont pu être connues de David et de son entourage alors que ce dernier était chef de bande et se mariait avec une riche veuve de la région (supra). Cependant, il nous semble impossible de préciser si cette tradition abrahamique calébite était antérieure à leur arrivée dans la région (ou à leur constitution en clans?), comme le propose R.E. Clements[29].

L'hypothèse d'une première rédaction aussi ancienne du cycle d'Abraham est-elle bien raisonnable? A-t-elle quelque vraisemblance historique? Quatre indices semblent l'indiquer:

1 – L'existence d'une culture écrite à Hébron même est maintenant attestée dès le Bronze Moyen par un fragment de tablette accadienne[30]. Il serait sans doute prématuré d'en déduire l'existence d'une tradition scribale locale continue jusque vers l'époque de David car le site d'Hébron semble avoir été abandonné au Bronze Récent[31] et la tradition scribale paléo-hébraïque alphabétique est différente de l'accadienne cunéiforme. Cependant, si le rôle central d'Hébron dans la montagne de Juda au XVII-XVIe siècle av. J.-C. y a entraîné la présence de scribes accadiens, on peut légitimement supposer que le rôle politique d'Hébron capitale du royaume de Juda, puis de celui de Juda et Israël, sous David y a entraîné la présence de scribes paléo-hébreux. Ceci paraît d'autant plus vraisemblable que l'écriture alphabétique paléo-hébraïque était beaucoup plus facile à maîtriser que l'écriture cunéiforme accadienne.

2 – Les pointes de flèche/javeline inscrites d'El-Khadr[32] semblent

---

28 Cf. déjà, par ex., A. Jepsen, "Zur Überlieferungsgeschichte der Vätergestalten", dans *Festschrift A. Alt, WZ, 2/3* (1953/4), pp. 139-155, spéc. 145ss; L.E. Axelson, *The Lord Rose up from Seir*, CBOTS 25 (Lund, 1987), pp. 87-91, 94-95, 179.

29 *Abraham and David* (London, 1967), pp. 39ss.

30 Cf. M. Anbar – N. Na'aman, "An Account Tablet of Sheep from Ancient Hebron", *Tel Aviv* 13-14 (1986/7), pp. 3-12; M. Anbar, "A Cuneiform Tablet of the 17th-16th Centuries BCE Discovered at Hebron", *Qad* 22 (1989), pp. 94-95.

31 Cf. A. Ofer, *Qad* 22 (1989), p. 90.

32 Cf. J.T. Milik – F.M. Cross, "Inscribed Javelin Heads from the Period of

assez clairement montrer que l'écriture n'était pas inconnue de l'élite militaire du sud de Jérusalem au XIe s. av. J.-C.

3 – Avant de devenir chef de bande, le jeune David semble avoir été formé un certain temps au service du roi Saül (1 S 16:14-23; 17:55-58) se liant d'ailleurs d'amitié avec son fils Jonatan (1 S 18:1-4; 19:1,7...). Il est probable que l'écriture n'était pas inconnue dans cet entourage immédiat du roi d'Israël, de ses fils et de ses serviteurs. David a pu, lui-même, y apprendre à lire et à écrire ou, au moins, y apprécier l'utilité de l'écriture au service de la politique et de l'administration royales.

4 – Lorsque David fuit la cour de Saül et devient chef de bande dans la région calébite de Ziph, Maôn et Carmel, il y est accompagné d'un survivant du sacerdoce de Nob, Abyatar (1 S 22:20-23), qui deviendra plus tard prêtre en chef de la royauté unifiée (2 S 20:25). Dès l'époque "calébite" de David, celui-ci eut souvent recours aux services de ce prêtre tout dévoué (1 S 23:6,9; 30:7-8; 2 S 2:1...). Alternativement, on peut aussi penser au prophète/voyant[33] Gad, ayant recommandé à David de se réfugier au "pays de Juda" (1 S 22:5) et le conseillant encore à Jérusalem (2 S 24:11-19), en notant que le chroniste lui a rattaché une partie des livres de Samuel (1 Ch 29:29; 2 Ch 29:25). Un tel personnage cultivé, ou quelqu'un de similaire, a très bien pu, dès cette époque, commencer à recueillir les traditions orales calébites en les développant et les adaptant au service des desseins politiques de son protecteur.

Il est clair que ces quatre remarques ne prouvent pas que la rédaction du cycle primitif d'Abraham remonte à la fin du XIe s. av. J.-C. mais elles suffisent à montrer qu'une telle hypothèse n'a, en soi, rien d'invraisemblable historiquement. Comme nous avons vu que le rôle d'Hébron dans les traditions abrahamiques anciennes

---

the Judges: A Recent Discovery in Palestine", *BASOR* 134 (1954), pp. 5-14; F.M. Cross, "Newly Found Inscriptions in Old Canaanite and Early Phoenician Scripts", *BASOR* 238 (1980), pp. 1-20; cf. aussi J.M. de Tarragon, "La pointe de flèche inscrite des Pères Blancs de Jérusalem", *RB* 98 (1991), pp. 244-251; F.M. Cross, "An Inscribed Arrowhead of the Eleventh Century BCE in the Bible Lands Museum in Jerusalem", dans *A. Biran Volume*, ErIs 23 (1992), pp. 21*-26*; id., "Newly Discovered Inscribed Arrowheads of the Eleventh Century BCE", *The Israel Museum Journal* 10 (1992), pp. 59-62.

[33] Pour le titre de Gad, cf. H. Haag, "Gad und Nathan", dans A. Kuschke-E. Kutsch (éd.), *Archäologie und Altes Testament. Festschrift für K. Galling* (Tübingen, 1970), pp. 135-143.

conduisait naturellement à cette solution, il nous semble que celle-ci s'impose, sauf preuve du contraire, même si on doit admettre que ce cycle a ensuite été réinterprété et complété à diverses époques de l'histoire d'Israël.

Sans entrer ici dans le détail de l'histoire probable de la rédaction du texte actuel, nous voudrions simplement montrer que cette datation haute du cycle primitif d'Abraham permet d'en mieux comprendre certains aspects:

1 – Le cycle d'Abraham n'est pas simplement clairement centré autour du sanctuaire de Mambré-Hébron: on remarque aussi qu'il n'y est fait nulle mention de Jérusalem/Sion. Ce fait est bien connu et s'étend d'ailleurs à toutes les traditions patriarcales[34]. Le fait est d'autant plus surprenant pour Abraham que, dans le texte actuel, celui-ci voyage du nord au sud de la Palestine et qu'il aurait été facile de le faire s'arrêter à Jérusalem pour y construire un autel comme à Bethel (Gn 12:8; 13:4) ou à Mambré-Hébron (Gn 13:18), ou encore pour y planter un arbre sacré comme à Béérshéba (Gn 21:33). Il est vrai que beaucoup d'exégètes voient une référence voilée à Jérusalem en Gn 14:18-20 (Melkisédeq, roi de Salem) et Gn 22:2 (le pays de Moriyya); cependant rien n'indique que cette interprétation du deuxième toponyme soit primitive[35]; le verbe *r'h*, "voir" est cinq fois répété en Gn 22 (vv. 4,8,13,14), ce qui conviendrait aussi bien au "désert de Yeru'el" (2 Ch 20:16)[36] qu'au sanctuaire de Mambré[37] ou au sanctuaire de Béér-Lahaï-Roï (Gn 16:14; 24:62; 25:11)[38]. La référence à Jérusalem en Gn 14 paraît beaucoup plus probable car "Salem" peut difficilement viser ici un autre lieu que Jérusalem[39]. Cependant, avec la plupart des commentateurs, il est assez clair que Gn 14:18-20 représente une insertion dans le texte

---

34 Cf. K. Baltzer, "Jerusalem in den Erzväter-Geschichten der Genesis?", dans E. Blum et alii (éd.), *Die Hebraische Bibel und ihre zweifache Nachgeschichte. Festschrift R. Rendtorff* (Neukirchen, 1990), pp. 3-12, spéc. 3.

35 Cf. I. Kalimi, "The Land of Moriah, Mount Moriah and the Site of Solomon's Temple in Biblical Historiography", *HTR* 83 (1990), pp. 345-363, spéc. 345-349.

36 Cf. H. Gunkel, *Genesis*, HK I,1 (1922), p. 241; K. Baltzer (1990), p. 9, n. 18.

37 Cf. déjà A. Alt, "Der Gott der Väter", dans *Kleine Schriften zur Geschichte des Volkes Israel I* (München, 1953), pp. 1-78, spéc. 54, n. 2.

38 Cf. déjà R. Kilian, *Isaaks Opferung*, SBS 44 (Stuttgart, 1970), pp. 99-113.

39 Cf. J.A. Emerton, "The Site of Salem, the City of Melchizedek (Genesis xiv 18)", dans J.A. Emerton (éd.), *Studies in the Pentateuch*, SVT 41 (1990), pp. 45-71.

primitif, insertion qui semble prendre tout son sens à l'époque de David roi de Jérusalem[40] et suppose que le texte primitif de Gn 14 soit, au moins, légèrement antérieur, datant, par exemple, du règne de David à Hébron.

2 – Un tel contexte historique permet de mieux comprendre certaines analogies entre la figure d'Abraham et celle de David[41]. On notera en particulier qu'Abraham fait allégeance au Philistin Abimélek (cf. surtout Gn 20:15) comme David s'était mis au service du roi philistin Akish de Gat (cf. surtout 1 S 27:5)[42] et que le guerrier Abraham se conduit de manière aussi noble que le chef David en 1 S 30[43]; on pourrait même se demander si les énigmatiques "318" guerriers d'Abraham (Gn 14:14) ne doivent pas être rapprochés des "quelque 400 hommes" partisans de David (1 S 22:2). Par ailleurs, Dieu promet de transmettre son héritage aussi bien à un descendant d'Abraham (Gn 15:4) qu'à un descendant de David (2 S 7:12) en employant le même expression hébraïque *'šr yṣ' mm'yk* qui n'est attestée que dans ces deux cas[44], tandis que Gn 13:15 et 2 S 7:16 précisent que ces deux promesses sont "pour toujours (*'d-'wlm*)". Le terme "alliance (*bryt*)" est commun aux deux figures avec lesquelles Yahvé fait alliance (Gn 15:18; cf. 2 S 23:5) et aussi bien Abraham que David concluent des alliances (*krt bryt*) avec d'autres hommes (Gn 14:13; 21:32; cf. 1 S 18:3; 20:8; 2 S 3:13,21; 5:3)[45]; on re-

---

[40] Cf. Id., "Some Problems in Genesis XIV", ibidem, pp. 73-102, spéc. 74, 75, 97-1O2; cf. déjà id., *VT* 21 (1971), pp. 421-426; K. Baltzer (1990), p. 10; cf. aussi indirectement les remarques de Th. Booij, "Psalm CX: 'Rule in the midst of your foes'", *VT* 41 (1991), pp. 396-407.

[41] Cf. surtout H. Schmid, "Melchisedek und Abraham, Zadok und David", *Kairos* 7 (1965), pp. 148-151; R.E. Clements (1967); M. Weinfeld, "The Covenant of Grant in the Old Testament and in the Ancient Near East", *JAOS* 90 (1970), pp. 186-188; J.R. Lundbom, "Abraham and David in the Theology of the Yahwist", dans C.L. Meyers – M. O'Connor (éd.), *The Word of the Lord shall go Forth. Essays in Honor of D.N. Freedman* (Winona Lake, 1983), pp. 203-209; malgré les réticences de N.E. Wagner, "Abraham and David?", dans J.W. Wevers – D.B. Redford (éd.), *Studies in the Ancient Palestinian World Presented to F. Winnett* (Toronto, 1972), pp. 117-140, spéc. 131-140; J. Van Seters (1975), pp. 151-153, 307.

[42] Cf. H. Cazelles, "Abraham au Négeb", dans M. Görg (éd.), *Die Väter Israels. Festschrift J. Scharbert* (1989), pp. 23-32, spéc. 31.

[43] Cf. V. Muffs, "Abraham the Noble Warrior", *JJS* 33 (1982), pp. 81-108, spéc. 93-95.

[44] Cf. M. Weinfeld, "The Promise to the Patriarchs and its Realization: An Analysis of Foundation Stories", dans M. Heltzer – E. Lipinski (éd.), *Society and Economy in the Eastern Mediterranean* (c. 1500-1000 B.C.), OLA 23 (Leuven, 1988), pp. 353-369, spéc. 360.

[45] Cf. déjà les remarques de D. McCarthy, "Compact and Kingship: Stimuli

marque, en particulier, que Gn 21:27 et 1 S 23:18 émploient la même expression hébraïque: *wykrtw šnyhm bryt*. De façon plus générale, la "dîme" du butin, versée par Abraham à Melkisédeq (Gn 14:20), "semble préfigurer David consacrant à Yahvé ses prises métalliques (II Samuel 8/11-12) qui forment le fonds du trésor du Temple salomonien (I Rois 7/51, administré par le clergé sadocide dont Melkisédeq est sans doute le 'type'"[46], tandis que la promesse faite à Abraham de devenir une *gwy gdwl*, source de bénédiction pour les familles de la terre, peut difficilement se comprendre autrement qu'une référence à l'empire davidique[47]. Cependant ces rapprochements doivent être interprétés avec prudence car il est clair que certains d'entre eux supposent l'existence du royaume davidique à son apogée et ont probablement été rédigés à Jérusalem un peu plus tard, vraisemblablement, en particulier, par une rédaction datant du début du règne de Salomon[48].

3 – Si la rédaction primitive du cycle d'Abraham a été contemporaine de l'unification par David des diverses composantes du royaume de Juda, on comprend qu'Abraham, représentant les clans calébites, ait été associé à Isaac, représentant les clans siméonites au sud-ouest d'Hébron, et à Loth, représentant les populations au sud et à l'est de la Mer Morte (Transjordanie)[49].

a) La plupart des exégètes s'accordent à reconnaître aux récits primitifs associant Loth et Abraham (Gn 13:14; 18-19) un caractère ancien[50]. Nous nous contenterons ici de quelques remarques:

---

for Hebrew Covenant Thinking", dans T. Ishida (éd.), *Studies in the Period of David and Solomon* (Tokyo, 1982), pp. 75-92, spéc. 78-80.

[46] Cf. A. Caquot, "L'alliance avec Abram (Genèse 15)", *Semitica* 12 (1962), pp. 51-66, spéc. 65.

[47] Cf. B. Mazar, "The Historical Background of the Book of Genesis", *JNES* 28 (1969), pp. 73-83, repris dans id., *The Early Biblical Period. Historical Studies* (Jérusalem, 1986), pp. 49-62; M. Weinfeld, "Old Testament—The Discipline and its Goals", dans J.A. Emerton (éd.), *Congress Volume. Vienna 1980*, SVT 32 (Leiden, 1981), pp. 423-434, spéc. 425; G.E. Mendenhall, "The Nature and Purpose of the Abraham Narratives", dans P.D. Miller et alii (éd.), *Ancient Israelite Religion. Essays in Honor of F.M. Cross* (Philadelphia, 1987), pp. 337-357.

[48] Il s'agit peut-être d'une rédaction "sadocide": cf. A. Lemaire, "Vers l'histoire de la rédaction des livres des Rois", *ZAW* 98 (1986), pp. 221-236, spéc. 231-232. Pour une rédaction à l'époque salomonienne, cf. récemment K. Berge, *Die Zeit des Jahwisten. Ein Beitrag zur Datierung jahwistischen Vätertexte*, BZAW 186 (Berlin, 1990), spéc. pp. 74, 313.

[49] Cf., par ex., R. Kilian, "Zur Überlieferungsgeschichte Lots", *BZ* 14 (1970), pp. 23-37, spéc. 27.

[50] Cf., par ex., E. Blum, *Die Komposition der Vätergeschichte*, WMANT 57

– Abraham et Loth, ainsi, d'ailleurs, qu'Isaac, sont présentés comme des pasteurs de grands troupeaux, ayant à leur service des bergers (Gn 13:2,5,7; 26:26). Cette présentation, qui reflète probablement l'économie régionale de l'époque, peut être rapprochée du fait que, par son mariage avec Abigaïl veuve de Nabal, David s'est probablement trouvé à la tête de troupeaux importants gardés par des bergers (1 S 25:2,7,14-16).

– David séjourna un moment au "désert d'Ein-Guèdi" (1 S 24:1), apparemment en compagnie de Gad (1 S 22:5) et d'Abyatar (1 S 23:6ss); c'est peut-être dès cette époque que l'entourage de David a commencé à rassembler des traditions locales, liées au sud de la Mer Morte, sur Loth.

– La légende sur l'origine des Moabites et des Ammonites (Gn 19:36-38) surprend par l'absence des Edomites qui habitaient au sud de la Mer Morte. Cette absence s'explique probablement par le fait que le royaume édomite n'a été créé que vers 846-841 av. J.-C.[51] et que la mise par écrit de cette tradition est antérieure à cette date[52].

– Cette légende semble impliquer que les populations transjordaniennes à l'est de la Mer Morte pouvaient être appelées "fils de Lot" (Ps 83:9) et que, à l'époque où cette tradition a été mise par écrit, les Moabites et les Ammonites étaient considérés comme des "frères" (cf. Gn 13:8) des Judéens. Ceci pourrait correspondre à l'époque de David qui, à ses débuts, semble s'être appuyé sur le roi de Moab (cf. 1 S 22:3-4) et sur le roi d'Ammon (cf. 2 S 10:2)[53].

– La tradition du bouleversement (*hpk*) des villes de la plaine (Gn 19:21-29), spécialement celui de Sodome et Gomorrhe, semble attestée en Amos iv 11 (*kmhpkt 'lhym 't-sdm w't-'mrh*; cf. aussi Is 13:19), et Is 1:9-10, tandis que la référence possible d'Osée 11:8 à Gn 14:2,8 reste plus incertaine. Ces mentions du prophète de Téqo'a (Am 1:1) et de celui de Jérusalem vers le milieu et la fin du VIIIe s. av. J.-C. semblent indiquer que cette légende était bien connue de leurs auditeurs.

(Neukirchen, 1984), p. 273; H. Gese, *Alttestamentliche Studien* (Tübingen, 1991), pp. 36-39.

[51] Cf. A. Lemaire, "Les territoires d'Ammon, Moab et Edom dans la deuxième moitié du IXe s. avant notre ère", dans *Studies in the History and Archaeology of Jordan* IV (Amman, 1992), pp. 209-214, spéc. 213.

[52] Cf. id., dans E. Laperrousaz (éd.), *La protohistoire d'Israël* (1991), p. 296.

[53] Cf. T. Ishida, *The Royal Dynasties in Ancient Israel*, BZAW 142 (Berlin, 1977), spéc. p. 64.

b) Les traditions sur Isaac se rattachent aux clans siméonites[54] et pourraient avoir été recueillies et mises par écrit pendant les seize mois du séjour de David à Ciqlag. L'intégration de cette région au royaume de Juda (1 S 27:6), liée à la proclamation de David roi d'Hébron, a vraisemblablement entraîné la fusion de ces traditions avec celles d'Abraham. On notera que cette tradition d'Isaac, centrée primitivement autour de Béér-Lahaï-Roï (Gn 24:62; 25:11) et de Béérshéba[55] (Gn 26:23-33) semble déjà connue d'Amos vii 9 qui pourrait viser ces deux sanctuaires (cf. Am 5:5; 8:14).

c) La signification des traditions sur Hagar et Ismaël (Gn 16; 21:9-21)[56] paraît, de prime abord, plus difficile à saisir. D'après Gn 25:12-18; 1 Ch 1:28-31; 5:10,19,20; 27:30-31 et le Ps 83, il est assez clair que la figure d'Ismaël était liée aux populations arabes, c'est à dire aux voisins méridionaux du royaume de Juda. Or, alors qu'il était à Ciqlag, David combattit vigoureusement les Amalécites qui ravageaient son territoire et tout le Négeb (1 S 27:8; 30; 2 S 1:1; cf. 2 S 8:12) et semblaient assez mal vus dans son entourage (cf. 2 S 1:8,13). Ismaël semble donc représenter les Amalécites occupant un moment et razziant le Négeb calébite et celui de Ciqlag mais que finalement, comme Abraham expulsa son fils illégitime Ismaël, David chassa de ce territoire.

Dans l'hypothèse d'une rédaction du cycle primitif d'Abraham sous le règne de David à Hébron, il apparaît donc qu'un tel cycle a déjà pu inclure des traditions sur Loth ("frère" d'Abraham), Isaac ("fils" d'Abraham) et Ismaël (fils illégitime expulsé). Même si ces traditions ont pu être, elles aussi, révisées et remaniées ultérieurement, leur intégration dans le cycle d'Abraham semble liée à l'histoire de l'unification des composantes du royaume de Juda.

Ainsi, d'après son contexte géographico-historique, c'est vraisemblablement peu avant l'an 1000 av. J.-C., à Hébron et dans l'entourage de David (Abyatar, Gad ou quelqu'un de similaire?) que fut rédigé le cycle primitif d'Abraham-Loth-Ismaël-Isaac.

---

[54] Sur la localisation de Siméon, cf., par ex., N. Na'aman, "The Inheritance of the Sons of Simeon", *ZDPV* 96 (1980), pp. 136-152.

[55] Cf., avec diverses nuances, H. Schmid, *Die Gestalt des Isaak* (Darmstadt, 1991), p. 36; A. Schoors, "The Bible on Beer-Sheba", *Tel Aviv* 17 (1990), pp. 100-109.

[56] Cf. récemment T.D. Alexander, "The Hagar Traditions in Genesis XVI and XXI", dans J.A. Emerton (éd.), *Studies in the Pentateuch*, SVT 41 (Leiden, 1990), pp. 131-148.

CITY-DWELLERS OR ADMINISTRATORS FURTHER LIGHT ON THE CANAANITES

by

NIELS PETER LEMCHE

Copenhagen

Old paradigms and young scholars

"The great scholars of the past have, alas, not been followed by scholars of their own standing". This complaint is commonly heard in conversations between present—day Old Testament scholars. Most countries once possessed such great personalities as, in Germany, Albrecht Alt (d. 1956), Martin Noth (d. 1968) and Gerhard von Rad (d. 1971), in North America William F. Albright (d. 1971), in France Roland de Vaux (d. 1971), and, from Scandinavia, scholars like Sigmund Mowinckel (d. 1965), Johannes Pedersen (d. 1976) and Ivan Engnell (d. 1962). All of these are easily remembered.

Further, all of these scholars were considered fathers of famous theories, hallmarks of scholarship as well as founders of "schools" (I realize that many of their disciples will object that they did not create schools; however, for all practical purposes, the circles of admirers surrounding the "great men" functioned like schools, and must—in the eyes of an outsider—rightfully be called so). The difference between masters and disciples is in fact that the latter mainly reformulated the theories of their masters; they never tried in a serious way to challenge the paradigms, that were formulated by their mentors.

This situation should be accepted without regret, and there is nothing suspicious or degrading about it. The masters of the past often presented their opinions in a provisional form and hard work had to be done by many scholars before standard paradigms of scholarship had safely manifested themselves.

However, new problems arise as soon as such paradigms begin to crack, which occurs either because they have reached unrealistic dimenions[1] or because they have become so commonplace that they simply invite young upstart scholars to contradict them.[2] In cases when old theories are severely attacked, the veneration of the old masters may be little more than an obsession reminiscent of the censureship of new ideas. In this way "the ideology of the great scholar" may prevent new ideas from appearing, not because reorientation is unwanted or unnecessary, but because it cannot be reconciled with the old paradigms.

Battles fought in the open between new ideas and old paradigms may be very fruitful to scholarship. However, when a young scholar tries to formulate his own ideas—although guided by old paradigms—the positive influence of the master may turn into something absolutely negative. Instead of creating fruitful syntheses between old and new theories in the well-known Hegelian style (although this is itself a procedure to be considered a *cul de sac* or graveyard of many a promising scholar, rather than an example of the golden mean between extremes), such an influence may eventually prevent a scholar from freeing himselves from the past. In this manner, ideas long dead elsewhere have quite often been able to survive in the field of OT studies.

In the following sections I intend to demonstrate how old and almost abandoned paradigms have led two modern scholars astray. In both cases the subject of concern will be the Canaanites of the Old Testament.

As I have recently published a study of the Canaanites,[3] I will not present the usual "Forschungsbericht" in this place. It should only be remembered that, according to the traditional paradigm, a state of war always existed between the Israelites and the Canaanites, and, further, that the origins of this schism between the

---

[1] The best example of this is perhaps M. Noth's amphictyonic hypothesis which served for decades as a kind of magic remedy that was held to explain every problem of ancient Israelite history. Another example is Sigmund Mowinckel's theory of a "Thronbesteigungsfest" in Israel in the period of the monarchy which similarly obtained almost incredible importance in spite of the very shakey basis of the theory within both the OT and other ancient Near Eastern sources.

[2] The present reaction against the stratification of the Pentateuch into several different sources covering more than half a millennium may be such a case, as is, of course, the almost unlimited number of "literary" studies of biblical narrative style.

[3] *The Canaanites and Their Land. The Tradition of the Canaanites*, JSOT SS 110 (Sheffield, 1991).

Israelites and the Canaanites can be traced back to Israel's most early history.

In this connection it was of no consequence whether scholars believed in Albright's conquest hypothesis or they accepted Alt's immigration hypothesis. Without exception scholars considered the Canaanites to have been the enemies of Israel, and Canaanite culture and religion to have been the very anthithesis of Israelite culture and religion. Furthermore, Canaanites and Israelites belonged to two different ethnic groups. Only in the course of history were the differences between Israelites and Canaanites to be toned down as a consequence of the continuous syncretism which in the period of the monarchy moulded Israelite and Canaanite religion into one and the same religion.[4]

The emperor's new clothes: The survival of old paradigms

My first example will be a scholar who—in spite of his intentions to present an updated view on the Canaanites—has been unable to free himself from the influence of earlier paradigms. In his recent article on Canaan and the Canaanites in a well-known theological dictionary,[5] the Swiss scholar Fritz Stolz reconstructs the history of Canaan on the basis of ancient Near Eastern documents. In general Stolz' handling of the Ancient Near Eastern evidence must be considered acceptable, although, when he has to choose between two different notions of Canaan, as either a vague geographical indication or a precise name of one of the Egyptian provinces in Asia, the author decides in favour of both options at one and the same time. Whether or not this is correct is not the point here. Important in this connection is his decision also to write a short history of Canaan, including a description of Canaanite society which is partly based on information contained in the Old Testament.

In spite of the possibility that "Canaan" in ancient times may have been no more than a vague geographical term which may therefore not be identified with a specific nation, Stolz accepts the biblical notion of Canaan as an adequate name for the pre-Israelite Palestinian world. In this way he also accepts the general picture of

---

[4] To mention but a single paradigmatic example: W.Dietrich, *Israel und Kanaan. Von Ringen zweier Gesellschaftssysteme*, SBS 94 (Stuttgart, 1979).

[5] F.Stolz, "Kanaan", *TRE* 17 (1988), pp.539-556.

the inhabitants of this area as that promulgated by many Old Testament scholars of the past, although he at the same time has to reorganize his description of the Canaanites in order to make it conform with more modern ideas. As far as his interpretation of the societal organization of the Canaanites is concerned, Stolz relies heavily on the positions of scholars like Mario Liverani, and, accordingly, he assumes that the Canaanite world should be divided into two fundamentally different spheres, on one hand being the city and on the other the countryside.[6] Up to a point, Stolz is clearly in harmony with, for example, the revolution hypothesis as formulated by, especially, Norman K. Gottwald.[7]

However, when it comes to Stolz' understanding of the emergence of Israel and the historical foundation of the difference between Israelites and Canaanites, the old paradigm of Alt emerges in the moment he turns to the role of the nomads in Syria and Palestine at the end of the Late Bronze Age. Thus the old paradigm survives although the old idea that Israel's origin can be traced back to the intrusions of nomads at the end of the Late Bronze Ages was totally discredited by Gottwald as well as, before him, George E. Mendenhall.[8] Stolz has evidently not been able to free himself from the ghosts of roaming Semitic bedouins who were to become the fathers of great civilizations. In this fashion he muddles up the whole question of the emergence of Israel[9] when he tries to reconcile such mutually contradictory hypotheses as, on the one hand, the theory of Alt and, on the other, the revolution hypothesis. It goes without saying that there is little prospect of success here.

It was to be expected that Stolz' reconstruction of the early history of Israel as well as its religious developments would follow the course marked out by German scholars of the first part of this century.

---

6 Several studies by, especially, Mario Liverani should be mentioned in this connection. I shall only refer to the recent description of this assumed conflict in M.Liverani, *Antico oriente. Storia, società, economia* (Rome, 1988), pp.546-552.

7 N.K.Gottwald, *The Tribes of Yahweh* (New York, 1979).

8 On nomadism, cf. especially N.K.Gottwald, "Were the Early Israelites Pastoral Nomads?" in: J.J.Jackson and M.Kessler (eds.), *Rhetorical Criticism. Essays in Honor of James Muilenburg*, Pittsburgh Theological Monograph Series 1 (Pittsburgh, 1974), pp.223-255, slightly revised in *The Tribes of Yahweh*, pp.435-463.

9 In his description of the early development of the Israelite people, Stolz is following the traditional German theories to a far greater extent than we are initially led to believe. However, this is not my theme here.

There is no need to elaborate on this here. However, the important part of the article is still to come. In his final section Stolz concentrates on the ideological aspects of the Old Testament understanding of the Canaanites as the antitheses of the Israelites. Stolz is able to show how this concept developed from at least the time of the prophet Hosea and until the early post-exilic period. This final part of Stolz' article is rich in perspective, and—as I have shown in my own study on the Canaanites[10]—it does not presuppose that the identity of the biblical Canaanites can be referred back to any historical reality of the late 2nd millennium BCE.

It would be easy to criticize Stolz's description of ancient Palestinian society in general. I shall, however, leave this subject and turn to my next case study.

The Canaanites: A new social setting?

A new and original theory concerning the terms "Canaan" and "Canaanites" in the Old Testament has recently been published by Karen Engelken.[11] In her article Engelken publishes precise statistics covering the occurrences of the two terms in the Old Testament as well as two new theories concerning the history of the terms: Engelken maintains that (p. 50) "The name of Canaan as well as the "Canaanites" were of no importance to the Israelites after the introduction of the Hebrew monarchy. In the late retrospective narratives (of P), however, the term *Eretz Canaan* has obtained quite a new dimension, and the Canaanites, too, were endowed with a different connotation." Furthermore, Engelken says, "'Canaan' is never used to describe an ethnic entity like Israel". Her conclusions are (pp. 62-63):

(1) "Canaan is never used to describe an ethnic group. In the Old Testament, as in other Ancient Near Eastern sources, the word may be used as name for a territorial unit or a part of Syria or Palestine.... We should, however, also pay attention to the instances where cuneiform writers associate the Canaanites with highwaymen."

---

[10] Cf. n.3 above.

[11] K.Engelken, "Kanaan als nicht-territorialer Terminus", *Biblische Notizen* 52 (1990), pp.47-63. A preliminary criticism of Engelken can be found at the end of my *The Canaanites*, pp.172-173. All quotations from Engelken have been translated from the German by this author.

(2) "In the Old Testament, whenever the names 'Canaan' and 'Canaanites' do not refer to a territorial unit they are always social terms. In the old source material in the Old Testament these names are especially used to characterize the way of life that was rejected by the Israelites, that is the life as citizens in the towns of Palestine. At a later date the connotation "merchant" was attached to the two terms ..."

The author's final point is equally important (p. 63):

(3) "Perhaps we may envisage a development of the terms which started in the territory of the Palestinian city-states and which, in the eyes of the early Israelites, turned the two terms into socially derogatory designations for the exploitative system of the city-states. This negative connotation led on to the understanding of the two terms as designating "exploitative merchants", and at the end of the day, when the city-states were no longer considered a problem to the Israelites, the terms reassumed their old territorial meaning."

It is evident that such a hypothesis could not have been formulated by a German scholar of the present time before a certain reorientation had taken place, one which disregards on the one hand the traditional view of Israelite history as expressed by the Old Testament itself and on the other the opinions that were held in the past by a majority of German scholars. It is obvious that Karen Engelken has given up the ideas of Alt and Noth according to whom the Israelites constituted an ethnic unit that was foreign to the Canaanite world of Palestine in the Late Bronze Age. According to Engelken the Canaanites and Israelites were never ethnically different. It also becomes obvious, when she speak about the differences between Canaanite exploiters who lived in the cities and exploited those Israelites who remained in the countryside, that the interpretation of the early history of the Israelites which led her to present this hypothesis must be some variety of the revolution hypothesis as put forward by Mendenhall and Gottwald.[12] The relationship between Engelken's ideas and the theories of Mendenhall and Gottwald becomes evident as soon as we realize that her theory is founded on the assumption that a kind of dichotomy existed in early Iron Age

---

[12] Cf. G.E.Mendenhall, "The Hebrew Conquest of Palestine" (1962), repr. in *The Biblical Archaeologist Review* 3 (New York, 1970), pp.100-120; idem, *The Tenth Generation* (Baltimore, 1973); N.K.Gottwald, *The Tribes of Yahweh* (New York, 1979).

society in Palestine between, on one side, the peasants and the nomads and, on the other, the city-dwellers. This assumption must be considered the very foundation of the revolution hypothesis, and without it the revolution hypothesis cannot be sustained.

It is obvious that it is possible to direct the same kind of criticism against Engelken's new interpretation of Canaan and the Canaanites in the Old Testament as was formerly launched against the revolution hypothesis by—not least—this writer.[13] However, it is not my intention to reopen the discussion of the heuristic value of, say Alt's description of the origin of the Israelites[14] (not to speak of Albright's or even Yehezkel Kaufmann's conquest models[15]). To the contrary, although we may question the validity of Mendenhall's and Gottwald's own hypotheses, they have contributed immensely to our understanding of the social process that led to the emergence of Iron Age society in Palestine.[16] That is to say that there is no reason to resort to old explanations of that hatred of the Canaanites which is conspicuous in most parts of the Old Testament, by maintaining that this animosity was caused by ethnic differences between two distinct populations or nations which lived in the same area in the Early Iron Age. To this extent, Engelken's hypothesis represents a definite advantage in comparison to older theories.

---

[13] In N.P.Lemche, *Early Israel. Anthropological and Historical Studies on the Israelite Society before the Monarchy*, SVT 37 (Leiden, 1985), cf. the conclusions to the socio-anthropological part, pp.198-201.

[14] On this, see *Early Israel*, pp.35-48.

[15] On Albright's reconstruction see *Early Israel*, pp.48-62. Cf. further Y. Kaufmann, *The Biblical Account of the Conquest of Palestine* (Jerusalem 1953).

[16] As correctly pointed out by J.Maxwell Miller in his "Is it Possible to Write a History of Israel without Relying on the Hebrew Bible?" in Diana Vikander Edelman (ed.), *The Fabric of History*, JSOT SS 127 (Sheffield, 1991), pp.93-102, the study of Palestinian history in the Iron Age is today beset with a number of terminological problems, as it would be incorrect, while affirming Israel's "Palestinian" or even "Canaanite" background, to continue to speak about *Israel's* history. Guidelines that may tell us how to escape this terminological impasse are developed in the same volume by Thomas L.Thompson ("Text, Context and Referent in Israelite Historiography", pp.65-92), and by Ernst Axel Knauf ("From History to Interpretation", pp.26-64). The present article is written under the spell of the old terminology, and its author begs forgiveness if he here and there should happen to sin against the new spirit.

A SOCIOLOGICAL CRITIQUE

We may, however, wish to penetrate deeper into the problem by evaluating the fundamental presupposition of Engelken, which is, at the same time, that of Mendenhall and Gottwald, namely the idea that a fundamental dichotomy existed between city and countryside in traditional societies like the early Israelite one. Another point that would have been worth discussing in this connection is the impact of modern pentateuchal studies on our problem as these studies are likely to deal a death-blow to the revolutionary hypothesis,[17] while they, at the same time, may be taken to support another view on the Canaanites of the Old Testament. This question must, however, be left out of consideration in this place.

Whereas Alt and his successors placed the important line of division in traditional Middle Eastern societies between nomadic and settled cultures, the line of separation has been moved by Mendenhall and Gottwald so that it now lies somewhere between urban and peasant society. Both scholars have made it sufficiently clear that nomads and farmers cannot be considered archetypical enemies; rather, they have to live, at least in the Middle East, in a kind of symbiosis because neither of the two groups can survive without the presence of the other group.[18]

Consequently, we now understand the old idea of "pure nomads" roaming about on endless treks without ever encountering settled peoples to be no more than a romantic stereotype which is not even valid as far as modern bedouins living in the driest parts of present day Saudi-Arabia are concerned. Furthermore, it is also clear, thanks to the rather intensive scientific social-anthropological study of Middle Eastern nomadic societies over the last forty years, which was more or less inaugurated by the Norwegian anthropologist Fredrik Barth, that the common-place distinction between nomads and semi-nomads is far too simple to have any explanatory power. As a matter of fact, we would do better to speak of a kind of socio-economic continuum which covers the whole range of occupa-

---

17 The advocates of the revolution hypothesis generally favour an understanding of the formation of the Pentateuch very close to the one formulated by Martin Noth. This is very pronounced in Gottwald's *The Tribes of Yahweh*, passim.

18 This theme has been more completely developed by Gottwald, in his *The Tribes of Yahweh*; cf. especially chapter 40 (pp.464-473): "Socioeconomic Morphemes in Canaan: Coexistence and Opposition".

tional niches from the almost-pure nomad, that is, the bedouin, on one side to the absolutely settled peasant who only leaves his farmhouse in order to till his fields, on the other. Along this line of continuum, several subspecies of nomadism and peasantry may be found, not necessarily all in the same area or at the same time. However, no important line of division can be traced between these occupations that would exclude one of them from society, at least not as far as socio-political points of view are concerned (ideology is another matter, but it is also a matter which has not yet been studied in an adequate manner).[19]

So far the available evidence seemingly supports Mendenhall and Gottwald: The real line of division must be sought elsewhere. However, a study of the relations between village and city in Middle Eastern traditional society makes it equally clear that the line of continuum also continues to include traditional urban society.[20] Social anthropologists have readily admitted that this is correct from a socio-economic point of view but also from an ideological angle. The central issue is investment. Well-to-do city-dwellers are likely to invest their surplus in landed property, whereas the wealthy peasants and farmers, as well as the rich nomads, may at the same time prefer to buy houses in nearby cities in order to become members of the societal elite that resides in the cities. Furthermore, it has been noted that the traditional oriental city is just as dependent on the production of the countryside as the peasants are on money flowing into their communities from the cities. And, finally, it has been realized that the most important single occupation to be found in the traditional oriental city is agriculture, a large part of the population being directly involved in the production of food, while an even greater

---

[19] On this see *Early Israel*, pp.84-163. In his well-informed study, *Das Image der Nomaden im Alten Israel und in der Ikonographie seiner sesshaften Nachbarn*, OBO 107 (Freiburg/Göttingen, 1991), Thomas Staubli devotes comprehensive sections to ideological matters, although these are mostly based on ancient, which is to say, rather one-eyed, sources.

[20] *Early Israel*, pp.164-201. It would, however, be wrong to say that Old Testament scholars have readily accepted this idea, which is mainly because they lack sociological sophistication, or so I am led to believe. The generally undramatic course of such societal changes may also make them less inviting for budding historians who are more interested in more dramatic developments. This also applies to such otherwise informed studies as Thomas L. Thompson, "Palestinian Pastorialism and Israel's Origins", *SJOT* 6 (1992), pp.1-13.

part is engaged in the preparation and distribution of the basic products of the countryside.[21]

It should now be evident that the very foundation of the revolution hypothesis, that is, the assumed antagonism between land and city, cannot be sustained, at least not on a sociological basis.

Neither can the old notion be upheld that the Israelites lived in the countryside and the Canaanites in the cities. Thus, when we read about the life of the Israelites in the Old Testament it is obvious that the whole context of Israelite culture as described by Old Testament authors was urban. First of all we have no information about Israelite nomads. The only nomadic peoples mentioned in the Old Testament are either foreigners like the Midianites or they are Israelites who have withdrawn from the settled life like the Rechabites, who originated in the period of the Hebrew kings. To mention only a few cases, the stories about the judge Gideon and his son Abimelech are definitely city-orientated. Gideon resided at Ophra, not in the countryside, and Abimelech went on to become the king of Manasseh with his residence at Shechem. Later on Samuel stayed at Ramah, and travelled, not between various villages or hamlets, but between the small towns of Benjamin. Also the Israelite high-places were, according to the Old Testament, situated either in the townlets or very close to urban communities; this applies to the sanctuary at Shechem, the one in Gilgal as well as the major one at Bethel. Real information about nomadic groups or groups living outside the city communities is hardly to be found in the Old Testament.

---

[21] This is, of course, based on information derived from traditional Middle Eastern cities in this century, and its relevance to ancient oriental cities may therefore be questioned. However, when we consider that such Late Bronze Age cities as Alalakh or Ugarit numbered as many as 5,000 to 10,000 inhabitants (i.e., between 10% and 20% of the total populations of the respective kingdoms), it would be ridiculous to imagine that all of them were engaged in the trading and business of the palace administration, or that they were all members of the palace household. The issue has never been properly studied, but it would certainly be important if a situation like that in present-day traditional cities also existed in ancient towns. In Late Bronze Age Palestine this must necessarily have been the case, as no, or at least very few, villages existed before the 12th century BCE (for further information, see Thomas L. Thompson, *The Settlement of Palestine in the Bronze Age*, TAVO B 34 (Wiesbaden, 1979), and, in spite of a different opinion as to the interpretation of events, Israel Finkelstein, *The Archaeology of the Israelite Settlement* (Jerusalem 1988), who, indeed, confirms the results obtained by Thompson).

THE CANAANITE-ISRAELITE CONTROVERSY: ANOTHER EXPLANATION

However, it may still be possible to refer the antagonism between the Israelites and the Canaanites back to premonarchical and early monarchical times. If we look at the social structure of Israelite society, it is obvious that Israelite families were united into a number of lineages and clans irrespective of whether or not they were at the same time citizens in one of the states in Iron Age Palestine. The basic social structure is unlikely to have changed in spite of the introduction of monarchic government in these states. However, the disappearance of the tribal system as such may be attributed to the emergence of the states. In the course of history it seems more than likely that tribal society was reduced in importance and finally disappeared. If we look at the information in the books of Kings we see that the tribal affiliations of the principal personalities are properly listed in the early phase of the two Palestinian kingdoms, whereas such information disappears after the Omrides.

This situation concurs very well with information presented by modern ethnographers and social-anthropologists, which informs us that tribal societies are likely to be crushed by states, whereas minor societal formations—including lineages or even clans—may survive or even be strengthened. We will, however, argue that state and tribe are mutually exclusive political formations which cannot exist simultaneously in one and the same society. In *Early Israel* I referred to the amusing story transmitted by Ian Lewis, an English social anthropologist, who wrote about the nomadic tribesmen of Somalia. According to Lewis, the communist government which seized power in Somalia in the 1960's abolished the tribal system by law. After that, the former tribesmen termed themselves ex-members of ex-tribes. In the end, the exasperated government also had to forbid the use of the word "ex-".[22]

However, I have also described the relationship between state and tribe as metaphorical. First, it should be realized that it is almost impossible to define a tribe in a satisfactory manner. According to the anthropological literature, a tribe may consist of a small number of related persons, as, for example 500 individuals. This is the situation among the bedouins of the Negev desert. However, the members of some African tribal societies may be numbered in the thou-

---

[22] See *Early Israel*, pp.226-227.

sands, tens of thousands or even hundred-thousands. The whole matter becomes absolutely absurd when the ethnographer Paul Bohannan argues that the society studied by him, the Tivs of Africa, cannot even be considered a tribe although it embraces about a million souls. It should be obvious that the term "tribe" is almost meaningless when it is understood to cover a social phenomenon alone.

The disappearance of tribal systems when incorporated into a state is, however, interesting. My argument says that no society can embrace both systems, tribes as well as a centralized state, at one and the same time. As a matter of fact, tribes and states are political, not social organisations. It is true that tribesmen belonging to one tribe acknowledge that they are all members of one and the same family system and that tribal genealogies are drafted in order to "prove" their membership of the tribe. It has, on the other hand, at the same time been noted that the tribe is unimportant from a social point of view. The smaller societal units like clans and lineages are far more important as far as the daily life of the tribesmen are concerned. In my short history of Israel, *Ancient Israel*, I have accordingly maintained that the concept of tribe is to be considered to be a metaphor covering the functions which in a state society are handled by the officers of the state, whereas in tribal society the tribal leaders have to handle these functions[23] The officers of the state are, however, administrators and public servants rather than members of tribes, and they derive their influence not from the membership of a certain tribe but from their position among the servants of the state (which does not, of course, preclude their favouring particular segments of their own society). This situation could well have been an everlasting source of conflict in family-orientated societies in the Middle East in ancient times, as it has been in modern times.[24]

---

[23] Cf. my *Ancient Israel* (Sheffield, 1988), p.102.

[24] It must therefore be accounted an idle question to ask: what was a Hebrew tribe? This also applies to the discussion in C.H.J.de Geus, *The Tribes of Israel*, Studia Semitica Neerlandica 18 (Assen, 1976), pp.133-150, as well as the paragraph devoted to the concept of an Israelite tribe in my own *Early Israel*, pp.274-290. As long as we fail to acknowledge that tribal systems and states are, from a political point of view, mutually exclusive political, rather than social, organizations, we shall have little chance ever to understand the processes which may transform the members of tribal societies into citizens of states, a development which also includes the ideological acceptance of the domination of the state.

Instead of a socio-economic dichotomy as envisaged by the advocates of the revolution hypothesis, I would like to propose that we speak about a *socio-political dichotomy* or *discontinuum*. The dividing line in a society like ancient Palestine should not be sought among the various social groups that constitute the society itself. Rather, the real division lies between the leaders of the traditional society and the officers of the state who act not on behalf of the family system, but as the representatives of a remote and exalted king who may or may not, once, himself have been a member of one of the social segments that belong to his kingdom.

It should also be recognized that in spite of the fact that the Davidic dynasty seems itself to have stressed its membership of the tribe of Judah, such claims were not heard when Omri and his sons reigned in Israel, or when Jehu and his followers exterminated the dynasty of Omri. It is my contention that the Old Testament writers were well aware of the conflict between tribal society and the state, their paradigmatic example of the conflict being the Nabot incident which they place in the days of king Ahab of Israel (1 Kgs. xxi).

If we assume that the anti-Canaanite sentiments expressed by Old Testament writers originated in historical circumstances connected with the (re-)appearance of centralized states in Palestine in the Iron Age, it may at the same time be possible to trace the hatred of the Canaanites back to even earlier times.

If we state that the Canaanites were the representatives of the governments of the city-states of Syria and Palestine already in the Late Bronze Age, who were considered to be foreign intruders by the members of the local societies, all of which were family-organized, then it would be wrong to think that ordinary man—nomad—peasant—or townsman (to use these stereotypes)—would have thought differently about these Canaanites, or that one of these groups would have held them in greater esteem than the two other groups.

In Iron Age Palestine, the tribes that arose after the downfall of Late Bronze Age civilization may have remembered the Canaanites/administrators as having been their enemies, and when, at a later date, the tribesmen were incorporated into the new states of Israel and Judah, they may for a second time have believed their oppressors, the king's servants, to be not Israelites but "Canaanites".

Although this theory may sound unusual, it cannot be ruled out.

To the contrary, it is possible to support it by additional arguments, for example by pointing out that the political power system of Late Bronze Age Palestine was imposed on the country and its population by its Egyptian overlords, and, as is well known, the Egyptians in the time of the 19th dynasty may have established a province which they called Canaan, although this province probably only have encompassed the southern part of the country.[25] The local inhabitants may therefore have used the term "Canaanites" to denote their foreign oppressors and especially their local lackeys.

When the historical narratives about the origin of Israel were drafted many centuries later, the Canaanites, who were always understood to be the enemies of Israel, were then turned into the original population of the land, whom the Israelites were to exterminate and drive away according to the will of their God, Yahweh.[26]

---

25 On this, see my *The Canaanites*, pp.25-52 (Ch.2, "The Canaanites and their Land: The Second Millennium") and the literature quoted there.

26 Although this model of pre-Israelite Palestinian society is seemingly in conflict with the model formulated by, in particular, Mario Liverani, (see above), it at the same time reveals the weak link in Liverani's construction. Liverani employs a model which covers two basic structures, the free persons and the "king's men", that is, the dependents of the royal palace, while he at the same time asserts that a dividing-line exists between city and countryside. In actual fact, what he has acknowledged is the basic dichotomy between familially-organized people, who are not paid by the palace (i.e., the state, in the Late Bronze Age), and people who were the immediate subjects of the king and whose social position was based on their dependence on the king, i.e., the state. In this connexion the assumed division between city and countryside is of secondary importance, as people living in the city but engaged in agricultural pursuits would presumably share the animosity and bad feelings of the rural population towards the officers of the state. Like most scholars, Liverani has overestimated the importance of social organization, and at the same time underestimated the role of the political network that existed in the small Syrian and Palestinian states.

THE IRON AGE OF NORTHERN JORDAN

by

MAGNUS OTTOSSON
Uppsala

When Professor Eduard Nielsen, Doctor *honoris causa* at the University of Uppsala in 1987, together with Joshua, Moses' assistant, assembled the tribes of Israel to Shechem, it was at dawn of the Iron Age in Palestine.[1] Although most of the people mentioned in the Book of Joshua belonged to the Cisjordanian area, there were some tribes which represented Transjordan. It must be regarded as an impossible task to reconstruct the historical reality behind the Day of the Covenant in Shechem, but the archaeological activity has been so intense in Palestine in recent years that we have got a rather clear picture of the history of settlement in the period in question. We do not know whether the Cisjordanian settlements could be called "Israelite" or not.[2] But as the Old Testament historiographers mostly had a good knowledge of tribal borders and areas, there is a good chance that the 218 villages or small towns in the region of Ephraim and Manasse may have belonged to people who could have taken part in covenantal ceremonies in Shechem.[3] Scholars are nowadays in any event very much aware of the difficulty of combining the archaeological results from the transition period between

---

[1] E. Nielsen, *Shechem. A Traditio-Historical Investigation* (Copenhagen, 1955). Although the space here does not allow more than a general note, I should like to emphasize how much Eduard's dissertation on Shechem methodologically meant for us in Uppsala during the fifties and sixties. Eduard has lectured here several times and his scholarly work was always discussed in Ivan Engnell's Higher Seminar. We regard Eduard as "one of us".

[2] In recent times, several monographs on early Israel have appeared. From a Scandinavian point of view I should like to mention N.P. Lemche, *Early Israel*, SVT 37 (Leiden, 1985) and G. W. Ahlström, *Who Were the Israelites?* (Winona Lake, 1986), further: *Toward a Consensus on the Emergence of Israel in Canaan*, ed. D. Edelman, *SJOT* 2 (1991), and Th. L. Thompson, "Palestinian Pastoralism and Israel's Origins", *SJOT* 6 (1992), pp. 1-13.

[3] See I. Finkelstein, *The Archaeology of the Israelite Settlement* (Jerusalem, 1988), pp. 65 ff.; 119 ff.; M. und H. Weippert, "Die Vorgeschichte Israels in neuem Licht", *Theologische Rundschau* 56 (1991), pp. 384 ff.

the Late Bronze Age and the Iron Age with the "history" told in the Book of Joshua and in the Book of Judges.[4] Whatever we should choose to call the settlers of this period, what we find is a new and concrete pattern of settlements, a pattern of villages which shows a way of life different in relation to that in the so-called "Canaanite" centres on the plains and further to the west. During this period there was an enormous change in the economy of Palestine which resulted in a stationary way of life concentrated in new settlements. Although they are small and not directly equipped with strong fortifications, they do not seem to have been either "poor" or wealthy; rather, they seem to have been founded by prosperous and—especially—numerous groups of people. The Iron Age could not have been introduced into this area in a more spectacular way.

The idea behind this short paper is not to enter into the historio-philosophical discussions on the transitional period which is now such a popular topic among scholars. I just want to describe how a small Scandinavian expedition in northern Jordan was lucky enough to find some remains of the period mentioned above, and, further, how they were able stratigraphically to investigate how the Transjordanian people of this time managed to start a settlement upon the Late Bronze Age ruins. They not only used the fortifications of this past period, but also, in the following Iron I A-period, were able to enlarge their settlement by building new walls combined with an elaborate gate system and citadel.

The site is Tell el-Fukhar[5], on the eastern side of the meandering Wadi esh-Shellale, situated around three kilometres west of Ramtha, the town on the border between Jordan and Syria. We were advised to dig here by Professors Siegfried Mittmann, Tübingen and Moawiyah Ibrahim, Irbid, if we sought to get a picture of the evolution of northern Jordan during the Iron Age. Together with Professor Svend Holm-Nielsen, the writer contacted the Secretary General of the Department of Antiquities of Jordan, Dr. Bisheh and his successor Professor, Dr. Safwan Tell, Amman. They gave us a permit for two seasons in 1990-91. Pro-

[4] See recently M. Ottosson, *Josuaboken—en programskrift för davidisk restauration*, Acta Universitatis Upsaliensis. Studia Biblica Upsaliensia 1 (Uppsala,1991), pp. 229 ff. English Summary, pp. 260-274.

[5] See the preliminary report in *AJA* 96 (1992), pp. 516-518 and M.Ottosson, "Tell el-Fukhar. Den skandinaviska expeditionen till norra Jordanien", *SEÅ* 57 (1992), pp. 7-27.

fessor Holm-Nielsen conferred his codirectorship on Dr. John Strange, Copenhagen. The latter concentrated his work on the top of the site in order to investigate a then-suggested "Hellenistic villa". Dr. Strange uncovered it in the Third Season, 1992. The main investigation of the Iron Age on Tell el-Fukhar was a Swedish project. In Uppsala we had started a project entitled "On the Arameans", and we suspected them to be the Iron Age settlers of northern Jordan, and naturally also of Tell el-Fukhar.[6]

Previous archaeological work in northern Jordan

Most of the archaeological work conducted in northern Jordan so far consists of surveys done at different times, and it is indeed interesting to compare the various results in order to follow the methods used for dating. Such a comparison first of all has to do with the pottery found on the different sites. A survey gives us what is only a very preliminary picture of the settlement of a site, and there may be accidental occurrences which affect our understanding of the different archaeological periods. The main and most detailed survey of northern Jordan was done by S. Mittmann in 1963-64.[7] He worked very systematically in making a useful division of northern Jordan using the points of the compass for orientation. For his area designated "der Norden" he used the asphalt road between esh-Shune-Irbid as the southern border, delimited by the Jordan to the west and the Yarmouk to the north. In this area he reported 88 sites; of these, 9 show LB II pottery, 22 Iron I and 22 Iron II-sherds. The last two numbers are interesting; there is, first of all, an enormous increase of settlements in Iron I compared with the number in LB II. "Iron II" is a fairly long period which is nowadays easily divisible into subdivisions. We are not told in Mittmann's report whether the sherds are of late or early provenience, and this may have been difficult to determine in the sixties. One thing in Mittmann's report is important to mention: on some sites, most of the sherds on the surface are of early Iron type, belonging to the 12th century B.C. "Iron II" is to be regarded as a general date, and we

---

[6] See M. Ottosson, "In Quest of the Arameans", (forthcoming in *Cahiers de la Revue biblique*).

[7] S. Mittmann, *Beiträge zur Siedlungs- und Territorialgeschichte des Nördlichen Ostjordanlandes*, Abhandlungen des Deutschen Palästinavereins, hrsg. von A. Kuschke (Wiesbaden, 1970).

will intuitively suggest that the term represents a late phase of the period. North of Irbid at least seven sites are reported to contain Iron I-II remains, and some of them are littered with pottery from Iron I. We thus get the impression that the most important settlements in the area belong to the early Iron I period. Irbid itself must have been a centre in ancient times. The entire site is now covered by the modern city, and salvage digs done by Dr. C.J.Lenzen reveal major gaps in the stratigraphic profile.[8] But also here it may be maintained that the site seems to have nurtured a large and wealthy population during Iron I A. The city wall had been built in LB II B and it was still in use in Iron I.

The Wadi esh-Shellale runs to the north around 10 km east of Irbid. Mittmann's survey of the sites concentrating around the wadi and representing the Iron Age gives the impression that pottery of the earliest period of the Iron Age preponderates.

Mittmann's survey of the region termed "der Westen" is impressive. In the area south of the road Irbid-Umm Qes down to Wadi Ragib on the western range of Aglun, 151 sites were surveyed. Four sites show LB II-sherds, 40 sites Iron I, and 23 sites Iron II-sherds. This area is just north of the Wadi Zerqa. In the beginning of the Iron Age, this valley and the area around it were densely settled, but the number of settlements in Iron II was reduced nearly 50 per cent.

Mittmann's area called by him "der Süden" lies east of Gerasa. 70 sites have been counted, namely those which were not visited by Nelson Glueck. It is difficult to get any reliable statistical material from here, as I do not know how many sites there really are. But of the sites visited one shows LB II sherds, 10 represent Iron I and 6 Iron II.

The area called "der Osten" covers the mountains north of the Medwar-Mafraq road and the plains next to Irbid. Here Mittmann counted 25 sites. One represents LB II and two sites show remains from Iron I, while a single one contains late Iron Age pottery.

Sketching Mittmann's survey results of the entire area north of the line esh-Shune-Irbid-Tell er-Ramith, we get the impression that the early Iron Age was a time when this area was densely settled. Written sources are so far missing, and the movements of people are

---

[8] C. J. Lenzen *et al.*, *ADAJ* 29 (1985), pp. 151-159; *Liber Annuus* 36 (1986), pp. 361-363; *BN* 42 (1988), pp. 27-35; *RB* 95 (1988), pp. 239-247.

not known, but the survey results nevertheless give a hint that there was then a stationary tendency in the social structure. People continued to settle on or in the layers of the LB II-cities. A pattern of new settlements on virgin soil like that in Cisjordan, which is supposed to have arisen through people abandoning the Bronze Age cities or arriving from elsewhere, i.e., the Israelites, is so far either not known or not observed in Transjordan. On the other hand, it is also very difficult to evaluate Mittmann's "Iron II". According to Mittmann's "Preface", the late Dr. Paul Lapp co-operated with him in reading the pottery. We may assume that Lapp at this time knew the Transjordanian Iron Age pottery from his excavations at Tell er-Rumeith.[9] Dr. Lapp was at the time completely sure that this site was identical with Ramoth Gilead, which is mentioned in the Old Testament. And he was also able to claim that the layers of destruction represented, now the Arameans and now the Israelites, according to the stories of shifting fortunes of war, as related in the Old Testament. Such statements were typical of the time.[10] Nowadays I think we have to be careful about reading OT-history out of the strata of northern Jordan. The Iron II A-B periods, which saw the battles of the Arameans and the Israelites, are certainly still to be looked for. The dating of the Iron II pottery, which was said to belong to these periods, was done about 30 years ago. According to modern pottery analysis, there is a clear trend in the area concerning the settlements during the Iron Age. They are early and/or late.

The East Jordan Valley Survey, conducted in 1975,[11] included 106 sites between the River Yarmouk and the Wadi Rajib, which is about six kms north of the Wadi Zerqa (the Jabbok). There was a clear decline in settlement from Middle Bronze Age II, (14 sites). Only 6 sites reveal remains from Late Bronze Age, but 19 sites are said to represent Iron I B, and nearly the same number of sites show continued settlement in Iron II. The Ghor was inhabited during the whole of this period. Most settlements were very prosperous. The area just north of the Wadi Zerqa seems to have been something of a crossroad. The main roads passing the Jezreel Valley reached the Ghor between the Wadi Zerqa and the Yarmouk, and here as in the valleys running up into the Gilead mountains there are many large

[9] *RB* 70 (1963), pp. 406-411; 75 (1968), pp. 98-105.

[10] Cf. B. Mazar *et al.*, "Ein Gev, Excavations in 1961", *IEJ* 14 (1964), pp. 1-49.

[11] M. Ibrahim *et al., BASOR* 222 (1976), pp. 41-66.

sites which were certainly important road stations and commercial centres. The Iron Age sites seem mostly to be spread along the Zerqa. The results of these important surveys have not yet been published in detail, but there have recently been extensive excavations on Tell Deir 'Alla, Tell el-Mazar, Tell es-Sa'idiyeh and, most recently, a Swedish expedition directed by Dr. Peter Fischer, Gothenburg. All these digs show that there were cultural relations with Cisjordan and the Ghor during all archaeological periods.[12]

The survey in the Maqarin area just south of and on the slopes of the Yarmouk included 31 sites.[13] Only one of these revealed Iron Age pottery, predominantly Iron I B. In using the term "Iron I B", the surveyors date the main settlements to around 1100-1000 B.C. As I have not seen the pottery, I dare not say in what way it corresponds to our "Iron I A" on Tell el-Fukhar (see below). The Maqarin survey gives the impression that the southern slopes of the Yarmouk and its adjacent valleys were very sparsely inhabited in the Iron Age. The land usable for settlements and cultivation is to be found north of the Yarmouk.[14] But just south of the Yarmouk, across from the Zeizoun railway station, there is a site of great interest, namely Tell el-Baidar.[15] Although the site is reported to be littered with pottery from the Late Bronze Age, the visible structures, a circular wall approximately 45 m in diameter which surrounds the hill, and a gateway of dressed basalt blocks, give associations to other sites both in Jordan, southern Syria and Golan which seem to have been important centres in the beginning of the Iron Age.[16]

The Iron I A period saw an enormous increase in settlements in central northern Jordan, but then there must have been a decrease,

---

12 See now R. G. Boling, *The Early Biblical Community in Transjordan* (Sheffield 1988).

13 *ADAJ* 22 (1977-78), pp. 114 f., 119-126.

14 A. Abou-Assaf, *Tell-Aschtara in Suedsyrien*. Erste Kampagne 1966, and *Tell-Aschtara*. Zweite Kampagne 1967, *Annales Archéologiques Arabes Syriennes* 18 (1968), pp. 103-122 and 19 (1969), pp. 101-108 and recently F. Braemer, *Syria* 61 (1984), pp. 219-25.

15 *ADAJ* 22 (1977-78), pp.122 f.

16 Cf. the layout of Tell Hadar in Golan (M. Kochavi, *IEJ* 39 (1989), pp. 1-17), and of Khanasiri and of Aidun, situated 20 kms resp. 3 kms west of Mafraq. See D. Homès-Fredericq-J.B. Hennessy (eds.), *Archaeology of Jordan II 1* (Leuven,1989), pp. 347 f. and pp. 125 f. For sites in southern Syria, see H. Sader, *Les états araméens de Syrie* (Diss. Tübingen, 1984), p. 287.

in some places an actual hiatus, until the Iron II C period. This impression is also reached through a reading of Ibrahim/ Mittmann's report from the excavations on Tell el-Mugayyir around 25 years after Mittmann's survey of northern Jordan.[17] The excavators found a lot of pottery belonging to the early Iron Age. The Persian period was also well represented, but then the report speaks of "unvermischte Keramik der mittleren Eisenzeit", and here I should like to have more details, as the Persian period must be regarded as the last phase of Iron II. According to the description of the structures excavated so far on Tell el-Mugayyir, the site seems to have had the same function and history as Tell el-Fukhar (see below). This means that the site served as a well-protected caravanserai to house a garrison, provide safety for the people, and to store necessaries. In his report of the survey of the last site, Mittmann mentions sherds belonging to Iron I-II (12th to 9th centuries) but no Persian.[18] The excavations brought to light Iron I A and Persian sherds—a mere three representing Iron II A-B. I will not force the question of a "gap" of Iron II in northern Jordan until more sites have been excavated. Commercial centres and caravanserai may have existed, but whenever we have so far looked for structures representing this epoch, we have looked in vain.

Tell el-Fukhar may not have been the most central town in northern Jordan, but situated as it was on a sharp bend of the Wadi esh-Shellale, it could easily be defended, as the northern, western and southern sides create natural glacis and an Iron I A gate system to the east made the place fairly safe. There are excellent water supplies in the valley to the southeast. A tunnel, the length of which is as yet not known, has been cut here into the hill next to the neighbouring site, Tell Umm er-Riglen, about 250 m southeast of Tell el-Fukhar. On top of the site, Hellenistic walls are visible on the surface, but to the northeast pottery and some small finds in the irregular baulks of robbers' trenches assured us that we could easily reach Iron Age levels here. Through his survey on the tell in 1963, Professor Mittmann was able to suggest that, according to the pottery finds, the site had been settled especially in the Late Bronze Age and in Iron Age I-II. When we started our excavations we could definitely see that it was the latest phase of Iron Age II, Iron II C, which was

---

17 *AfO* 33 (1986), pp. 167-172.
18 Mittmann (1970).

represented on the site. Sherds from this period were found mixed with Iron I A pottery on the northern slope. Structures from the Iron Age II A-B were totally missing. Only three sherds from these periods have been found so far. Although erosion has been extensive on the site, the lack of remains from Iron II A-B cannot be accounted for by this fact alone.

The stratigraphy of the Iron Age was very easy to follow, and we were surprised to see that the Iron I A people were aware of the structures of the previous periods. They had reused the defensive walls and widened their settlement to the east in such a way that it fit into the previous layout. Some sherds found in the fill were datable to Early Bronze Age I-III. The Middle Bronze Age was not represented at all.[19] The first town with a defence system on the site was built in Late Bronze II A. In this period a heavy outer defensive wall, around 150 cm wide, was made out of large boulders with cobble chinking. The small section of the wall which we were able to lay bare in the First season 1990 seems to have belonged to a citadel. The wall was preserved to a height of 320 cm, but in this period it was not equipped with glacis and moat. The wall section found by us ran east-west, but another wall, now very much robbed, ran to the south and formed a corner with it at an angle of 90 degrees. On both sides of this wall there were well-laid stone pavements. The find of a "Hyksos" scarab from around 1550 B.C. dated the pavements definitively, and this date was in congruence with the pottery types.[20]

Late Bronze Age—Iron Age

About half a metre above the stone pavement of the Late Bronze II A period there was another pavement of the same type. Although a robber's trench of modern date had spoiled a part of it, so much of the layout was preserved that we could reconstruct a so-called Four Room House. One column built up of two circular stone rings, (one was fallen), about 40 cm in diameter, was found *in situ*, and an elliptical "hole" in the pavement two m away gave us the impression

---

[19] J. Strange reports some MB II B or LB I A sherds found in Area C during the third season 1992 "Tell el-Fukhar 1992: Third Season", (report to the department of Antiquities of the Hashemite Kingdom of Jordan to be published in *ADAJ*).

[20] This scarab was lost.

that there had been a line of columns here belonging to a house. On the pavement were remains of at least two ovens *(tabun)*, and next to them an enormous ash pit. It was not possible to determine the size of the "house", but when we found other house installations belonging to the same level in the square west of it, we understood that the transition between the Bronze and Iron Ages was spectacular on our site. Next to the "house" and stone pavement 3 was a basalt column, preserved to a height of 110 cm and half a metre in diameter. The stones had been reused, and the postament seems to have been a capital in a previous life. This type of column has been found on Tell el-Husn (Beth-Shan). The area has been very much sacked, but a standing stone, 123 cm high, 39 cm wide and 20 cm deep, well cut on all sides, had been placed adjacent to a house wall, (B 21). Two flat rocks, each measuring ca. 65 × 55 cm, were placed in line in front of the standing stone. Wall B 21 was of some interest, as it in its exact centre formed a narrow niche. It is very difficult to reconstruct the layout of the installations, but all of them belong to the crucial transitional period which has been so much debated in Palestinian archaeology. It seems likely that the wall mentioned above is the rear wall of a rectangular building of the so-called "Migdal Temple" type, and it is indeed tempting to judge the area cultic.[21] But so far only one piece of an oblong fenestred incense burner decorated with crawling snakes (compare the burners at Beth Shan) has been found in the area.

The types of pottery are of greatest interest. There is a clear mixture of Bronze Age and Early Iron Age types in manufacture and style. Painted pottery such as Chocolate-on White and Mycenean III are mixed with coil-made storage jars and cooking pots. Some sherds of the "Collared rim jar" type indicated that jars so typical for the period all over Palestine were also used on Tell el-Fukhar. The transition period, LB II-Iron I, is usually held to have been a time of newcomers in this area of Palestine who settled in the mountains and in places with sufficient moisture. However, it would be difficult to argue that "newcomers" dwelled in this level, as the pottery traditions from the Bronze Age are so strong. Although the

---

21 Naturally, we were tentatively thinking in cultic categories, suspecting that the "niche" belonged to a "Migdal" temple; see M. Ottosson, *Temples and Cult Places in Ancient Palestine* (Uppsala, 1980). Cf. also G. Loud, *Megiddo II* (Chicago, 1948), Figs 247 and 248.

settlers of the period reused the fortification wall and certainly the building behind the standing stone and erected the basalt column, they did not reuse the well-laid stone pavements of the previous period. Naturally, they must have been aware of these structures, but they did not spend any time to get through half a metre of clay and *terra rossa*. It may be that, the clay which often appears in tumbles all over the site was too hard to penetrate. They laid new pavements instead, in the process not seldom using large and heavy flat rocks. One interesting thing is that the enormous ash pit mentioned above was "levelled out" when the Iron I A walls were laid above it. New walls were built in the transitional period of fairly large rocks, the stones laid directly on the ground without any foundation trenches at all. According to such small finds as mortars and pestles in great number, the citizens of the period were farmers who cultivated the fields in the area and kept sheep and goats. It is important to note that they used exactly the same domestic area as the people of the Late Bronze Age II A had done.

The Iron I A period

The structures belonging to the Iron I A period were found just above and in relation to the latest Bronze Age layer and everywhere on the northern and northeastern slopes of the site just below the humus level. Sometimes the lines of the walls were visible on the surface. We noted that there had been heavy erosion through the ages. Some sections of the walls were definitely gone. The walls had also been looted of their stones. But the remains nevertheless made quite an impression on the excavators. The tumbles of hard yellow clay here and there seem to have prevented the stones from being eroded away or looted. Also in this period, stone pavements were laid another half a metre above the previous level, and finds of lamps and ovens made from two storage jars, one inserted into the other, were common. The large ash pit mentioned above could still have been in use. Some typical Iron I A pottery was found in it. When we widened the trenches on the slope to the northeast we still found remains of Iron I A close to the surface, but below them there were no structures from the Bronze Age. The inhabitants of the Iron I A town had reused the LB II A-B fortification wall, B 2, running east-west on the northern slope, but they also built a continuation of it to the east around eight metres in length, and from there it made a turn to the south at an angle of 90 degrees. This wall was well built, and it runs up to a gate with gate house. Further digging has to clarify the layout of the gate area, but so far it is very impressive, with a possible glacis of a heavy layer of cut limestone. The Iron I A town was thus bigger than its forerunners, and its defence at least in the gate area looks very strong. It is possible that stones were taken from the Bronze Age walls inside the new fortifications, but as far as we could make out, this activity was done by a new generation of inhabitants. The newly built-up area was nicely fitted to the previous smaller town. The north-south wall of the city gate mentioned above ran parallel with a Late Bronze Age II A wall, which had been largely robbed in Persian times. It seems probable that also this wall ran up to a city gate of that time. The walls of the Iron I A gate house were robbed down to their very foundation. But this looting must not have happened later than in the Iron II C period, as the stratification lines in the baulks are straight. The inner wall of the gate running around ten metres to the north continued also to the south and to the summit of the site, from where a citadel or palace governed the area in both the LB II A-B and Iron I A periods.

The Iron II C period

Remarkably enough, there were no remains of the Iron II A-B periods on Tell el-Fukhar. As said above, only three sherds of the red polished ware typical for this time were found. There could have been enormous erosion through the centuries, as also the Iron I A-walls just below the surface were robbed in places. But the last phase of the Iron Age was represented through several nicely stone-dressed silos. These silos were everywhere dug into the Iron I and LB II layers. There was not a single structure that could be referred to Iron II A-B. There was no town on the site in the Iron II C period. There was only a threshing-place and the silos offered good facilities for storage. There are good winds here most of the day, especially in the summer. Grains of wheat were sometimes found in the deep silos. The pottery indicates that the threshing-place was in use in the Persian period. From the end of the Iron I A period, the site seems to have been uninhabited and used as a quarry for more than 500 years. It was first in the Hellenistic period that there was a wealthy settlement on top of the site in the form of a large "villa". A coin of Ptolemy III (245-221 B.C.), found directly on a floor together with beautiful pottery of the time, offered an exact date.

The investigation of the Iron Age in northern Jordan is still in its beginning phases, even though work started nearly 50 years ago. It may be that the area has not been regarded as very important for the history of Palestine, as it has been "hidden" south of the curving Yarmouk. Thanks to its position on the side of the main crossroads north of Irbid there are now possibilities to find "virgin" sites with pottery and structures of great interest. Their content can now be compared with the enormous material excavated on hundreds of sites to the south and west. Through its isolation the settlers of the different periods formed a pottery culture, at least at the end of the Bronze Age and in the beginning of the Iron Age, which must be studied and restudied. So much is certain at least from the results obtained so far from the excavations on Tell el-Fukhar: the Late Bronze Age II A-B and Iron I A consist of a single cultural block. This may be recognized first of all through the layout of the site, which was used from the LB II A-B periods into Iron I A. The same kind of stone-paved floors were used, and the defensive wall built in LB II was in use in the Iron I A period, when it was also extended to the east. This block is stratigraphically easy to discern, as the LB II A marks the beginning of town-planning on the site and Iron I A the end. The cultural unity is also shown through the coil-building manufacture of pottery.

Usually, Iron I A is understood as the period when iron tools appeared for the first time. Recent excavations in Jordan show that this date can be pushed back into the LB II B period[22] On Tell el-Fukhar a mason's tool which was certainly made of iron was found below an Iron I A wall in 1991 and from the latest season in 1992, Dr. John Strange and Dr. Patrick McGovern report the find of a crucible bottom in an LB II B context. The crucible appears to have contained melted iron from a refining operation. Metallurgical activity is thus to be proposed for Tell el-Fukhar already at the end of the Bronze Age.

Certainly there were no newcomers in the Iron Age. The settlers had performed a reconstruction and an enlargement of the previous

---

[22] P. E. McGovern, *The Late Bronze and Early Iron Ages of Central Transjordan: The Baq'ah Valley Project, 1977-1981*, University Museum Monograph 65 (Philadelphia, 1986), p. 340.

Bronze Age town. They were agriculturalists who used dry farming and shepherds who kept sheep and goats, like their forerunners on the site. Finds of tools including hundreds of pestles, mortars and grinding stones, together with animal bones, prove this. The main repertoire of pottery consists of cooking pots and storage jars.

* * *

It is not easy deciding how to judge the Old Testament texts about northern Jordan in the light of the results of the excavations and surveys in the area. But we are told that Gileadites, Macirites and Jairites, just to mention some groups of people, lived here. In the OT texts these peoples appear very much schematically and the historical setting is very diffuse. There are also towns which were placed in northern Gilead, Num. 32:39 ff., but very few were known by name. In the wars fought between Israel and Aram, the area of northern Jordan is often mentioned as the main battlefield. Archaeologically speaking, we are then in the period of Iron II A-B. But we have put a question-mark above for this period. It is very strange that remains of Iron II A-B in northern Transjordan are either missing or very thin when there are plenty of them in Cisjordan.[23] Much research on the problem has still to be done. And as excavations continue on very few sites, we have no possibility to fill in the chronological gap. Such a long lacuna of settlement would seem to be historically impossible. But as the OT-texts are so silent concerning the names of the many Early Iron age towns, the splendour of which the now-ruined sites still give evidence, we must assume that the OT authors knew very little about the history of the area. But it could at least be said that there was a great density of settlements during the Iron I A period.[24] We do not know whether there was in northern Jordan a settlement pattern like that in Cisjordan, with hundreds of small, undefended villages. The surveys have mostly been done on clearly visible ruined sites, and so the excavations are very few in number. It is a strange coincidence that the archaeological results on Tell el-Fukhar, so far, offer chronological possibilities to understand the early history of the area which the texts of the OT try to describe. In the transitional period between

---

[23] See recently D. Ussishkin *et al*, "Excavations at Tel Jezreel 1990-1991", *Tel Aviv* 18 (1991), pp.72-92 and 19 (1992), pp. 3-70.

[24] See R. G. Boling, *The Early Biblical Community in Transjordan* (Sheffield, 1988).

the Bronze Age and the Iron Age, people lived there who continued and developed the previous culture and also became the initiators of the subsequent Iron I A period, the people who broke the framework of the old town and created a large settlement founded on the old traditions. Their town must have been very short-lived, and no new generations of Iron II A-B continued city life on the site. The Iron I A people were the last citizens in the Iron Age and were surely no newcomers. They had to leave their town for an attacking enemy or something else. They did not return, and their site was left open to erosion and stone—,looting through the centuries. Modern robbers have dug several deep trenches on Tell el-Fukhar in order to find the treasure of gold which is said to have been hidden here in old days. The site still keeps this secret. But the people of Iron I A were mighty enough to send a large and representative delegation to the Day of Covenant at Shechem, if it was held in their days.[25]

---

[25] This statement does not mean that Jos 24 is regarded as an historical report, but rather as an ideological pivot in the framework of the composition of the whole Book of Joshua. See Ottosson (1991).

THE PROMOTING MOTHER
A LITERARY MOTIF IN THE UGARITIC TEXTS AND IN THE BIBLE

by

BENEDIKT OTZEN

Aarhus

One of the more conspicuous features in modern Old Testament scholarship is scholars' growing awareness of literary form and literary motifs in biblical texts. In earlier scholarship, the historical dimension was dominant in any treatment of biblical problems, and when it came to matters pertaining to literary form, they were most often dealt with along the lines of ''literary criticism'', in the classical, Germanic sense of the expression; of ''form criticism'', of ''tradition history'', or, in more recent times, of ''history of redaction''.

When, forty years ago, Eduard Nielsen instructed me in the exegesis of the Old Testament at the University of Copenhagen, he was to us students a representative of the then-modern ''history of tradition'', and, with his emphasis on the importance of oral tradition, one might think that he would not pay much attention to the literary form of a tradition as it has been preserved in a literary context. However, this was not the case. With a developed sense of form-critical issues, Nielsen invariably emphasized that one cannot take a shortcut back to an oral tradition: one has to respect the tradition as we have it, in literary form, in the actual Old Testament. It is exactly the scholar who is interested in moving back to the hypothetical oral tradition underlying the literary shape who must pay due attention to the forms and motifs of the literary product.

While conducting a seminar on the Ugaritic texts and the Old Testament, I came upon a literary motif that has a certain resemblance to a motif which crops up several times in the Old Testament, and even in the New. However, before revealing my observations I am bound to present my reservations: I am not a Ugaritologist, and ''literary reading'' of the Old Testament, in the contemporary sense, is not really my field. So the following observations are presented with appropriate modesty. My situation may be compared with that of Mr. Pott, one of the friends of Mr. Pickwick, who, when asked to write an article on Chinese Metaphysics, knew nothing about the topic, but took down his encyclopaedia, read the articles entitled "China" and "Metaphysics", respectively, after which, as Dickens has it, he "combined his informations". *Mutatis mutandis*: When I encountered the figures of the usurping Athtar and the mother figure behind him in the Ugaritic texts I combined my Ugaritic observations with my Old Testament knowledge.

Since the Ugaritic texts were found, numerous attempts have been made to trace connexions between these Canaanite documents and the Old Testament. In the beginning, many scholars were tempted to delineate solid historical links between the Ugaritic records, and biblical stories and history. It is well known how Charles Virolleaud and René Dussaud found biblical places and persons to be mentioned in the Keret Legend. These highly-respected pioneers of Ugaritic scholarship were speedily forced to abandon these far-fetched interpretations, not least under the influence of the understanding of the Keret Legend as a dynastic myth or cultic myth, as was maintained by, for example, Sigmund Mowinckel, Johannes Pedersen, and Ivan Engnell—if I may be allowed to "promote" some Scandinavian scholars.[1]

The French approaches are merely examples of how connexions between the Ugaritic texts and the Old Testament should *not* be established. But this does not mean that such connexions are not many and various. Particularly the mythical and religious texts have yielded a richness of ideas that crops up in the Old Testament in a transformed shape which accomodates them to the development of Israelite religion.

I do not intend to pursue these general lines here, but shall instead concentrate on a single, specific literary motif which seems to be present both in the Ugaritic texts, the Old Testament and, perhaps, the New Testament; this is the motif I have termed the "promoting mother". In the case of the Ugaritic texts we find the motif in the stories about the god Athtar, who usurps the throne of Baal or of one of the other leading gods. In the Old Testament we encounter this motif in both the patriarchal stories and in the Davidic narrative cycle.

---

[1] Henri Cazelles, "Ras Schamra und der Pentateuch", *Theol Quartalschrift* 138 (1958), p. 30, mentions other scholars who have criticized Virolleaud and Dussaud.

If we tried to find a common denominator for the conflicts in the mythological texts from Ugarit it would probably not be far wide of the mark to say that all of them are about power, about who has the right to be the king of the gods and to have his royal palace built. This holds good both for the texts about Baal and Yam and for those about Baal and Mot. The texts about Anat and Baal, and about Baal's temple or palace also have the same centre of gravity. In this play of intrigues and struggles we meet the god Athtar, not as a principal character, but as a figure whose attempts to obtain power, though unsuccessful, are typical of the development of events. At some point further back in ancestry of the myth he may have played a more important role as a sort of "substitute king", but in the form in which we have the texts now he is merely a pawn in the game, a pawn in the hands of a powerful, but not entirely beneficent mother, the goddess Athirat.[2]

Right at the beginning of the text dealing with the fight between Baal and Yam (CTA 2, col. III) we meet Athtar as king. However, he cannot maintain his power: Shaphash, the sun-goddess, tells him that El has decided that Yam is to be king, and Yam is in turn himself overpowered by Baal. Unfortunately, the part of the text that tells us about Athtar is heavily damaged, so that we cannot see just who is arriving at the abode of El to complain about Yam and to stand up for Athtar's cause. If the verbs in question are to be understood as masculine singular, it may be Athtar himself who speaks, but if they are plural, then it may be Athtar's speakers. However, it could just as easily be the messengers of his mother, Athirat, so that already in this text it is possible that we find the mother who attempts to promote her own son. Certainty, however, is impossible.[3]

However this may be, the role of Athirat in the various conflicts in the mythological texts is somewhat ambiguous.[4] Sometimes she

---

[2] For Athtar: Caquot-Sznycer-Herdner, *Textes ougaritiques*, I (Paris, 1974), p.95; F.O.Hvidberg-Hansen, *Kana'anæiske myter og legender*, I (Aarhus, 1990), p.30; further: A.Caquot, "Le dieu 'Athtar et les textes de Ras Shamra", *Syria* 35 (1958), pp. 45-60; J.Gray, "The Desert God 'Attar in the Literature and Religion of Canaan", *JNES* 8 (1949), pp. 72-83. On Athtar as "substitute king", see A.S.Kapelrud, *Baal in the Ras Shamra Texts* (Copenhagen, 1952), p.76, and Th.H. Gaster, *Thespis* (1950) 2nd ed., (New York, 1961), pp.216-19.

[3] See Hvidberg-Hansen (1990), p.52, on the various possible translations; he himself thinks of either Athtar or his messengers.

[4] For new literature about Athirat, see O.Loretz, *Ugarit und die Bibel* (Darmstadt, 1990), p.83 n.195; cf. Kapelrud (1952), pp.75f; and Hvidberg-Hansen (1990), pp.40-43.

acts as Baal's enemy, as we shall see later, but in another text (CTA 4, col. II) she seems to help Baal to have his temple built. On the other hand, she hardly does so on her own account, but rather out of fear of Baal and Anat. When these two gods arrive at her home, she is so frightened that it has the most catastrophic and embarrassing consequences for her.[5] She is afraid that they have come to kill her sons, and her ensuing willingness to help Baal is apparently due, not only to their bribing her with rich gifts, but also to her fear. By helping Baal, she protects her sons against the belligerent gods, Baal and Anat. Eventually, Athirat and her sons are invited to the banquet at which Baal inaugurates his temple (CTA 4, col. VI, 46).

Instead of being grateful for this, Athirat and her sons seem to be highly exhilarated and jubilant when Baal is forced to surrender his power and descend to Mot in the underworld (CTA 6, col. I, 39-42). In the first place, it is El, the one responsible for the world-order, who suggests that some other god will have to ascend Baal's throne; the gods may not be without a king. As Athirat is the mother of the gods it will, naturally, have to be one of her sons. El seems to want the strongest (oldest?) of Athirat's sons to be king, one that could tolerate comparison with Baal (CTA 6, col.I, 49-51). Athirat, however, has different plans: she wants the cleverest of her sons to be king. El appears to intimate cautiously that the one in question might be too weak, but Athirat seeks to secure a career for her (favourite?) son, who, as it develops, is Athtar, the god of the young goats. She gets her way.[6]

But alas, Athtar is a failure: "his feet did not reach the foot-stool, his head did not reach its top. And Athtar the terrible spoke: 'I cannot be king in the recesses of Zephon'. Athtar the terrible came down, he came down from the seat of the mightiest Baal, and became king over the whole broad earth".[7] We do not hear about the reaction of his ambitious mother, as at least 30 lines of text are

---

5 Provided, that is, that one follows the translation of Caquot-Sznycer-Herdner (1974), pp.197f.: "Son excrément couvre sa chair; elle répand son ordure dans la mer, l'urine, son excrément dans les fleuves". Other translations find references to various parts of Athirat's apparel behind the enigmatic words.

6 The problems of the translation of the conversation between El and Athirat are treated in most translations. See e.g. J.C.L.Gibson, *Canaanite Myths and Legends* (Edinburgh, 1978), p.75; Caquot-Sznycer-Herdner (1974), pp.256f.; Hvidberg-Hansen (1990), pp.113f. (with notes in vol. II, pp.82f.).

7 Translation in Gibson (1978), p.76.

missing, but we may imagine that she reacted violently when she acknowledged the fiasko.

We leave the lofty world of the gods and their far too worldly skirmishes. We turn instead to some Old Testament stories about ancient times, when human passions were no less strong and unabashed than the divine emotions. The stories are more well known than are the Ugaritic tales, so that we may be briefer and concentrate on the motif of the mother.

As is well known, scholars have often seen parallels between the Ugaritic Keret Legend and the biblical story of the Davidic succession. In his doctoral thesis *David the Chosen King* (1964), Agge Carlson mentions the obvious connexions and claims that "accepted literary patterns have provided a basis for the form given the Davidic story". He emphasizes what he calls the *hieros gamos* motif in both the Ugaritic and the biblical cycles, respectively: Keret's marriage to Hurriya and David's to Bathsheba, and he remarks that the latter plays a "distinctly negative role" in the ensuing Succession Narrative.[8]

Henri Cazelles also concentrates upon the Keret Legend. He draws our attention to the conspicuous detail that the eighth of Keret's daughters, the youngest of all his children "is to be given the first-born's blessing". He refers to the biblical stories in which the younger child obtains the right of the first-born, and he observes "die Rolle der Frauen" in these stories and mentions the mother Rebecca who secures her youngest son Jacob the right of the first-born, the mother Bathsheba, who prepares the way to the throne for her son Solomon, and so on.[9]

However, Cazelles also finds a mother figure who plays a special role in the Baal cycle. Cazelles seemingly combines CTA 5,V18-25 (Baal's intercourse with the heifer and the birth of his son) with CTA 10,III,25-38 (Baal's intercourse with Anat/the heifer and the birth of Baal's son). According to Cazelles Anat adopts the child, clothes it and brings it to Mount Saphon where, eventually, Baal entrusts the throne of his dominion to his child. Cazelles emphasizes the suc-

---

[8] R.A.Carlson, *David, the Chosen King* (Stockholm, 1964), pp.190-93; cf. Hvidberg-Hansen (1990), pp.204f., and Stan Rummel, *Ras Shamra Parallels*, III (Roma, 1981), pp.299-317.

[9] Henri Cazelles, *Theol. Quartalsschrift* 138 (1958), pp.31f.

cession motif in the Ugaritic texts, and he pursues this motif on into the Old Testament. He, too, mentions Isaac, who obtains the succession instead of the first-born, Ishmael; Jacob, who obtains it instead of Esau; and Judah, who is the fourth son of Jacob, but who nevertheless comes to possess both sceptre and throne. And in all these connexions, he adds, in both the Ugaritic texts and in the Old Testament, the role of the women is predominant. He apparently thinks that in the story about the child Anat bears to Baal Anat acts as the promoting mother, who brings her last-born child to Saphon so that he may inherit the throne (at the expense of Baal's older sons?).[10]

Of course, it would be interesting if we also had an instance in which Anat acts as the promoting mother in a manner parallel to the figure of Athirat in the text dealt with above. But however willing I might happen to be to accept more "promoting mothers" in the Ugaritic texts, I am not sure that Cazelles is right in his interpretation of Anat's role in the texts just mentioned—always assuming, that is, that I have understood his rather brief presentation correctly. But the Old Testament parallels that he adduces to this motif are valuable, and he is certainly right to claim that the female members of the royal family in the Keret Legend (Hurray, the queen; Thitmanat, the daughter; and Sha'taqat, the demon, whom Cazelles identifies with Thitmanat) act independently and sometimes importantly in the plot, just as the women do in the biblical stories.

As far as I can see, however, it is *only* in the records of the goddess Athirat and her son Athtar in the Baal cycle that we have a fully developed Ugaritic parallel to the biblical "promoting mother" stories. I said above that all the stories in the Ugaritic myths and legends are about "power". In the Baal cycle the mother intervenes, as Athirat attempts to determine who is to possess power and become king of the gods. Similarly, the Old Testament stories are also about "power". They settle such questions as who will become the ancestor of the future Israel, Isaac or Ishmael? Jacob or Esau? Or, who will become king of Israel, Solomon or Adonijah? Here, too, the mother attempts to decide the issues.

More recently, another scholar has dealt with the relationship

---

10 Cazelles (1958), pp.35-37.

between the Ugaritic texts and the Old Testament narratives. In the lavishly published third volume of *Ras Shamra Parallels* (1981), Stan Rummel has a section entitled "Narrative Structures in the Ugaritic Texts".[11] The first 60 pages are about the combat between Baal and Yam as reflected in Exod 15, Judg 5 and certaim psalms which contain the combat theme, some Deutero-Isaianic passages, and so forth. The last part of the section, however, concentrates on the Keret Legend and its similarities with the patriarchal stories, and with the succession story within the Davidic cycle.

Rummel systematically examines the views of such other scholars as Engnell, Gordon, Fisher, and Carlson (strangely enough, though, not Cazelles). He first focuses on Keret's vow in its parallel relationship to Jacob's vow in Gen 28. After all, both vows are made in the course of the hero's journey to secure a wife for himself in a foreign country. He also discusses some general considerations relating to the respective structures of the Keret Legend and the patriarchal cycle. When he comes to the Davidic cycle, Rummel criticizes Engnell's cultic interpretation of the Keret Legend. He treats Carlson's rather short exposition in some detail. We have already mentioned Carlson's views, and we shall return to some of the material in Rummel's work below, when we deal with the motif of the promoting mother in both the patriarchal cycle and in the Davidic cycle.

Roger Syrén has discussed some of the tales we shall meet in the following in his forthcoming book, *The Forsaken Firstborn*. Syrén does not adduce Ugaritic material for comparison; nor is he especially interested in the roles of the various mother-figures. But he does provide a thorough analysis of the tales of the first-born who fails to obtain his rightful inheritance: Ishmael, Esau, Reuben, and Manasseh. He carries out a literary analysis of the texts and finds that a theological trend underlies them. We meet the attitude behind this theology in the post-exilic generations which were confronted with the problem of foreigners in the time of the reforms of Nehemiah and Ezra. Syrén's treatment contains a wealth of valuable observations, and we shall return to it in the following.[12]

---

[11] Rummel (1981), pp. 221-332.

[12] Roger Syrén, *The Forsaken Firstborn. A Study on a Recurrent Motif in the Patriarchal Narratives.* The book will be published in 1993 in Sheffield. Roger Syrén has very kindly placed the manuscript of his book at my disposal; naturally, I can only refer to it meaningfully by section.

We shall take the Succession Narrative first. These narratives have often been treated; I have already mentioned Agge Carlson's study above, and in general I shall refer to David Gunn's excellent analysis in *King David*. Gunn, too, it may be remarked, has an eye for the role played by women in the record. Among other things, he mentions the remarkable way in which "a woman is so often an important catalyst in the plot" (Rizpa, Bathsheba, Tamar, Abishag): "The Woman who Brings Death".[13] The Succession Narrative is about royal power, and it thus comes close to the story of Athtar's trying to usurp Baal's throne. The obvious difference between the Ugaritic version of the story and the biblical one is, of course, that there is a "happy ending" in 1 Kings 1, at least in the sense that Solomon and his promoting and intriguing mother are the winners. By contrast, in the Ugaritic narrative, Athtar and his otherwise powerful mother, who is mother of all the gods, are the loosers.

We know the situation as it is depicted in 1 Kings 1: David is dying and bedridden. His oldest son, Adonijah, wants to be king after him and arranges for his coronation to take place in the Kedron Valley. Nathan and Bathsheba manipulate the senile David to let the younger son, Solomon, who is David's son by Bathsheba, become king, and to this end they arrange a competing ceremony also in the Kedron Valley. As we have mentioned, Bathsheba and Solomon come out as the victors. The succession to the throne in Jerusalem is arranged (so the story-teller intimates) in accordance with the will of the good God—and of Bathsheba.[14]

We encounter more or less the same features in the story of Rebecca. By manipulating Isaac, who is also senile and bedridden, she ensures that Jacob, her younger son, obtains the blessing of the firstborn. Of course Jacob, the ancestor of the twelve tribes, has to emerge victorious. We need not dwell upon the Jacob-Rebecca narrative[15]; as far as the motif of the promoting mother is con-

---

13 D.M.Gunn, *The Story of King David. Genre and Interpretation*, JSOT SS 6 (Sheffield, 1978), p.43.

14 Cf. Rummel (1981), pp.295-317 (the discussion mentioned above, mainly with A.Carlson, about the Keret Legend and the Succession Narrative).

15 In his introduction to his chapter about the Jacob-Esau relationship (ch.3), Syrén makes several observations on the similarities between the Ishmael narrative in Gen 21 (and 16) and the Jacob-Esau tale in Gen 27 (and 25): the pre-natal oracles; the mothers favouring the younger, the fathers the elder son. There is also an

cerned, this narrative goes by the book, and Rebecca is exactly as we should expect her to be: enterprising, strong-willed, headstrong—and not overly scrupulous.

The same may be said of Genesis 21. Sarah is childless and, although it may be humiliating to her, she is forced to let Abraham have a son by her Egyptian slave-girl. When, later, miraculously, Sarah conceives and bears her own son Isaac, she seizes a silly pretext to drive out the slave-girl: the older boy laughs at the younger! But officially she says that the slave-girl's son, Ishmael, "shall not share the inheritance with my son Isaac". Once again the narrative is about power: who shall inherit the legacy of the mighty Abraham? En passant, we should note that the role of the mighty Abraham is somewhat pathetic in this story; he is apparently uneasy at the conflict between his two wives. But to Sarah her son's interests are far more important than anything else: she gets her way, and Hagar and Ishmael are sent—by Abraham—into the desert[16].

The outcome of each of these three stories, whether about Solomon, Jacob or Isaac, is obvious and inevitable. But it is important that these stories be told, even if they are obvious, in the first place because they throw the power and greatness of the protagonist into relief; secondly, because they reflect the actual balance of power in the mythology or in the historical tradition of the people in which they are told. Solomon, Jacob and Isaac are dominant figures in Israelite tradition, whereas Adonijah, Esau and Ishmael are not. Just as Baal is a major figure in the Ugaritic pantheon, and hence is victorious by definition, while Athtar is a minor god.

---

example of the "deliberate variation of narrative analogy": Jacob flees, whereas Esau stays at home, while in the other cycle Ishmael flees and Isaac remains with his parents. In later sections, Syrén develops his idea that these stories reflect the relations of post-exilic Jews to foreigners (e.g. section 3.2.3.5, and the final section of the book, entitled "A Historical *Sitz* for the Motif", section 6.4). Also C. Westermann *Genesis 12-36,* BKA I/2 (Neukirchen, 1981), p.541, has observed the relationship between Gen 27 and 21; J.P.Fokkelman, *Narrative Art in Genesis* (Assen, 1975), p.101, has studied a parallel feature in the two accounts about the ageing, bedridden fathers, Isaac and David. Fokkelman shows the conspicuous structure of the whole chapter on p.98. See also Rummel (1981), pp.284-95 for material from the Keret Legend.

[16] Roger Syrén's treatment of Gen 21 is found in section 1.3. He presents his observations of the relations of the Ishmael cycle to the post-exilic congregation in the chapter entitled "The Ishmael-Motif Applied to a Post-Exilic Context" (section 2). J. Van Seters, *Abraham in History and Tradition* (New Haven, 1975), pp.192-202, cf. 309-12, likewise dates these traditions to the exilic or post-exilic periods. Syrén refers throughout to Van Seters' study.

I am not sure whether the story of the mother of the sons of Zebedee in Matthew 20 provides a good parallel to the other stories. She does not engage in intrigue, but she does promote, indeed. She begs that, if her sons may not become kings in the divine kingdom, then at least some kind of viceregents. As we all know, the mother is unsuccessful; the sons of Zebedee are offered suffering instead of royal glory.

Looking back upon these various stories, we need not emphasize yet again the obvious similarities between them, nor the differences, which no one could fail to see. I think it has become clear that I am not trying to establish any connexion between them, whether historical or literary, in the sense that one version is supposed to be dependent on one or more of the others. As Liverani says, when he traces a specific literary motif common to an Egyptian legend, to the story of kign Idrimi of Alalakh, to the legend of king Keret of Ugarit, and to the story of king David of Israel: "we should not try to look for the origin of the motif, and in which context it is secondary or derived from elsewhere. We can talk about different but parallel use of the same pattern which corresponds to certain psycho-social phenomena that have been known all over"[17]. Agge Carlson says the same in different words in his treatment of the relationship between the Keret Legend and the Davidic story: "the Davidic traditions describe history while making literary use of traditionally accepted motifs and patterns"[18].

Matters are more or less the same, as far as our motif about mothers and sons is concerned. I shall offer a few hints about the way such observations as I have imparted above may prove useful to Old Testament scholarship.

It is well known that one of the biblical stories we have dwelled upon, namely the story about Solomon's way to the throne, has been treated by Edmund Leach along structuralist lines. Even if Leach is not an Old Testament scholar, he has nevertheless made some valuable observations on the story of David, leading up to Solomon's accession to the throne. He finds a pattern of "polar oppositions" in the narrative: Saul-David; David-Nabal; David-Uriah; Amnon-

---

[17] Mario Liverani, "Partire sul carro, per il deserto", *AION* NS 22 (1972), p. 404. Niels Peter Lemche has kindly drawn my attention to Liverani's utterance.

[18] Carlson (1964), p.192.

Absalom; Adonijah-Solomon[19]. And all the way through he sees "the female intermediary right in the middle", that is, between the male oppositionary figures: Saul's daughter Michal, Abigail, Bathsheba, Tamar, and Abishag. According to Leach, all of it deals with endogamy and exogamy, about mixed marriages and about the right to the Land of Israel of those of pure blood.[20]

Maybe Leach goes too far in his conclusions; that is not under discussion here. But I think he has detected a pattern in the stories, and it is fundamentally correct to interpret family relations as an expression of social or political realities. In Leach's own words, "details of past kinship and affinal connections are 'remembered' only as justification for the assertion of rights".[21]

Such narratives have mostly to do with fathers and sons, or else with the mutual relationships of brothers. When women are involved it is mostly as conjugal or sexual partners, and in this event the texts attempt to say something about endogamy and exogamy. Of course, the mother role is implied here; but the mother-son relationship, as is illustrated by our examples, is rare.

It is easiest for non-structuralists to see the value of the structuralist approach when we have to do with mythological texts. When Leach says that "the biblical story of the succession of Solomon to the throne of Israel is a myth which 'mediates' a major contradiction",[22] this is, of course, confusing. But it is useful for exegetes to observe how a mythical pattern or, as in this case, part of a mythical pattern, can make its way into an historical text (or what we are prone to call an historical text). Such observations can cast light on the historical record: one realizes that the historical record is, to a certain degree, stylized according to a certain pattern, and that its message may be more important than the question of its historical accuracy.

---

[19] Edmund Leach, "The Legitimacy of Solomon. Some Structural Aspects of Old Testament History", in Edmund Leach, *Genesis as Myth and Other Essays* (London, 1969), pp.25-83, esp. pp.74ff. Cf. R.C.Culley, "Some Comments on Structural Analysis and Biblical Studies", in *Congress Volume: Uppsala 1971*, SVT 22 (Leiden, 1972), pp.129-42. Rummel (1981), pp.317-20, gives an account of Leach's ideas, with criticisms.

[20] Leach (1969), p. 64.

[21] Leach (1969), p. 80.

[22] Leach (1969), p. 31.

DIVINE NAMES AND EPITHETS IN GENESIS 49:24b-25a SOME METHODOLOGICAL AND TRADITIO-HISTORICAL REMARKS

by

MAGNE SÆBØ

Oslo

In the recent study of the Old Testament there seems to be a growing tendency to focus on the history of the religion of Israel. To a great extent, this has been done within the framework of the early social and cultural history of Israel. Studies of this kind are not new, but it may be characteristic of the present situation—partly prompted by recently discovered archaeological evidence—that the focus is now fixed on *the question of God* in early Israel, and on *early Yahwism.*[1]

Within these perspectives, new attention has also been paid to the very complex and significant text Gen.49:24b-25b, not least because of its unique repleteness of divine names and epithets of archaic character in vv. 24b-25aαβ. Earlier scholars often studied the composition of Gen.49:3-27 with a view to its general historical background,[2] but some scholars have in recent times focused more

---

[1] Cf. W.F.Albright, *Yahweh and the Gods of Canaan* (London, 1968); F.M.Cross, *Canaanite Myth and Hebrew Epic. Essays in the History of the Religion of Israel* (Cambridge, MA, 1973); D.N.Freedman, "Divine Names and Titles in Early Hebrew Poetry", in F.M.Cross et al. (eds.), *Magnalia Dei. The Mighty Acts of God. Essays . . . in Memory of G.Ernest Wright* (New York, 1976), pp.55-107; J.A.Emerton, "New Light on Israelite Religion: The Implications of the Inscriptions from Kuntillet 'Ajrud", *ZAW* 94 (1982), pp.2-20; K.Koch, "Die Götter, denen die Väter dienten", in E. Otto (ed.), *Studien zur alttestamentlichen und altorientalischen Religionsgeschichte* (Göttingen, 1988), pp.9-31; M.Köckert, *Vätergott und Väterverheißungen. Eine Auseinandersetzung mit Albrecht Alt und seinen Erben* (Göttingen, 1988); J.C.de Moor, *The Rise of Yahwism. The Roots of Israelite Monotheism* (Leuven, 1990); S.M.Olyan, *Asherah and the Cult of Yahweh in Israel*, SBLMS 34 (Chico, 1988); M.S.Smith, *The Early History of God. Yahweh and the Other Deities in Ancient Israel* (San Francisco, 1990); J.H.Tigay, *You Shall Have no Other Gods. Israelite Religion in the Light of Hebrew Inscriptions*, HSS 31 (Chico, 1986).

[2] See H.-J.Kittel, *Die Stammessprüche Israels. Genesis 49 und Deuteronomium 33 traditionsgeschichtlich untersucht* (Theol. Diss. Kirchliche Hochschule, Berlin, 1959); A.H.J.Gunneweg, "Über den Sitz im Leben der sog. Stammessprüche (Gen 49

strongly on different religious aspects of the text. This has been done to a large extent within the broader context of Canaanite religion, especially as it has been revealed by the Ugaritic texts of Ras Shamra.[3] However, in historical, religio-historical and other respects there is much divergence in the modern scholarly discussion, not least with respect to vv. 24b-25b. Given this state of affairs, it might prove useful, as well as methodologically sound, to pay close attention to the text in its own literary context. This should include comparison with similar texts, and, first of all, with its "parallel" in Deut. 33:13.[4] Therefore a fresh look at this complex and multifaceted text may start with some of its text-critical and form-historical problems.

1. The *Hebrew text* of Gen.49:24b-25aαβ presents problems of two different kinds. First, there are two well-known *cruces* in this small text cut, namely *miššām* in v. 24bβ and *wᵉʾet* in v 25aβ. In commentaries and monographs for over a century and more there have been numerous proposals for emending the Massoretic text in vv. 24-25, some of which are merely witnesses to scholarly arbitrariness.[5]

Second, the form and the syntactical relations of vv. 24b-25aαβ to their immediate context in vv. 24a and 25γδb(-26), within the framework of the rest of the Blessing of Joseph (vv. 22-26), involves some problems that require due attention. However, as far as the usual handling of textual probelms and *cruces* is concerned, a basic methodological problem is involved which may be briefly commented upon here. In cases of this kind modern interpreters have often mixed text-critical arguments with literary and other sorts of argu-

Dtn 33 Jdc 5)", *ZAW* 76 (1964), pp. 245-55; H.-J.Zobel, *Stammesspruch und Geschichte*, BZAW 95 (Berlin, 1965); F.M.Cross, D.N.Freedman, *Studies in Ancient Yahwistic Poetry* (Missoula, Montana, 1975), esp. pp.69-122; H.Seebass, "Die Stämmesprüche Gen 49,3-27", *ZAW* 96 (1984), pp.333-50; idem, "Erwägungen zum altisraelitischen System der zwölf Stämme", *ZAW* 90 (1978), pp.196-220; C.H.J. de Geus, *The Tribes of Israel* (Assen, 1976), esp. pp.70-96; for further references cf. C.Westermann, *Genesis 37-50*, BKAT I/3 (Neukirchen, 1982), pp.243-46.

[3] Cf. i.a. J.Coppens, "La bénédiction de Jacob. Son cadre historique à la lumière des parallèles ougaritiques", *Volume du Congrès: Strasbourg 1956*, SVT 4 (Leiden, 1957), pp.97-115; Freedman (1976), pp.63-66; Smith (1990), pp.16-24.

[4] Cf. J.D.Heck, "A History of Interpretation of Genesis 49 and Deuteronomy 33", *Bibliotheca Sacra* 147/585 (1990), pp.16-31.

[5] As an *exemplum instar omnium* note the radical emendation by M.Dahood, *Biblica* 40 (1959), pp. 1002-07. The extensive emending procedure was heavily criticized by H.S.Nyberg, *Studien zum Hoseabuche* (Uppsala, 1935) p.12 and passim.

ment, instead of distinguishing carefully between them.[6] One may indeed dispute whether such a procedure actually contributes to the accurate understanding of the text, all the more so since the text-critical discussion should in the first instance be based on text-historical evidence, as the ancient textual history has proven to be a tradition history in its own right.[7] Therefore, special heed will be given to this side of the textual problems.

Turning to the evidence for the ancient textual history of Gen.49:24b-25aαβ, it may be said in general that the Versions present a very variegated and somewhat perplexing picture of the text.

The Septuagint (LXX), to begin with, differs very much from the MT of Gen.49:22-26, and hence also in vv. 24-25. It is hard to form any clear opinion as to what the Hebrew *Vorlage* may have been like, but it might have been rather different from the present MT. Also, the LXX may, as usual, include elements of interpretation. The LXX text of v 24-25 (with vv. 24b-25aαβ underlined) runs as follows:

24 *καὶ συνετρίβη μετὰ κράτους τὰ τόξα αὐτῶν,*
καὶ ἐξελύθη τὰ νεῦρα βραχιόνων χειρῶν αὐτῶν
διὰ χεῖρα δυνάστου Ἰακώβ,
ἐκεῖθεν ὁ κατισχύσας Ἰσραήλ.
25 *παρὰ θεοῦ τοῦ πατρός σου,*
καὶ ἐβοήθησέν σοι ὁ θεὸς ὁ ἐμός,
καὶ εὐλόγησέν σε εὐλογίαν οὐρανοῦ ἄνωθεν
καὶ εὐλογίαν τῆς ἐχούσης πάντα
ἕνεκεν εὐλογίας μαστῶν καὶ μήτρας, . . .[8]

With the use of the verbs *συνετρίβη* and *ἐξελύθη*, the LXX has strengthened the martial tone of v. 24a, as compared with the MT. By connecting these verbs tighter than in the MT with "the hand of the Mighty One of Jacob" in v. 24bα the LXX has linked God more immediately with the victory in Joseph's battle than is the case

---

[6] Cf. i.a. V.Maag, "Der Hirte Israels", in *Kultur, Kulturkontakt und Religion* (Göttingen, 1980), pp.111-44, p.121 and n.19. Westermann exemplifies a host of modern commentators when he makes valuable literary remarks within the context of his text-critical section; cf. (1982), p. 249.

[7] Cf. M.Sæbø, *Sacharja 9-14*, WMANT 34 (Neukirchen, 1969), pp.25-28 for the theoretical discussion; idem, "From Pluriformity to Uniformity. Some Remarks on the Emergence of the Massoretic Text. . .", *ASTI* 11 (1978), pp.127-37.

[8] J.W.Wevers, *Genesis*, Septuaginta I (Göttingen, 1974), ad loc.

in the MT. Further, by rendering v. 24bα *literatim*, the LXX confirms the MT (*mîdê 'ᵃbîr ya'ᵃqob*). It also confirms the form *miššām* in v. 24bβ. However, it is uncertain what was read and rendered in the case of the two words in the MT *ro'eh* and *'eben*, since they have no direct rendering.[9] If, by employing the form *ὁ κατισχύσας* the LXX intended to draw a parallel with the verb in v. 25aα (*wᵉya'zrekkā*), this would entail combining v. 24bβ with v. 25aα, which would in turn imply a weakening of the transition from indirect to direct address of Joseph in v. 25aα. While it confirms the MT in v. 25aα, the LXX completely deviates from the MT in v. 25aβ, not only with regard to *wᵉ'et*, which may actually have read *wᵉ'el*, as we see reflected in *ὁ θεὸς ὁ ἐμός*, but also with regard to the divine name *šadday*, which is not rendered at all.[10]

In short, some interesting characteristics of the LXX version may be noted: 1) By and large, the LXX seems to reflect the same text form as the MT, although there are some deviations; obviously, the Hebrew text of vv. 24-25 presented some substantial difficulties to the LXX translators. 2) It is most interesting that *some of the difficulties seem to relate specifically to the divine names and epithets in vv. 24b-25aαβ*. For, on the one hand, the LXX has applied divine names of a commonly known character, those which contain the element *θεός* in *θεός τοῦ πατρός σου* and in *ὁ θεός ὁ ἐμός*, while, on the other hand, such apparently specific titles and epithets as Hebrew *ro'eh*, "shepherd", *'eben*, "stone", and especially *šadday*, which is otherwise translated in a variety of ways in the Greek Old Testament, have no equivalents here. Only the rare *'ᵃbîr ya'ᵃqob* has been "preserved" as *δυνάστης Ἰακώβ,* and may be in a mediating position.[11]

---

[9] On the probably erroneous listing in the Hatch/Redpath *Concordance*, p.751b, E.Tov (*The Text-critical Use of the Septuagint in Biblical Research* (Jerusalem, 1981), p.151) remarks that it "records *κατισχύειν* as the equivalent of אבן, even though from a formal point of view the Greek verb reflects both רעה and אבן"; cf. also S.Olofsson, *God is my Rock. A Study of Translation Technique and Theological Exegesis in the Septuagint* (Stockholm, 1990), pp.94f.

[10] The LXX has at least 6 renderings of *šadday*, among which especially παντοκράτωρ and κύριος παντοκράτωρ are known. However, one also finds ἐπουράνιος, ὁ θεός τοῦ οὐρανοῦ, ἱκανος and ὁ τὰ πάντα ποιήσας; and once (*qol*) *'el šadday* is only partially translated as the (φωνὴ) θεοῦ Σαδδαι (Ez. 10:5); cf. Hatch/Redpath, *Concordance*, III, p. 267a, with references, although the listing of Gen. 49:25 on p.631b (cf. p. 630) is disputable. See also Weippert, *THAT* II, c.874; Olofsson, *God is my Rock*, pp. 111-116.

[11] The rendering here is singular; otherwise the divine name is mostly translated as *θεός* (Is. 40:16; Ps. 132:3,5) and *ἰσχύς* (Is. 49:26); Is. 1:24 is dubious; cf.

The question may be raised as to what the reason for this might be. 3) Last but not least, this significant state of affairs may be taken to indicate that the procedure of transmitting and translating an ancient text was largely one of an interpretative nature.

The phenomenon of tradition may be demonstrated by the other ancient versions, now more in brief.

If we ought above all to pay due attention to the interpretative element in the translating process, this element is, as expected, particularly prevalent in the various Targumic traditions. It takes a relatively modest form in Targum Onkelos in connexion with the entire pericope, and with respect to vv. 22(-23) specifically it is excessive in the Palestinian Targums, as represented by *Neophyti* (N) 1.[12] In N 1 "Joseph, my son", depicted as a pious and invincible person, is the principal character in vv. 24-25. In the first part of v. 24 we read that "he placed his confidence in the Strong One" (ואשרי בתקיפה רוחצניה); that "he stretched out his hand and his arms to beseech mercy from (למבעיה רחמין מן) the Strong One of his father Jacob (תקיפא דאבוי יעקב)..." It is most interesting in this connexion that here the divine name *'abîr ya'aqob* is used twice, once in a full and idiomatic translation and once in a freely abridged form as well. On the other hand, the difficult v. 24bβ of the MT is wholly missing except for the word "(the tribes of) Israel".[13] In v. 25a N 1 has preserved the first divine name when it says in its characteristic fashion "May the Word of the God of your Father be at your aid". Of even greater interest than this is its rendering of *'el* (sic!) *šadday*: "and may the God of the heavens (ואלה שמיא) bless you", as this form is identical with one of the LXX translations (Ps. 90:1/91:1; cf. ἐπουράνιος Ps. 67:14/68:15).[14] Targum Onkelos likewise spiritualizes, but does so without focusing on the person of Joseph as in N 1, and in the process confirms the divine names in vv. 24ba and 25aα. Like N 1, it has no reference to *miššām ro'eh 'eben* in v. 24bβ, but only to "(the descendants of) Israel". However, unlike

---

Hatch/Redpath, *Concordance*, III, p.219b (with references); S.Olofsson, (1990), pp.87-94.

[12] Cf. A.Sperber, *The Bible in Aramaic* I (Leiden, 1959), ad loc.; A.Díez Macho, *Neophyti I* (Madrid-Barcelona, 1968), pp.334-37; 637-38.

[13] One might wonder, however, whether there is not an allusion to v. 25aα in the last part of v. 24: "with the strength of whose arm all the tribes of Israel are sustained".

[14] See note 10 above.

N 1 it confirms *literatim* the *w^e'et* of the MT in v. 25aβ, in the form of the *nota accusativi* (*w^eyat šadday*).

A stronger tendency to confirm the MT is shown by the Peshitta (P) in v. 24-25, which includes direct translations of the divine names in v. 24bα and in v. 25aα, and even for a substantial part in v. 24bβ. As far as both *cruces* are concerned, P departs from the MT, as it reads *šem*, "name", for *šam*, "there", and *'el*, "God", for *'et*. P also omits the preposition *min* at the beginning of v. 25.[15] Whether and, in the event, how P may have been influenced by the LXX or the Targums cannot be discussed here.[16]

The LXX exercised more influence in the western tradition with respect to the Old Latin (L), the translation style of which, with minor variants, approaches that of the LXX.[17] The influence of the LXX may ultimately be also traceable in the Vulgate (V), even though V is the version that comes closest to the stabilized MT: (24) *sedit in forti arcus eius et dissoluta sunt vincula brachiorum et manium illius per manus potentis Iacob inde pastor egressus est lapis Israhel (25a) Deus patris tui erit adiutor tuus et Omnipotens benedicet tibi benedictionibus*. . .[18] As we see, vv. 24b-25a follow the MT rather closely, as they literally confirm *šām* in v. 24bβ, as well as the words "shepherd" and "stone". However, in v. 25aβ V, like P, omits the preposition *min*, and in v. 25aβ it might have read "God", or at least it seems to have avoided *'et* by letting the divine name *Omnipotens* alone serve as subject of the following verb.

We are thus entitled to conclude that, in the course of the textual history of Gen.49:24b-25a the divine names and epithets seem to have been stumbling-blocks in the process of transmission and translation of the text.

As far as the conjectural Hebrew *archetype* of vv. 24b-25a is concerned, it might have been fairly close to the present MT. This may

---

15 *The Old Testament in Syriac. According to the Peshitta Version* I/1 (Leiden, 1977), ad loc.

16 Cf. M.D.Koster, "Which Came First: the Chicken or the Egg? The Development of the Text of the Peshitta of Genesis and Exodus in the Light of Recent Studies", in P.B.Dirksen and M.J.Mulder (eds.), *The Peshitta: Its Early Text and History* (Leiden, 1988), pp.99-126, esp. pp.119-25.

17 In the transition from v. 24bβ and v. 25aα L reads *inde convalescens / qui praevaluit Istrahel (25) a deo patris tui et adiuvit te deus meus et benedixit te*. . .; cf. *Vetus Latina*, 2. *Genesis* (Freiburg, 1954), p.514.

18 *Biblia Sacra iuxta Vulgatam Versionem*, rec. R.Weber OSB, I (Stuttgart, 1969), ad loc.

apply to the crucial form *miššām* in v. 24bβ, all the more so as it is witnessed by the LXX, which is the earliest version and which otherwise deviates here. Apart from this there are no inner-Hebrew variants at this point. On the other hand, the original text could well have read *wᵉ'el šadday*, since this form is not only attested by such major versions as G, P, Targum N 1 (and V), but also by Sam. and important Hebrew manuscripts like Ken 150.[19] All these witnesses may represent a significant non-Massoretic reading. In this instance, the existence of a dual inner-Hebrew tradition may have had other reasons than the vagaries of transmission. As for the rest of v. 24bβ (*ro'eh 'eben yiśrā'el*), we should note that it is this part that has been regarded as problematical by the LXX and other witnesses, and which has been dealt with so differently. It may be held that v. 24bβ is the *lectio difficilior*.

2. The *literary* and *formal* character of Gen.49:24b-25 seem to be every bit as complex as the text has turned out to be in text-historical terms, as is evident from modern critical research. In the scrutiny of this passage, much attention has been paid to the analysis of the literary *composition* as well as to the definition of the *form* and *genre* of Gen.49:3-27. Within this larger framework of undertakings, also an analysis of the literary and formal character of Gen.49:24b-25a will have to be carried out,[20] although here only in brief.

The transition from the rather obscure v. 24a to v. 24b represents a shift in style; and the last half-verse seems to begin a new section. While v. 23-24a are narrative in style and contain five verbal tense-forms, vv. 24b-25aα contain a structural sequence of *nominal* character, including three nominal constructions, all of which are introduced by the preposition *min*. Further, this sequence is followed by another one which also consists of three *nominal* constructions, v. 25aγδb in which the repeated *nomina regens* is the noun *birkot*, "blessings" (but v. 26a has different constructions).

---

19 B. Kennicott, *Vetus Testamentum Hebraicum, cum variis lectionibus*, I (Oxonii, 1776), p.102 (Mss 84 and 150); cf. also J.B.De-Rossi, *Variae lectiones Veteris Testamenti*, I (Parmae, 1784), p.46b; and C.D.Ginsburg, *The Old Testament*. I, *The Pentateuch* (London, (1911) 1926), ad loc.

20 See n.2 above. In his recapitulation of earlier research and in his own analytical efforts, Westermann (*Genesis 37-50*, pp. 246-78) has masterfully analysed the form and traditio-historical problems of the chapter. As for vv. 24b-25a, however, he seems to be in a quandary; one notes that v. 24b is lacking from his diagram on p. 276.

As for the *cruces* within this context, the adverb *šām* in v. 24bβ deviates from the other words introduced by *min* (*mide*, v. 24bα, and *me'el*, v. 25aα) in being related, not by person (viz. "hands", resp. "God"), but by locale ("there"). It is hard to discern exactly the relation of the adverb to the rest of v. 24bβ, even though it is probably not unintelligible. As for *w^e'et* in v. 25aβ, this lexeme seems to be ambiguous. It may, as in *Targum Onkelos*, be a *nota accusativi*, but what would the transitive verb then be? Or it might be the preposition *'et* (i.e., "(together) with"), but such prepositional usage would break off the possible link to the three preceding *min*'s. In either case, the lexeme in question is difficult to understand.[21] The syntactical position of these two *cruces* seems to be as difficult as their text-historical one, even though they have quite different contexts.

The small unit comprising vv. 24b-25aαβ seems to have a mediatory position between vv. 23-24a, which is of a somewhat martial character, and to which v. 24b may be related, and the section of "blessings" in vv. 25aγδb-26a, to which v. 25aβ seems to be a link. Additionally, vv. 24b-25aαβ are of divergent character as well. They point in opposite directions, v. 24b to the preceding and v. 25aαβ to the following. There is also a corresponding formal gap between v. 24b and v. 25aαβ, since v. 24b, together with vv. 22-24a, seems to speak in the third person, whereas v. 25aαβ addresses Joseph in the second person, in company with v. 26a. Targum Neophyti 1, which preserves the formal shift here, has direct address in the first half of v. 22 as well, and seems to have smoothed out this formal opposition in the transmitted text. Finally, the listing style of v. 24b differs from that of v. 25aαβ, where a similar enumeration of divine names (*'el 'ābîkā* and (*'el*) *šadday*) has been expanded by brief verbal clauses, namely *w^eya'zrekkā* in v. 25aα and *wîbār^ekekkā* in v. 25aβ.

These observations may argue for the probability of what is at least in part a new explanation of the literary composition and growth of the verses in question. First, the Blessing of Joseph seems to have been composed of small units, consisting of vv. 22, 23-24a, 24b, 25aαβ, 25aγδb, 26a and 26b, respectively, all differing in many respects. The composition will have been completed (long) before the later text history attested by the LXX onward. Second, the combination of the separate units may have been primarily made by an *additive and associative procedure of linking*, which is to say, between the

[21] See, however, the discussion of J.Blau, *VT* 4 (1954), pp. 7-19; N.Walker, *VT* 5 (1955), pp. 314-315; and, finally, J.Blau in *VT* 6 (1956), pp. 211-212. Cf. also H.P.Müller, *ZDPV* 94 (1978), p. 66 n.64; *HAL*, pp.1320a and 1321a.

words *yādāw* in v. 24aβ and *y*^{e}*dê* ("hands") in v. 24bα; further, between the sequence of the preposition *min* in v. 24b and, across the formal gap, *min* in v. 25aγ, i.e., between *wîbār*^{e}*kekkā* and *birkot*. In the third place, the existence of small units that are combined in this way corresponds at least partly to what Westermann has defined formally as *Stammessprüche*, consisting of brief "sayings", like proverbs, about individual tribes.[22]

As has often been observed in modern research, the individual "tribal sayings" of Gen.49:3-27 are very heterogeneous, as they vary considerably both in length and formal character. The longest "sayings" are those dealing with Judah (vv. 8-12) and Joseph (vv. 22-26). Their length may be regarded as an indication of their special significance. When comparing the composition of Gen.49 with its "parallel" in Deut. 33, some of their literary and form-historical problems, as well as their respective *traditio-historical* profiles, appear in stronger relief.[23] In the first place, it is significant that in Deut. 33 the inner relationship between Judah and Joseph has changed noticeably to Judah's disadvantage (as is shown by v. 7, compared with vv. 13-17), and that the "saying" about Levi in Gen.49 (vv. 5-7) has been totally transformed in a positive sense and expanded in Deut. 33 (vv. 8-11). On this occasion, however, it might be more interesting to compare Gen.49:24b-25a with Deut. 33:13, and in this connexion a synoptic arrangment will prove useful:

Gen.49:24b-25:	Deut. 33:13:
	(ûl^{e}*yôsep 'āmar)*
mîdê '^{a}*bîr ya'*^{a}*aqob*	
miššām ro'eh 'eben yiśrā'el	
me'el 'ābîkā w^{e}*ya'zrekkā*	
w^{e}*'et šadday wîbār*^{e}*kekkā*	*m*^{e}*boreket YHWH 'arṣô*
birkot šāmayim me'āl	*mimmeged šāmayim miṭṭāl*
birkot t^{e}*hôm robeṣet tāḥat*	*ûmitt*^{e}*hôm robeṣet tāḥat*
birkot šādayim wārāḥam	

The differences between the two texts are apparent. First of all, the various divine names and epithets in Gen.49:24-25 have "disappeared" in the Joseph "saying" of Deut.33:13-17; in their place, Deut has "Yahweh" alone (v. 13). This is not unexpected, as Deut.33 is as a whole a more markedly theological composition than Gen.49, and it clearly concentrates on Yahweh. By contrast, Gen.49 has the name of Yahweh in but a single place, and it does so in a way that breaks with the rest of the context (v. 18). Deut. 33 not only has

22 Westermann, *Genesis 37-50*, p.250.

23 Cf. n.2 above.

> Yahweh in the individual "sayings" (vv. 7, 13, 21, 23), but also in its framework (vv. 2-5 and 26-29), where Yahweh is first described in theophanic terms (v. 2; cf. Hab.3:3ff) and then (vv. 26-27) is also assigned special epithets like "God of Jeshurun", "rider of heavens . . . and clouds" (*rokeb šāmayim / šeḥāqîm*),[24] probably also "eternal God" (*'elohê qedem*).[25] Finally, in v. 29 Yahweh is even metaphorically described as "the shield (*māgen*) of your help, and the sword (*ḥereb*) of your triumph" (RSV). However, when such divine names, epithets and metaphors are used in the framework of Deut.33 one may well ask as to why the divine names and epithets of Gen.49:24b-25a are totally lacking in v. 13.

Westermann may be perfectly justified in defining the original "tribal sayings" as being brief, like proverbs. When he further maintains that the "sayings" of Gen.49 are "profane" except for those aspects of them which have been further "elaborated" or "developed", this, too, may be right for the most part, but not wholly so. For it is at least disputable with respect to vv. 24b-25a. More than that, in view of the Gen.49's variegated compositional history, what do the words "profane" and "elaborated" or "developed" really mean? Would such sharp distinctions as these be at all appropriate here? Even though Gen.49 does not use the name of Yahweh, with the exception of the late addition of v. 18, this hardly implies that the composition is "profane". The "sayings", or most of them, may well have been of this character; but the final result is not without theology. On the contrary, the divine names and epithets in vv. 24b-25aαβ constitute an essential part of the theological character of the composition. Moreover, it is the *very accumulation or "clustering" of names and epithets which represents a real challenge to the study of this chapter*, and this fact requires a better explanation than it has up to now received.

Hermann Gunkel posed this problem in his commentary on Genesis, in terming the phenomenon here a "solemn accumulation of divine names" and comparing it to a similar form in Gen.48:15.[26]

---

[24] See Ps.68:5; cf. A.Cooper (and M.H.Pope), "Divine Names and Epithets in the Ugaritic Texts", *Ras Shamra Parallels* III (Rome, 1981), No.40, p. 458.

[25] So, traditionally, the RSV. The text, however, is somewhat ambiguous. Now the NEB and RevNEB have "who humbled the *gods of old*". Likewise, the New RSV has "he subdues the ancient gods".

[26] *Genesis übersetzt und erklärt*, GHAT I/1 (8. Aufl.; Göttingen, 1969), p.486; and on Gen.48:15 he says, p.473, "Häufung der Gottesnamen bei feierlicher Anrufung vgl. als Parallelen etwa Ps 80_2 50_1. In solchem Fall nennt der Polytheist alle die Götter, die er verehrt. . ., der antike Monotheist alle die Namen Gottes, die er

However, the problem might be more precisely defined as determining the *formal and theological function of these divine names and epithets* in the context of the Joseph "saying" and of the composition as a whole.

3. The *names and epithets* of Gen.49:24b-25aαβ are, as is generally recognised, of various kinds. They have often been analysed,[27] so that brief remarks on each of them will suffice here. The most problematic features are the epithets in v. 24bβ, so we shall dedicate somewhat more effort to them.

3.1 אביר יעקב, *'abîr ya'aqob*. The first name is rare and, in its other contexts, only late (Ps.132:2,5; Is.49:26; 60:16 and, with "Israel", also Is. 1:24). However, since Albrecht Alt's epoch-making study of the subject in 1929,[28] it has commonly been held that the name is very old and belongs to a specific type.[29] This may still be maintained, in spite of recent criticism in favour of a younger date.[30] In addition, there has been some discussion about the exact meaning of אביר, discussion based on two alternate readings: either *'abîr*, used solely as a divine name in the Old Testament, "the Mighty One" (6 times, as listed above); or *'abbîr*, meaning mainly "strong" (17 times), but sometimes (3 or 4) "bull".[31] Even though the latter sense is rather restricted, some scholars also relate it to Gen.49:24b, in part with reference to 1 Kings 12:25-33.[32] In the

---

kennt". Like Gunkel, Westermann, too, speaks of "die Häufung der Gottesnamen, die an 48,15-16 erinnert", but he calls it "eine ebenfalls späte Bildung".

27 For bibliographical references, see Westermann, *Genesis 37-50*, p.273 (*Exkurs*), and *Genesis 12-36* (1981), pp. 133-35; cf. also W.H.Schmidt, *Exodus 1-6*, BKAT II/1 (Neukirchen, 1988), pp. 147-52 (with references).

28 A.Alt, "Der Gott der Väter", now in idem, *Kleine Schriften* I (München, 1953), pp. 1-78, esp. pp.24-29; cf. his response to early criticism, "Zum 'Gott der Väter'", *Palästinajahrbuch* 36 (1940),pp. 53-104. See also H.Weidmann, *Die Patriarchen und ihre Religion* (Göttingen, 1968), pp. 126-67; and n.30 below.

29 Cf. i.a. Zobel, (1965), pp. 22f; R. de Vaux, *The Early History of Israel* I (London, 1978), p.272; Seebass, *ZAW* 96 (1984), pp. 337-39; Koch, (1988), p. 13.

30 See i.a. J. Hoftijzer, *Die Verheißungen an die drei Erzväter* (Leiden, 1956), pp.95f.; J.Van Seters, "The Religion of the Patriarchs in Genesis", *Biblica* 61 (1980), pp. 220-33; Köckert (1988), pp. 63-67; 147-61; cf. also H.Vorländer, *Mein Gott* (Kevelaer/Neukirchen, 1975), pp. 203-14; R.Albertz, *Persönliche Frömmigkeit und offizielle Religion* (Stuttgart, 1978), pp.77-96.

31 Cf. H.H.Schmid, *THAT* I, cc.25-27; and esp. A.S.Kapelrud, *ThWAT* I, cc.43-46 (with references).

32 Cf. J.Coppens (1957) (see n.3 above), pp. 101f.; F.Dumermuth, *ZAW* 70 (1958), pp.85f.; M.Weippert, *ZDPV* 77 (1961), p. 105; H.Vorländer, *Mein Gott*, p. 186; M.S.Smith, *Early History*, pp. 16f.

present context, as well as in the context of the other instances of *ᵓbir*, this sense is definitely unlikely; nor has it any textual support. The theologically motivated distinction expressed by these words need not at all be late.[33]

3.2. רעה *ro'eh*. The word is generally taken to be a noun, "shepherd",[34] all the more so as the title was an ancient epithet of both gods and kings outside of Israel as well.[35] However, it is noteworthy that in the closely related text Gen.48:15bβ the same form is used verbally as a *participle*, equipped with the *nota acc.* Moreover, it is the predicate in a relative clause that has no relative pronoun, whereas the parallel relative clause in v. 15bα has the relative pronoun:

האלהים אשר התהלכו אבתי
האלהים הרעה אתי מעודי

It is furthermore remarkable that the LXX has a participle (ὁ κατισχύσας) in Gen.49:24bβ, while at the other end of the textual development, the V has a noun (*pastor*).[36] It might be worth considering, then, that in its original setting *ro'eh* in v. 24bβ may not have been a noun, but a verbal form like the similar form in 48:15b, even though it will have been as a nominal form, namely a *participle*, that became understood as a noun at an early date.[37] If this was the case, then v. 24bβ may furthermore be regarded as a sentence in its own right, in which the next two words represent the subject, and *ro'eh* the predicate. As for the relationship to the crucial form *miššām*, finally, the sentence may, in analogy with the construction in 48:15bβ, be held to constitute an asyndetic relative clause, that is, without the relative pronoun.[38] Some such syntactical under-

---

[33] See esp. Kapelrud *ThWAT*, I, c.45; Olofsson, *God is my Rock*, p. 90.

[34] Cf. Maag (1980) (see n.6 above); Ph.de Robert, *Le berger d'Israël* (Neuchâtel, 1968), esp. pp. 41-44; Vorländer, *Mein Gott*, pp. 196f.; J.A.Soggin, *THAT* II, c.793; G.Wallis, *ThWAT* VII, cc.572-74; also Olofsson, *God is my Rock*, pp. 94f.

[35] For the OT see n.34; for Israel's environment see D.Müller, *ZÄS* 86 (1961), pp. 126-44; I.Seibert, *Hirt-Herde-König. Zur Herausbildung des Königtums in Mesopotamien* (Berlin, 1969).

[36] A similar development may be observed for *nôšā'*, Zech.9:9; cf. Sæbø (1969), pp. 51f.

[37] Wallis, *ThWAT* VII, c.573, indicates that as far as the kings are concerned the verbal aspects prevail: "Eher als das nominalisierte Ptz 'Hirte' hat das verbum finitum 'weiden' in übertragenem Sinne Eingang gefunden". This may even be seriously considered in connexion with God as well; see Ps. 23:1 and esp. Ps. 80:2, where there are interesting references to both 'Israel' and to 'Joseph': *ro'eh yiśr-ā'el/noheg kaṣṣo'n yôsep*.

[38] Cf. C.Brockelmann, *Hebräische Syntax* (Neukirchen, 1956), § 146.

standing of v. 24bβ as this would solve a number of problems: there would be no inner opposition between two unrelated nouns (*ro'eh* versus *'eben*) which would then have to be explained away as either a double tradition or a conflation which was later understood as being in apposition; the relation to *miššām*, or, originally, perhaps to *šām* alone, would be easier to explain; and, last but not least, an early shift from verb to noun would also render the text-historical problems both more intelligible and more explicable. On the other hand, an absolute use of a transitive verb is surely a serious problem; but also as a noun *ro'eh* is unrelated here.

3.3 אבן ישראל *'eben yiśrā'el*. The use of *'eben* in this construction is unique in the Old Testament. It has been questioned, all the more so since *ṣûr* is otherwise used, both rather often and especially in the Psalms, as the specific divine epithet designating God as the 'Rock'.[39] However, as is indicated by a Ugaritic parallel, this is not unique in a broader context,[40] and there is in any case a usage of *'eben* in Is.8:14 that is similar, though not identical, to the use here. There might very well have been religious reasons for the striking 'disproportion' between *'eben* and *ṣûr* as divine epithets. On the one hand, *'eben yiśrā'el* may be connected with specific Bethel traditions.[41] But, on the other hand, there also existed broad, mostly prophetical polemics against the worship of sacred stones as well as of gods of stone,[42] and that might have had a negative effect on the use of a divine epithet of this kind. Nevertheless, *'eben yiśrā'el*, when used as a divine epithet, represented a highly metaphorical usage and conception; at the same time, however, it may well have been on the fringe of what was considered theologically tolerable in Israel.

---

[39] Cf. M.P.Knowles, "'The Rock, his work is perfect': Unusual Imagery for God in Deut xxxii", *VT* 39 (1989), pp. 307-22; S.Olofsson, *God is my Rock*, pp. 94f.; otherwise A.S.Kapelrud, אבן, *ThWAT* I, cc.50-53; H.-J.Fabry, צור, *ThWAT* VI, cc.968-83 (with further references); also J.Gamberoni, מצבה, *ThWAT* IV, cc.1064-74. Without any text-historical support, D.N.Freedman (1976) (see n.1 above), p. 65, contents that "The word *'bn* may be understood as by-form of *bn*, 'son', and that "it should be read as plural", whereby he renders v. 24bβ, "Shepherd of the sons of Israel", as does A.S. van der Woude (*THAT* II, cc.538-43), c.542; for yet another radical emendation by Dahood—which denies that *'eben* in this context is a divine epithet—see n.5 above.

[40] Cf. Cooper, *Ras Shamra Parallels* III (1981), pp. 336f.; B.Vawter, "The Canaanite Background of Genesis 49", *CBQ* 17 (1955), pp. 1-18, esp. pp. 7-16.

[41] See Gen. 28:11.17-19; 35:14-15; cf. esp. Kapelrud, *ThWAT* I, c.53.

[42] See Lev. 26:1; Deut. 4:28; 16:22; Is. 37:19; Jer. 2:27; 3:9; Ez. 20:32; cf. Kapelrud, *ThWAT* I, c.53; Olofsson, *God is my Rock*, p.95.

In any case, all this is testimony to the early age of the epithet in question.

3.4 אל אביך *'el 'ābîkā*. The character of this divine name is compatible to the first one, *'abîr ya'aqob*. Both of them belong to the ambit of Patriarchal religion and represent one of its most specific characteristics, which indicates the intimate almost familial relationship of the faith expressed.[43] There is a religio-historical problem as to the exact understanding of *'el* as part of this name, and in similar cases like Gen.46:3, namely whether it is to be understood generically, as in the usual anonymous rendering, "God of your father", or as the specific divine name El, hence "El your father".[44] This may not actually be relevant to the matter at hand, even though in this context the former example may be the more appropriate.[45] The problem is, however, made more delicate by the next name.

3.5 (אל)שדי (*'el*) *šadday*. The name *šadday* is generally (40 times out of a total of 48, mostly in Job) used alone;[46] and a discussion of its use in Gen.49:25aβ, which is presumably the oldest instance,[47] would not seem to be dependent on solving the crucial problem of *we'et* versus the variant *we'el*, which can claim considerable text-historical support. Yet it is noteworthy that *šadday* never occurs alone in Genesis, but only "in the full construct form" *'el šadday*.[48]

---

[43] Cf. Alt (1953) (see n.28 above), pp. 13-24, esp. p. 19; de Vaux (1978) (see n.29 above), p.272: "This religion of the god of the father is the earliest form of patriarchal religion of which we can have any knowledge"; further, i.a. K.T. Andersen, "Der Gott meines Vaters", *StTh* 16 (1962), pp. 170-88; Vorländer (1975), pp. 184-214; E.Jenni, *THAT* I, cc.9-11; W.H.Schmidt, *THAT* I, cc. 145.157-58; H.Ringgren, *ThWAT* I, cc.10-12.298-99; F.M.Cross, *ThWAT* I, c.273.

[44] Cf. N.Wyatt, "The Problem of the 'God of the Fathers'", *ZAW* 90 (1978), pp. 101-04, and the rebuttal by Seebass, (1984) (see n.2 above), p. 337, n.19.

[45] Cf. i.a. W.H.Schmidt, *THAT* I, c.146; also R. de Vaux, "El et Baal, le Dieu des Pères et Yahweh", *Ugaritica* VI (Paris, 1969), pp. 501-17; J.C.de Moor (1990) (see n.1 above), pp. 229-34.

[46] Among many studies see E.Burrows, "The Meaning of El Šaddai", *JThS* 41 (1940), pp. 152-61; F.M.Cross, *Canaanite Myth and Hebrew Epic* (Cambridge, MA, 1973); and esp. K.Koch, *"Šaddaj"* (1988) (see n.1 above), pp. 118-52 (= *VT* 26 (1976), pp. 299-332); and M.Weippert, *THAT* II, cc.873-81; Olofsson, pp.111-16; *HAL* pp.1319b-1321a (with references).

[47] See Burrows, *JThS* 41, p. 159; Koch (1988), p. 151; cf. also Weippert, *THAT* II, c.880.

[48] Cf. M.Haran, "The Religion of the Patriarchs: An Attempt at a Synthesis", *ASTI* 4 (1965), pp. 30-55, and see esp. p.47, n.10; Weippert, *THAT* II, cc.873f, distinguishes between the "Kurzform" (*šadday*) and the "Langform" (*'el šadday*). When Koch (1988), p. 26, says that "die direkte Zusammenstellung von El und

Therefore the question may be raised as to whether the *crux* in v. 25aβ might somehow be grounded in the parallelisation of the anonymous name *'el 'ābîkā* with the proper name (*'el*) *šadday*. Whatever the case may be, *šadday* is rather often connected with other divine names.[49] Moreover, it is likely that it was linked with Bethel, among other sacred places,[50] and that it was related to the giving of "blessing", in particular the "blessing" of fertility.[51]In the first place, then, the name of *šadday* in Gen.49:25 may be more closely related to the following section than to what precedes, a fact which only serves to intensify the literary problems.

4. The *divine names and epithets of Gen.49:24b-25a* seem to have been very significant, especially seen in a religio-historical perspective, as each of them has a history of its own. After the preceding brief remarks on the individual epithets and names, the discussion which was inaugurated in section 2 as to the key question of *what function the specific accumulation of these names and epithets might have in their context* must now be pursued. This may be done in a tripartite way, beginning with the literary composition.

4.1 *Syntactically*, the specific position of the individual epithet or name may contribute to a better understanding of the growth of the composition. In particular, it may prove possible to differentiate somewhat further the phenomenon of additive and associative linking of smaller units which was noted above. The structural sequence of three *min*-units in v. 24b-25a varies to a greater extent than is immediately apparent: the sequence not only bridges the formal gap between v. 24 and 25, but also includes, on the one hand, a unit (v. 24bβ) which is possibly not a nominal unit, but a self-contained sentence in its own right, the original form of which was *šām ro'eh 'eben yiśrā'el*. The insertion of an introductory *min* into this sentence seems to have transformed it into an asyndetic relative clause. On the other hand, it includes v. 25aαβ, two parallel divine epithets or

---

Schaddai nur in P auftaucht", he also includes in P (Gen. 17:1; 28:3; 35:11; 48:3; Ex. 6:3) the "full form" in Gen. 43:14 which is otherwise assigned to J (*HAL*, p. 1319b) or E (cf. O.Eißfeldt, *Hexateuch-Synopse*, p. 89*), cf. p.124; and in Gen 49:25a he prefers the MT reading. Both are disputable.

49 See the listing in Koch (1988), pp. 125-26.129; cf. Weippert *THAT* II, c.880.

50 See Gen.28:18-19, esp. 35:11-15 and 48:3; cf. Koch (1988), pp. 146f.

51 See the *birkot*-sequence of vv. 25b-26a, and cf. Koch (1988), pp. 142-46.151.

names that have been expanded by the addition of parallelised sentences promising protection and blessing, the last of which has been extended through a sequence of "blessing" descriptions (v. 24aγδb-26a).

In this complex composition, the formal combining element is represented by the sequence of three *min*'s which here unifies some fairly disparate materials. The different divine epithets and names constitute the unifying element with respect to the contents. In all their diversity and in a unique way, the names and epithets hold the variegated materials together. A tentative translation of vv. 24-25 which also indicates their structure, may now be given:

But his bow remained steady
  and flexible were his strong arms—

from (by/because of) the *Mighty One of Jacob*,
from where the *Stone of Israel* is guarding (/protecting),
from the *God of your father*,
    who will help you,
  and *God Almighty*,
    who will bless you:

blessings of the heavens above,
blessings of the deep that crouches below,
blessings of the breasts and the womb.[52]

4.2 The *religio-historical* study of the divine epithets and names in Gen.49:24b-25aαβ has concentrated more on them in isolation from one another than in their present combination in the context. In his study on *Šadday*, however, Klaus Koch has commented on the various connexions of this divine name with other divine names and epithets as representing "*Ketten von Gottesbezeichnungen*",[53] but in his interesting study he has given the priority to the possible relationship and identity of the deities in question than to the form-historical and religio-historical problem of what Gunkel, referring to Gen. 48:15, called the "feierliche Häufung der Gottesnamen", as mentioned above. The question is whether we find anywhere else a similar phenomenon that may be able to shed some light on this unique structure.

In the Akkadian creation epic, *Enūma eliš*, there is a form which

---

[52] See the different translation of Cross/Freedman (1975) (see n.2 above), pp. 75-76.89-92.

[53] (1988), p. 125.

seems to be analogous, but which, as far as I am aware, has not been included in any discussion of Gen.49, namely the listing of the *fifty names of Marduk* which was recited with due solemnity on the fourth day of the Near Year's festival (tablets vi 122-vii 144).[54] With its hymnic style and unique abundance of divine names, this "proclamation" has as one of its goals the broad glorification of the victorious god, as is also announced in the framework of the list (vi 121-23 and especially vii 143-44). The multiplicity of names are intended as an expression of Marduk's supreme position and of his great honour—although the inner relationships of the names involves many problems of "identification".[55]

In a similar way, unique in the Old Testament, we find that a broad and 'solemn' expression of divine assistance and protection, as well as the blessing of a tribe like Joseph's, is made by a special 'listing' of ancient divine names and epithets. The prime *raison d'être* for this 'listing' and accumulation, may be not so much the narrative and assurance of divine help and gifts in itself, which are often and quite variously expressed in the Old Testament, as it is the unparalleled way in which it has been done in this instance. The "proclamation" of ancient divine names and epithets here may therefore be understood as an *exclusive expression of the power and steadfast reliability of the patriarchal God*. It may not be just an incidental circumstance that this takes place within the framework of the "saying" of the tribe of Joseph, but it is more likely that this "saying" of this dominant tribe was regarded as the most "strategic point" for the proclamation of the dominating position of the ancient God of Israel.

4.3 In *traditio-historical* and *theological* perspective, the accumulation of different divine epithets and names in Gen.49 may involve

---

[54] See *ANET* (^{3}1969), pp.60.69-72; cf. esp. F.M.Th. de Liagre Böhl, "Die fünfzig Namen des Marduk", *AfO* 11, (1936), pp. 191-218, reprint in *Opera Minora* (Groningen/Djakarta, 1953), pp. 282-312.504-08; also K.Tallqvist, *Akkadische Götterepitheta* (Helsingfors, 1938), esp. pp.362-72.

[55] Note also the other important aspect observed by Böhl (1953), p. 284: "Die Zahl gehört zum Kosmos, im Gegensatz zum Chaos. Wenn Marduk als die Summe seiner Funktionen fünfzig Namen hat oder erhält, so bedeutet das, dass er den Kosmos regiert und umfasst". See, further, W.G. Lambert, "The Historical Development of the Mesopotamian Pantheon: A Study in Sophisticated Polytheism", in H. Goedicke/J.J.M. Roberts (eds.), *Unity and Diversity* (Baltimore/London, 1975), pp. 191-200; W.G. Lambert, art. "Babylonien und Israel", *TRE* V (1980), pp. 67–79, esp. "7. Babylonischer Monotheismus", pp. 77-78.

a deep tension between their mutual diversity and respective history, on the one hand, and the fact of their being "united" in a composition of this kind, on the other. In spite of their individual history and character, however, the very combination of divine names and epithets may be understood as a witness to the "unity" of the patriarchal God, or the other way round: some notion of the divine "unity" may have been a kind of *conditio sine qua non* for the special composition of Gen.49:24b-25aαβ.

This supposition may be additionally substantiated by a triangular comparison of Gen.49 with Deut. 33 and Ex. 6:2b-3, which represent different traditio-historical strata.[56] When we note, as mentioned above, that Deut.33:13 has "replaced" the divine names and epithets of Gen.49 by the one name, *Yahweh*, this may be seen as not only a contrast with the earlier names and epithets—*Yahweh* being now the exclusive name for the God of Israel—but even to some extent as a continuation of the ancient tendency towards what might be termed a "pluralistic" way of expressing the "unity" of God. Both in Ex. 3 and, above all, in the P-context of Ex. 6:2b-3, it is just this that has become a programmatic theological stance and "dogma".[57] Seen in this perspective, the "proclamation" of names and epithets in Gen.49:24b-25a may, in its specific way, represent an early contribution to the monotheistic trend and tendency in Israel's faith and theology.

5. *In conclusion* it may be stated in all brevity that the accumulative concentration of divine names and epithets in Gen.49:24b-25a may be regarded as an old and important stepping-stone in the long traditio-historical process of the indigenous theological apprehension of God in ancient Israel.

---

[56] When J. Van Seters (1980) (see n.30 above), p.226, evaluates Gen. 49:25-26 as having "been borrowed, with a few changes, from the Blessing of Moses", i.e., from Deut. 33:13-16, he is not doing justice to the ancient character of Gen. 49:25. In contrast, M.S.Smith, *The Early History of God* (see n.1 above), p. 17, finds that the "phrase *šadayim wārāḥam* in verse 25e echoes Ugaritic titles of the goddesses Asherah and Anat", and concludes, p. 22, that "Genesis 49:25-26 possibly points to an early stage when Israel knew three deities, El, Asherah, and Yahweh". However, such a linkage of the materials breaks with the whole trend and tendency demonstrated above, and is not likely.

[57] See n.1 above; and N.Lohfink, "Die priesterschriftliche Abwertung der Tradition von der Offenbarung des Jahwenamens an Mose", *Biblica* 49 (1968), pp. 1-18; idem, "Zur Geschichte der Diskussion über den Monotheismus im Alten Israel", in E.Haag (ed.), *Gott, der einzige. Zur Entstehung des Monotheismus in Israel* (Freiburg/Basel/Wien, 1985), pp. 9-25.

GENESIS KAPITEL 34. EROS UND THANATOS

by

J.A. SOGGIN

Roma

1. Daß diese Stelle in der hebräischen Bibel "eine äußerst bewegte ("turbulent") Geschichte" (wie sich der Jubilar ausdrückt)[1] hinter sich hat, ist wohlbekannt. Nicht nur hat man versucht, im Text das Zusammenfließen zweier Überlieferungen zu entdecken: einer, welche sich mit Familienangelegenheiten befaßt, und einer, deren Gegenstand stammesgeschichtliche Begebenheiten bilden; man hat auch hier und da (z.B. in den Versen 25-26 und 27-29) Duplikate entdeckt. Und aus dem angeblichen Zusammenfließen dieser beiden Überlieferungen soll endlich unsere Erzählung entstanden sein. Dabei sollte aber eines außer Zweifel stehen: daß die Gegenwart im Bericht von Simeon und Lewi als Hauptpersonen zum ursprünglichen Bestand gehören muß, sind sie doch die leiblichen Brüder Dinas, während die anderen nur Halbbrüder sind.

Doch wir wollen uns hier nicht weiter mit der Forschungsgeschichte abgeben: dafür siehe, u.A., die erwähnte Abhandlung des Jubilars und den Kommentar von C. Westermann, z.St. Dazu erhebt sich aber die Frage, ob derartige Betrachtungen nicht künstlich an den Text herangetragen wurden: von stammesgeschichtlichen Begebenheiten zu reden, z.B., hieße einen geschichtlich-politischen Hintergrund für unseren Bericht vorauszusetzen; daß es einen solchen gegeben habe, müßte aber erst einmal bewiesen werden, bevor man davon redet; und was dann die Beziehungen zwischen dem Familienbericht und dem politischen gewesen wären bleibt alles andere als klar. Daraus sollte hervorgehen, daß man den Zweck und den Gegenstand der Erzählung anderswo zu suchen hat, und dies möchte ich zu Ehren des Jubilars und Freundes hier versuchen.

2. Ich brauche die Erzählung nicht zu wiederholen, sie ist

[1] Eduard Nielsen, *Shechem* (Copenhagen, 1955), p. 242: "Among literary critics Gen. 34 has had a most turbulent history".

genügend bekannt: es handelt sich um eine Art von hebräischer *Cavalleria rusticana*, bei der Liebe, Gewalt und Tod in fast tragischer Konsequenz auf einander folgen. Sie ist besonders gut aufgebaut und enthält einige glaubwürdige Elemente, z.B. die von V.21 hervorgehobene, freundliche, wenn auch eigennützige Einstellung der Stadtbewohner den alles andere als mittellosen Wanderhirten gegenüber. Was man eher hervorheben sollte, sind die verschiedenen Merkwürdigkeiten, welche dem aufmerksamen Leser nicht entgehen sollten. Der zweite Teil dessen, was Jos 24,32 und Jdc 9,28 als *'anšê ḥămôr* bezeichnen, ist hier, zusammen mit dem Namen der Stadt, zu einem Personennamen geworden; die Beschneidung als unverzichtbare Vorbedingung zu einem Bund setzt Gen. Kap. 17, "P", voraus, denn nur dort ist von diesem Brauch in dieser extremen Form die Rede. Das geht auch aus dem Ausdruck *'ašer jalĕdāh lô*, V.1 hervor, der, wie C. Westermann richtig bemerkt, als typisch für "P" gilt. Aus diesen beiden Tatsachen läßt sich ziemlich objektiv folgern: unser Text kann keinesfalls als alt gelten, man sollte ihn als frühestens zu "P" gehörig oder vielleicht noch später ansetzen.

3. Der Text scheint verhältnismäßig korrekt überliefert und für Einzelheiten darf ich wohl auf die Kommentare und auf E. Nielsen verweisen.[2] Nur zu V.29 möchte auch ich mit dem Jubilar, auf Grund der Lesung der LXX (*ὅσα τε ἦν ἐν τῇ πόλει καὶ ὅσα ἦν ἐν ταῖς οἰκίαις*), eine Korrektur *'et kål 'ašer bā'îr wĕ'et kål 'ašer bĕbêtām* vorschlagen.

4. Die Unternehmung Simeons und Lewis gegen Sichem wurde oft als eine vom Zusammenhang der Erzvätererzählungen getrennte Überlieferung betrachtet: vielleicht habe man es sogar mit einem unabhängigen Bericht über die sogenannte Landnahme zu tun. Ja, es könnte sich um einen (gescheiterten) Versuch gehandelt haben, in der mittelpalästinischen Hochebene Fuß zu fassen, wie vielleicht auch aus dem Text Gen 49,5-6 hervorgeht. Doch das Problem erweist sich als viel verwickelter, sobald man zu den Einzelheiten übergeht. Ein Personenname *šĕkem* und ein Personenname *ḥămôr* sind nirgens, weder in der Hebräischen Bibel noch außerhalb, belegt; und während die Bezeichnung *'anšê ḥămôr* in Jos 24,32 und Jdc 9,28 als *nomen gentilicium* vollkommen an ihrem Plazt ist, mutet sie hier bestenfalls merkwürdig an: die Bezeichnungen für ethnische und politische Größen sind hier zumindest konfus und stammen

---

2 Eduard Nielsen (1955), pp. 241-259.

wohl aus einem Mißverständnis der älteren Texte! Dies sollte aber nicht verwundern, denn es ist nicht der Zweck der Erzählung, etwas über den vorisraelitischen Stadtstaat Sichem oder die sich dort niederlassenden Stämme Israels, sondern romanhaft über eine Familienangelegenheit zu berichten, zu der eventuell sozio-politische Elemente hinzukommen.

5. Dies geht m.E. nicht nur aus der verhältnismäßig späten Datierung des Textes, sondern auch klar aus der von den Brüdern Dinas aufgestellten Bedingung für das Zustandekommen eine Bundes, der Beschneidung, ohne weiteres hervor. Was dem Leser hier entgegentritt ist nicht nur die Beziehung zu Kap. 17, auf die schon hingewiesen wurde, sondern die Tatsache, daß die Beschneidung zu einem grundlegenden, als die Israeliten von den anderen Völkern unterscheidenden Merkmal dargestellt wird: nur wer beschnitten, also zum Judentum gehört oder übergetreten ist, darf mit dem weiblichen Mitglied eines israelitischen Stammes eheliche Beziehungen unterhalten. Ob überhaupt, und eventuell inwiefern, im Bericht Erinnerungen an eine vergangene Episode erhalten sind, kann heute nicht mehr ermittelt werden.

6. Die Zeit, in die uns die Erzählung führt ist also die der Konversionen zum Judaismus, ob diese nun spontan, also durch die Mission bewirkt zustande kamen, oder ob sie erzwungen wurden (z. B. die Idumäer unter Johannes Hyrkan I.).

7. Jeder Zusammenhang mit der "Landnahme" und mit den *ḫapīru* der el-'Amarna Zeit sollte deswegen fallen gelassen werden. Wenn man eine Parallele suchen möchte, dann könnte man vielleicht die der Entführung Helenens nach Troja in Betracht ziehen, ein in hellenistischer Zeit auch im Nahen Osten weitverbreitetes Motiv[3].

---

[3] Weitere Literatur: E. Blum, *Die Komposition der Vätergeschichte*, WMANT 57 (Neukirchen, 1984); M.M. Caspi, "And his Soul Clave unto Dinah (Gen 34)", *AJBI* 11 (1985), pp. 16-53; S.A. Geller, "The Sack of Shechem", *Prooftexts* 10 (1990), pp.1-15; H.S. Hoffner, "The Hittites and the Hurrians", in D.J. Wiseman (ed.), *Peoples from Old Testament Times* (Oxford, 1973), pp. 193-228; J. Skinner, *A Critical and Exegetical Commentary on Genesis*, ICC (2nd ed., Edinburgh, 1930); J.A. Soggin, *A History of Israel* (London-Philadelphia, 1984-85), pp. 143f.; deutsch: *Geschichte Israels und Judas* (Darmstadt, 1991), pp. 114f.; C. Westermann, *Genesis 12-36*, BKAT I/2 (Neukirchen, 1981).

THE BOOK OF JOSHUA
A HASMONAEAN MANIFESTO?

by

JOHN STRANGE

Copenhagen

I have always wondered why the hill-country of Epraim and Manasse, that is, the central hill-country and also the most important part of the double monarchy, Israel and Judah, is not represented in the Book of Joshua.

We have, in the first part of the book, an account of the conquest of the south, centered on the territory of Benjamin, concluding with a short story about the subjugation of Judah after the battle in the valley of Aijalon (Jos. 2-10), most of which has been classified as aetiological legends[1]; later there is an account of the conquest of Galilee in connection with a battle at Merom and the destruction of Hazor (Jos. 11,1-15), but nothing in between[2].

This is puzzling, as in later tradition the core of Israel was in Ephraim and Manasse with Shechem as its principal city (cf. Jos. 24; 1. Kings 12; 13,25), or Shiloh (1. Sam. 1-4), or even later Tirzah (1. Kings 14,17; 15,21-16,9; 16,15-18.23) or Samaria (1. Kings 16, 24-28).

The account in Jos. 1-11 is followed up in 12,1-6 by a sort of resumé of the conquests in Transjordan, clearly derived from Deuteronomy and perhaps Numbers. This resumé is in ch. 12,7-24 followed by a list of conquered kings in what is considered the ideal Israel. Again only a few cities of Epraim are mentioned (Tirzah, Hepher, Tappuah and Apheq), whereas the cities of Judah/Benjamin and Galilee are more fully represented. The list seems to be a summary of ch. 1-11 with some additional names[3], and as such cannot be earlier than the rest of the book. To my mind, it would

---

1 M. Noth, *Das Buch Joshua*, HAT I,7 (Tübingen, 1938), p. XI.

2 It is easiest to see it on a map of Joshua's conquests, see e.g. J. Strange, *Stuttgarter Bibelatlas* (Stuttgart, 1989), maps 33/34.

3 Cf. Y. Aharoni, *The Land of the Bible* (London, 1969), pp.208-11.

be futile to look for an historical setting which could accomodate this short list.

Another summary is found in ch. 13,1-6 where we have the list of "The Land that Remained". This is the area of the Philistine settlement, plus Geshur, to the east of the Lake of Gennesaret, and a great part of the Lebanon and Damascus, extending all the way to Lebo-Hamath. The text may have been taken from Judg. 3,1-3[4].

The summary is followed by a description of the division of the land east of the Jordan which is given to Reuben, Gad and Manasse, 13,7b-32. And then comes the long section on the division of the land west of the Jordan in ch. 14-19. This section consists partly of border descriptions[5], partly of lists of cities. But again there is the curious fact that whereas the south, represented by Simeon, Juda, Benjamin and Dan, and the North, represented by Asher, Naphtali, Zebulon and Issakar, are described with many names, the void is almost complete in the central part of the country, as may be seen on any map[6].

And for good measure the same thing is apparent in the list of Levitical cities in ch. 21 (parallel to 1. Chron. 6,39-69) which again may be easily seen on the map[7]. The few cities mentioned from the central hill-country apart from Shechem and Shiloh, both of which play prominent roles in the book, lie in the vicinity of Shechem and are mentioned in connection with a border description. Finally, it should be mentioned that Joshua's burial place, Timnat-Serah, is mentioned in the last chapter of the book.

The reason for these oddities is probably to be found in the date of the book, as it may be assumed that names mentioned in the book were either known—or of interest—to the author or final redactor of the older material.

Now the Book of Joshua has recently been classified as a "program-

---

[4] Noth (1938), pp.48f considers it an addition. For the extent of this area see Y. Aharoni and M. Avi-Yonah, *The MacMillan Bible Atlas* (Rev. ed.; New York and London, 1977), map 69.

[5] See the fundamental paper by A. Alt, "Das System der Stammesgrenzen im Buche Joshua", *Kleine Schriften zur Geschichte des Volkes Israel I* (München, 1953), pp. 193-202.

[6] Cf.e.g., Strange (1989), maps 35-36.

[7] Aharoni and Avi-Yonah (1977), map 108.

skrift'' (manifesto) for the restoration of the Davidic empire[8], and this seems to tally very well with the geographical scope of the book. Or, as seems more likely to me: the Solomonic empire in all its glory. Consequently, we should look for a period when dreams of the re-creation of the glory of the Davidic-Solomonic empire were active.

I can think of no other period than the early part of the Hasmonaean monarchy, i.e. the reigns of John Hyrcanus, Aristobolus and Alexander Jannaeus (135/4-76 BC)[9]. Of course, this would make it the youngest part of the Old Testament.

Without being able to prove it, I venture to suggest this dating because it produces plausible answers to a number of questions relating to the Book of Joshua:

1) The absence of names from the central hill-country in the onomasticon.

In the period of the Hasmonaeans, the Jews were living primarily in Judah and the Galilee, while the central hill-country was inhabited by the Samaritans[10]. A text describing the Israelite conquest and settlement would consequently consist of names from these areas, in particular, while there would be no suitable onomasticon from areas inhabited by the ''unclean'' Samaritans. This would also explain the concentration of the Book of Joshua on the Cis-Jordan, when we consider that the Transjordan has many Hellenistic cities.

2) The extreme feeling of hatred towards the ''Canaanites''.

In contrast to the prevalent attitude toward strangers in the Old Testament and the usually liberal view on marriage with foreigners which is attested in numerous cases, except in the very late books of Ezra and Nehemiah, we find expressed in the Book of Joshua the view that all Canaanites ought to be killed; there is a ''*herem*'' on them. The terminology used in the relevant passages might in fact point to a very early date, because it is the same terminology found in royal propaganda inscriptions from the end of the Late Bronze

---

[8] M. Ottosson, *The Book of Joshua—A Program of Davidic Restoration* (Uppsala 1991).

[9] See, e.g., for John Hyrcanus: W. Stewart McCullough, *The History and Literature of the Palestinian Jews from Cyrus to Herod* (Toronto and Buffalo 1975), pp. 129-133; and in general: V. Tcherikover, *Hellenistic Civilization and the Jews* (New York, 1959), pp. 235-265.

[10] For the Samaritans see e.g. McCullough (1975), pp. 76-80.

Age[11]; but no serious student would today assign such an early date to the book. Somehow, the terminology has survived and come into Israelite texts at a later date. Also the frequent use of the term "Canaanites" points to a late date[12].

If we date the book to the Hasmonaean period, the terminology would fit in perfectly with the bloody conquests of cities, not least the Hellenistic cities of Transjordan[13].

3) Although the Book of Joshua is considered part of the Deuteronomic History[14], the whole book is permeated with a terminology ussually assigned to P[15]. M.Ottosson even has a paragraph entitled "The Priestly Collector"[16]. Nevertheless, he is sceptical towards a dating of the book to the exilic or postexilic period[17], and is consequently forced to question the relative dating of D and P [18]. Naturally, this testifies to the weighty presence of P in the Book of Joshua.

Especially important are passages like Jos. 5,15, a nearly verbatim quotation of Ex. 3,5, because, as has been pointed out, the P-material in the Book of Joshua is connected with Moses[19]. In my opinion this makes the whole composition late.

At this point it should be asked why the prevalent dating of the Book of Joshua, that is, to the time of king Josiah, cannot be sustained. If we take a closer look at the traditions around Josiah, there is actually no hint of a programme aiming to restore the Davidic-Solomonic empire. All we hear is that Josiah destroyed the altar at Bethel (2.Ki. 23,15-18), that he demolished the temples in the cities

---

11 See M. Liverani, *Prestige and Interest* (Padova, 1990), pp.126-34 with a reference to *ḥerem* on p. 129.

12 For the term "Canaanites", see now N.P. Lemche, *The Canaanites and their Land* (Sheffield, 1991).

13 E.g. Pella which was demolished, AntJud XIII,15,4.

14 Soggin speaks of the Deuteronomic historical work as "a commonplace of Old Testament scholarship" (A. Soggin, *Joshua* (London, 1972), p.7).

15 See e.g. M. Noth, *Überlieferungsgeschichtliche Studien* (Darmstadt, 1967), pp. 182-190; O. Eissfeldt, *Einleitung in das Alte Testament* (Tübingen, 1964), pp. 333-339; E. Cortese, *Joshua 13-21*, Orbis Biblicus et Orientalis (Freiburg, Göttingen, 1990).

16 Ottosson (1991), pp.32-36.

17 Ottosson (1991), pp.36f.

18 Ottosson (1991), pp. 41f.

19 Ottosson (1991), p. 23; see also M. Rose, *Deuteronomist und Jahwist*, AThANT 67 (Zürich, 1981), pp. 78-90. I am not taking any stand as to priority of either of the texts.

of Samaria (2.Ki. 23,19), and that he was killed at Megiddo by the Egyptian king. But the actual extent of his dominion is not referred to, and apart from the notice of his death the sole interest centres on his religious reforms. The very area of his supposed interest, Samaria, is furthermore conspicuously lacking in the Book of Joshua, so the reason for the assignment of the book to the time of Josiah must be its connection with the Deuteronomic work of history, a connection which is not so certain. Finally the interest in Transjordan (ch. 13,8-29; 22,1-34) is supicious, because in this period Israel proper was apparently considered to be only the land west of the Jordan, as witnessed by Ez. 47-48, whereas interest in Transjordan was vivid in the Hasmonaean period.

4) The Book of Joshua has an awkward place in the present Bible.

If we look at the flow of the text, no one would actually miss the Book of Joshua, if it were not there. It parallels the other (admittedly incomplete) description of the conquest of the land in Judg. 1. Of course, it could just as easily be the other way round: Judg. 1 may be superfluous, but it seems to me that especially the P-material makes it probable that if any part is to be viewed with suspicion, it must be P.

The question might be asked: is the Book of Joshua a part of a "Hexateuch", as previously "asssumed?" [20] Or should Noth's Deuteronomic History prevail? Probably the latter, but the excision of Joshua would certainly make things easier. We would then have an older Deuteronomic work of history and a younger "Tetrateuch", only subsequently augmented by the Book of Joshua.

5) The position of Shechem in the Joshua traditions.

Although the area of the central hill-country, the area of Manasse and Ephraim, is only represented by a few names (see above under 1), one place certainly stands out as of central importance: Shechem[21]. Why is this place so important for the author/redactor/instigator of the Book of Joshua? Especially when we consider that

---

[20] Cf. first and formost J. Wellhausen, *Die Composition des Hexateuchs und der Historischen Bücher des Alten Testaments* (2nd. ed., Berlin, 1889), pp.118-136; and now Cortese (1990).

[21] At this point it is appropiate to refer to Eduard Nielsen's doctoral work: *Shechem. A Traditio-Historical Investigation* (Copenhagen, 1955).

the main sanctuary of the despised Samaritans was situated precisely here, on Mount Gerizim[22].

It is possible that it was exactly the strong religious traditions of Shechem which were the factor which secured Shechem a place in the Book of Joshua. Apparently there existed old traditions of an early pact concluded at Shechem between Israelites and the local inhabitants in connection with the "Migdol-temple" there, and the holiness of Shechem persisted because there probably was some connection between these traditions and the shape of the Solomonic temple[23]. Old traditions certainly existed among the Samaritans and exist even today. As these traditions could not be ignored by anyone writing on early Israel and the Conquest, the only thing to do was to ursurp them, so that any traditions belonging to the Samaritans were answered by the Book of Joshua: they belong to us, not to the Samaritans.

This again fits very well into the period of the Hasmonaeans; probably the Samaritan Pentateuch, which claims the traditions to be Samaritan, already existed, and we know that the temple of the Samaritans on Mount Gerizim was destroyed by John Hyrcanus in 128 BC[24].

The foregoing attempts to establish a plausible date for the composition and writing of the Book of Joshua; however, it leaves one important question open, namely the matter of historicity. It goes without saying that the book as such does not relate any actual conquest and division of the promised land to Joshua. Everybody agrees on that. However, the possibility that certain parts may contain historical facts or that certain parts of the lists may not be wholly fictitious must be examined.[25] But this task lies outside the scope of this essay in honour of to-day's septuagenarian.[26]

---

[22] McCullough (1975), pp. 78f.

[23] See J. Strange, "Theology and Politics in Architecture and Iconography", *SJOT* 1 (1991), pp.23-44.

[24] AntJud XIII, § 254-6; cf. McCullough 1975 p. 79.

[25] I am aware that I once again commit myself to a quite traditional view of Israelite history, as it has been expressed with regard to an earlier paper of mine: J. Strange, "The Transition from the Bronze Age to the Iron Age in the Eastern Mediterranean and the Emergence of the Israelite State", *SJOT* 1 (1986), pp.1-19.

[26] I wish to give my sincere thanks to Ms.Lise Lock at the Insitut for Bibelsk Eksegese for her attempts to improve my English.

THE BAN ON THE CANAANITES IN THE BIBLICAL CODES AND ITS HISTORICAL DEVELOPMENT

by

MOSHE WEINFELD
Jerusalem

Laws regulating the relations of the Israelites to the inhabitants of the land of Canaan who preceded them are found in the three law codes of the Pentateuch:

(1) In the so-called large Covenant code of Exodus 21-23, which is the most ancient code,[1] and in the law of the small Covenant code in Exodus 34:11-17.
(2) In the law of the priestly code in Numbers 33:50-56.
(3) In the Deuteronomic code: Deuteronomy 7:1-5; 20:10-18.

The order of the laws—i.e., the Covenant code, the priestly code, and Deuteronomy—seems to be the actual chronological order of these writings, as we shall attempt to demonstrate by what follows.

We shall analyze here the different attitudes toward the pre-Israelite population as they are represented in the aforementioned codes. However, before we begin the scriptural analysis, we shall preface a few words concerning the fundamental understanding of the idea of "dispossession"[2] which is common to all sources. All three sources are based upon the assumption that even though the dispossession is done or ought to be done by the Israelites, in reality

---

[1] The most important clue for the antiquity of the code is the law in Exod. 22:27: "You shall not curse/revile God nor put a curse upon a *chieftain* (*naśi'*) among your people".

In the Biblical books referring to the monarchic period we hear about cursing/reviling God and king (1 Kgs. 21:10, 13; Isa. 8:21 and compare Prov. 24:21), and not about cursing God and chieftain. Chieftain (*naśi'*) usually occurs in the context of the wandering in the desert (the book of Numbers) and in the period of the settlement (Jos. 9:22) as well as in the genealogical lists of the tribes of nomadic character such as Reuben (1 Chr. 5:1) and Simeon (1 Chr. 4:38). Cf. M. Weinfeld, "Chieftain", *Encycl. Judaica*, V (Jerusalem, 1974), cols. 420-421.

[2] In general we shall use the term 'dispossession'. Only when necessary, to be specific, shall we use 'expel' (*grš*), 'exterminate' (*ḥrm*) etc.

it is done by the hand of God.[3] Therefore we find ambiguities in the chapters with which we are concerned: On the one hand, God expels (*grš*), dispossesses (*hwryš*), sends away (*šlḥ*), annihilates (*hkḥyd*), thrusts out (*hdp*), drives out (*nšl*), destroys (*h'byd*), exterminates (*hšmyd*), and cuts off (*hkryt*) the Canaanites (Ex. 23:29; 34:11,24; Lev. 18:24; Deut. 4:38; 6:19; 7:1, 22, 23; 8:20; 9:3, 5; 11:23; 31:3, 4); and on the other hand the Israelites are commanded to do this (Ex. 23:31; Num. 33:52, 55; Deut. 7:2, 16; 20:17).[4]

The most prominent expression of the point of view that the dispossession is accomplished by God is found not just in the law codes themselves but in the literature which depends on them. Thus, for example, Joshua 24:12-13, which depends on pentateuchal sources (Ex. 23:28; Deut. 6:10-11), says: "I have sent the hornet before you and it drove them out before you . . . not by your sword or by your bow (*l' bḥrbk wl' bqštk*). And I have given you a land in which you have not labored and cities which you did not build and you have settled in them; vineyards and oliveyards which you did not plant, you are enjoying."

The first clause in this passage: "I have sent the hornet before you and it drove them out before you" draws on Exodus 23:28, and its conclusion: "not by your sword or by your bow" (24:12) is an elaboration of the author[5], while verse 13: "the land in which you have not labored and cities which you did not build .." overlaps Deuteronomy 6:10-11.

A more radical statement which expresses this theological view is available in Ps. 44:3-7: "You [God] dispossessed nations by your hand and you planted them; you distressed them and drove them out (*wtšlḥm*);[6] it was not by their sword that they took the land;

---

[3] For the combination of divine and human factors in Biblical historiography see I.L. Seeligmann, "Menschliches Heldentum und Göttliche Hilfe", *Theologische Zeitschrift* 19 (1963), pp. 385 ff.

[4] In addition to these references in the legal sources, we find the view about God's dispossession of the Canaanites in Deut. 33:27; Jud. 2:3; 6:9; 11:23-24; Amos 2:9; Ps. 78:55; 80:9; 1 Chr. 17:21; 2 Chr. 20:7. On the duty of the Israelites to dispossess the Canaanites in non-legal sources cf. Jud. 1:21, 27-28, 29, 30-31, 33. (On the sin of not dispossessing of the Canaanites in Jud. 1:1-2:5 cf. my article "The Period of the Conquest and the Judges as seen by the Earlier and Later Sources", *VT* 17 (1967), pp. 93-113, and see also Ps. 106:34-35).

[5] This is in contrast to Gen. 18:22: "Which I took from the Amorites with my sword and bow" (for an apologetic view of this verse cf. the Targums.)

[6] For *šlḥ* (pi'el) in the sense of expelling see below.

their arm did not save them but your right hand and your strength and the light of your face, because you liked them ... so I will not trust in my bow nor will my sword save me.''

In the law codes in the Pentateuch, God's intervention is expressed by the removal of the Canaanites in various forms: (1) God by himself expels the Canaanites (Ex. 23:29, 30; 34:11). (2) God sends his angel to expel the Canaanites and bring the Israelites into the land of Canaan (Ex. 23:20-23; 33:2). (3) God sends the hornet which expels the Canaanites (Ex. 23:28; Deut. 7:20; cf. Josh. 24:12).[7] It must be emphasized that these texts belong to the rhetorical/homiletic framework of the laws and not to the laws themselves. The laws of dispossession themselves, which we are examining, are formulated in terms of commandments and as such constitute instructions to be executed by the people.

Let us now take up the evidence in the Pentateuch on the commandments connected with the ''expulsion'' of the pre-Israelite inhabitants by Israel:

(1) In the large Covenant Code (Ex. 21-23) we read:

> When my angel goes before you and brings you to the Amorites and the Hittites and the Perizzites and the Canaanites, the Hivvites and the Jebusites[8] and I will annihilate them. You shall not bow down to their gods; nor shall you serve them; nor shall you follow their practices, but you shall destroy them and smash their pillars ... I will deliver the inhabitants of the land into your hands and you will drive them out before you. You shall make no covenant with them and their gods. They shall not dwell in your land lest they cause you to sin against me, for serving their gods will prove a snare to you (Ex. 23:23-33).

The verb which we find here for the ''dispossession'' of the Canaanites for both God (vv. 29, 30) and the Israelites (v. 31),[9] is *grš* = expel. This verb is used in the scriptures for ''divorce'' (*grš ʾšh* Lev. 21:7, 14; 22:13) and it is parallel to the verb *šlḥ ʾšh* elsewhere

---

[7] Cf. E. Neufeld, ''Insects as Warfare Agents in the Ancient Near East'', *Orientalia* 49 (1980), pp. 30-57.

[8] For the different lists of the Canaanite peoples, and for ethnic distinctions of these peoples, see T. Ishida, ''The Structure and Historical Implication of the Lists of the Pre-Israelite Nations'', *Biblica* 60 (1979), pp. 461-490.

[9] The reading of the LXX and the Vulgate of this verse: *wĕgerašti̇mō*, ''And I will drive them out'' is not anchored in the context which addresses Israel. See A. Dillmann, *Exodus und Leviticus* (Leipzig, 1897), ad loc.

in the scriptures (Deut. 24:1, 3; Jer. 3:1).[10] Indeed, even with the expulsion of the Canaanites we find the expression (*šlḥ*—pi'el) in Leviticus 28:24; 20:23 ("The nations which I sent away (*mšlḥ*) from before you"). And just as *grš* is accompanied by the preposition *mpny: grš "mpnyk/mpnykm"* (Ex. 23:1, 29, 30, 31), so also *šlḥ* is accompanied by this preposition in connection with the Canaanites (Lev. 18:24; 20:23).[11]

The argument for expulsion is religious: "lest they cause you to sin against me, . . . for it will prove a snare/trap (*lmwqš*) to you" (Ex. 23:33). The expressions "sin" (*ḥt'*) and "snare" (*mwqš*) as perpetuated in later sources, apparently draw from ancient traditions. In fact, all the laws concerning the "dispossession" of the Canaanites are combined with warnings against worshipping idols, and these latter occurrences are even used as a point of departure for the commandments for dispossession, like the passage which we have analyzed here (Ex. 23:24-25), as well as in Exodus 34:12-13 (cf. Deut. 7:5; 20:18; Num. 33:52).

(2) The second source in which we find laws which deal with relations with the pre-Israelite population is Exodus 34:11-16:[12]

> I will drive out before you the Amorites, the Canaanites, the Hittites, the Perizzites, the Hivvites, and the Jebusites. Guard yourself lest you make a covenant with the inhabitants of the land . . . lest it be a snare in your midst. But their altars you shall dismantle, and their monuments you shall smash and their sacred trees you shall cut down . . . lest you make a covenant with the inhabitants of the land and lust (*znh*) after their gods and sacrifice to their gods and he call you, and you eat his sacrifice; and you take his daughters for your sons and your daughters lust after their gods and they make your sons lust after their gods.

Here the emphasis comes upon a prohibition affecting social contact with the Canaanites: the making of covenants and marriage ties,

---

10 Compare Gen. 3:23 in connection with the expulsion of Adam from the garden of Eden: *wyšlḥhw* parallel with *wygrš* in v. 24.

11 *hwryš*, which will be discussed later, is also accompanied by *mpny*; see Exod. 34:24; Num. 32:21; 33:52, 55. Although the command "They shall not dwell in your land" (Exod. 23:33) could be interpreted in various ways (including extermination), the phrase "And you will drive them out" in v. 31 certainly means expulsion and not extermination.

12 For a thorough analysis of this pericope cf. J. Halbe, *Das Privilegrecht Jahwes Ex. 34:10-26. Gestalt und Wesen, Herkunft und Wirken in Vordeuteronomischer Zeit*, FRLANT 114 (Göttingen, 1975), pp. 119 ff.

and not a word is said about the expulsion or dispossession on the part of Israel (God alone will expel the Amorite and the Canaanite, etc. before Israel [v. 11]). In the large Covenant Code which we mentioned previously, expulsion is emphasized, therefore no mention is made of marriage ties. After the Canaanites are expelled and they are no longer living in the land of Israel (''they shall not dwell in your land''—Exod. 23:33), there is no place for prescriptions concerning marriage with the Canaanites. In contrast with this, in the present pericope, in which no mention is made of a commandment to expell the Canaanites, the view emphasized is the prohibition of marriage.[13] It seems that the source in Exodus 34 draws on Shechemite tradition such as the one in Genesis 34, which is concerned with covenant bonds with the inhabitants of the land and marriage ties (*connubium et commercium*) in language similar to that of Exodus 34:16: ''and we shall give our daughters to you and your daughters we shall take for ourselves'' (Gen. 34:16; cf. 34:9, 21; see also Judg. 3:6). Like in Exodus 23:20-33, so also in Exodus 34:11-16, warnings against relations with the Canaanites are combined with the warnings against idolatry: ''lest it be a sin'', ''and they cause your sons to lust after their gods'' (vv. 12, 16).

(3) Another series of laws which touches on relations between the Israelites and the inhabitants of the land of Canaan is found in Numbers 33:50-55:

> When you cross the Jordan into the land of Canaan, you shall dispossess all the inhabitants of the land, you shall destroy all their figured objects, you shall destroy all their molten images and all their high places you shall demolish. You shall inherit the land and take possession of it. And you shall apportion the land by lot among your families . . . clan by clan. And if you do not dispossess the inhabitants of the land, those whom you allow to remain shall be stings in your eyes and thorns in your side and they shall harass you in the land in which you live.

What we have before us is a passage of the priestly code, as we learn not only from the style,[14] but also from the fact that it incorporates

---

[13] Cf. J. Milgrom, ''Profane Slaughter and the Composition of Deuteronomy'', *HUCA* 47 (1976), p. 6, n. 21.

[14] Note the following phrases: *wydbr YHWH 'l Mšh* (v. 50); *'rṣ Kn'n* (v. 51); *mśkyt* (v. 12, comp. Lev. 26:1); *ṣlmy* (v. 52, cf. Gen. 1:26-27; 5:3; 9:6); *whtnḥltm* (v. 54, compare Lev. 25:46; Num. 32:18; 34:13); *wṣrrw 'tkm* (v. 55, compare Num. 25:17-18).

here a law of the division of the land by lot, which is the main concern in the priestly conquest tradition which originated in Shiloh (Josh. 18:1-10; cf. Num. 26:52-56). Another indication of the priestly tradition which occurs here is the pagan cultic objects mentioned in the section. In contrast to the other sources, which mention altars, pillars, and sacred trees or poles (*mzbḥwt, mṣbwt* and *'šrim*) (Ex, 23:34; 34:13; Deut. 7:5; cf. Judg. 2:3), which are generally found in open fields (see Deut. 12:2-3; 1 Kgs. 14:23; 2 Kgs. 16:4; 17:10), the source before us mentions cultic objects characteristic of temple enclosures. Here we find "figured objects" (*mśkyt*)[15] and molten images (*mskwt*) which appear in other places in the priestly writings (Lev. 19:4; 26:1; cf. Lev. 26:30-31). Also appearing here are "high places" (*bmwt*) which are mentioned together with the "incense-stands" (*ḥmnym*) alongside sanctuaries in Leviticus 26:30, and which we do not find in other sources in the Pentateuch.

The verb utilized here concerning the dispossession of the pre-Israelite inhabitants of the land is not *grš* "expel" but *hwryš* "dispossess". This verb literally means "to cause to possess/to inherit", and shows a gradual transition to extermination (Num. 14:12 [*'knw bdbr w'wršnw*]; Josh. 13:12; Zech. 9:14-15).[16] The use of this verb expresses an intermediate stage between expulsion (*grš*) in the ancient sources, and *hḥrym* meaning extermination in the book of Deuteronomy, as will be shown later. *Hwryš* can mean either expulsion or extermination.[17]

The reason mentioned here for dispossession is not religious but political: "They shall harass you in the land in which you live" (Num. 33:55). In the historiographic source of the Deuteronomic school (Joshua 23:13)[18] the threat has a slightly different form:

---

15 See Ezek. 8:12; Prov. 25:11 (*mśkyt ksp*); Lev. 26:1 (*'bn mśkyt*, which means bas-reliefs). Cf. the Panamua inscription: "whqm lh mšky" (H. Donner, W. Röllig, *Kanaanäische und Aramäische Inschriften* I (Wiesbaden, 1962), no. 215, 18).

16 Cf. N. Lohfink, "Die Bedeutung von hebr. yrš qal und hif.", *Biblische Zeitschrift* NF 26 (1982), pp. 14-33.

17 The ambiguity is reflected in the Targums: Onkelos and Ps. Jonathan translate *hwryš* 'expel' (trk), while Targum Neophyti translates 'extermination' (*šyṣy*) and so the LXX (ἀπόλλυμι, ἐξαιρέω, ἐξόλλυμι). In Deuteronomy and in the Deuteronomic school *hwryš* indicates extermination as may be learned from 9:3, where *hwryš* appears next to *hšmyd* and *h'byd*. Compare also 2 Kgs. 21:2 (*hwryš*) with verse 9 (*hšmyd*). *yrš* in Deuteronomy also implies extermination, see 2:12, compare 2:21, 22; 12:2, 29-30; 18:14; 19:1; 31:3.

18 For the nature of this farewell speech in the Deuteronomic school, see my book: *Deuteronomy and the Deuteronomic School* (Oxford, 1972), pp. 10-14.

Instead of "for stings (*lśkym*) in your eyes and thorns (*lṣnnm*) in your sides" (ibid.), here it appears as "and for stings (*lšṭṭ*) in your sides and thorns (*lṣnnm*) in your eyes", beside *mwqš* (= snare) which is attested in the earlier source (see above). *Mwqš* in the religious sense is coupled with national punishment in Judges 2:3: "They shall become as traps (*lṣdm*) at their sides and their gods be a snare (*mwqš*) to them." These expressions: *śkym, ṣnynm, šṭṭ* (= *šwṭ*), and *ṣdym* in Judges 2:3,[19] mean prickly thorns that cause pain and distress to those who sit on them. In this case they express the harassment which the alien remnants cause to the settlers of the land of Israel (cf. Ezek. 28:24: "Inflicting briars and painful thorns (*qwṣ* from all around you who will despise (*hš'ṭym*) you"). This motif, found in so many sources, may allude to the existence of an ancient tradition on the topic of the relations of the Israelites with the native population.

In contrast to other sources which, in similar contexts, list the particular peoples in detail (Ex. 23:23, 28; 34:11; Deut. 7:1; 20:17), here the lawgiver characteristically speaks about "all the inhabitants of the land" without designating the peoples in question. This principle opens up the way for Nahmanides to understand that it does not necessarily refer to the seven peoples of the land of Canaan, but to all those who are not Israelites. Additionally Nahmanides learned from this passage that the commandment was eternal: "That we were commanded to inherit the land which God gave . . . in every generation . . . to inherit is applicable forever, undertaken by every one of us, even after the exile" (Criticisms on the Book of Commandments of Maimonides, commandment 7). According to the opinion of Nahmanides, and in this case he is unique, the commandment to the Israelites in all generations is not only to inherit the land but also to dispossess its inhabitants.

However this is not the plain meaning of the scripture; the scripture refers only to those who went out of Egypt and who were about to enter into the land of Canaan to divide it into inheritances. This is not an "eternal statute" (*ḥq 'wlm*). One has to add that the general expression "inhabitants of the land (*ywšby h'rṣ*)" is found also in the sources of the book of Exodus (23:31; 34:12, 15) which refer to the expulsion of the Canaanites and is not unique to Numbers 33.[20]

---

19 Unless we accept the reading of the LXX: *ṣrym* (συνοχάς) = enemies; (compare Targum: *lm'yqyn*).

20 See my book: *Deuteronomy and the Deuteronomic School* (Oxford, 1972), pp. 342-343.

(4) The final source concerning the ban on the Canaanites to be discussed is Deuteronomy 7:1-2; 20:10-18. In Deuteronomy 7:1-2 we read:

> For the Lord shall bring you to the land whither you are going to inherit, and he shall make fall mighty nations before you, the Hittite and the Girgashite, and the Amorite, and the Canaanite, and the Perizzite, and the Hivite, and the Jebusite, seven mighty nations which are mightier than you. And the Lord your God will deliver them to you; and you shall smite them; you must annihilate them (*hḥrm tḥrymm*); you shall not make a covenant with them and you shall not spare them (*l' tkrt lhm bryt wl' tḥnm*). And you shall not marry them, you shall not let your daughter marry his son, and his daughter you shall not take as a wife for your son. For she will draw your son away from me and they shall serve other gods . . . but thus shall you do to them: Their altars you shall dismantle and their steles you shall smash; and their sacred trees you shall chop down; and their idols you shall burn with fire.

As far as making covenant with the Canaanites, the prohibition of contracting marriages with them and of dismantling their altars are concerned, the author of the book of Deuteronomy depends on Exodus 23:20-34, but he adds the commandment concerning the burning of idols which is unique to him (see Deut. 7:25).[21] The most important innovation by the author of Deuteronomy is the *ḥerem* of the seven peoples, which we shall discuss presently.

In a more legalistic passage in Deuteronomy 20:16-18 we read:

> But in the towns of these peoples (the Canaanites) which the Lord your God has given to you for an inheritance, you shall not let a soul remain alive, for you must annihilate them (*hḥrm tḥrymm*): the Hittite, and the Amorite, and the Canaanite, and the Perizzite and the Hivite, and the Jebusite, as YHWH, your God, commanded you, so that they do not lead you to do all the abominations which they have done for their gods and sin against YHWH, your God.[22]

---

21 See Halbe (1975), pp. 119 ff. This commandment occurs here for the first time in the book of Deuteronomy. Indeed David did not enforce this law; he just 'carried them (the idols) off' (2 Sam. 5:21). The Chronicler who follows the Deuteronomic law has David ordering 'to burn the idols' (1 Chr. 14:12) instead of 'carrying them off'.

22 These verses constitute a reinterpretation of an older law pertaining to the imposition of corvée upon a Canaanite city which makes peace with the Israelites (vss. 10-14). The author of Deuteronomy, who demands absolute and unconditional *ḥerem* on the Canaanites, interpreted the old law of 20:10-14 as applying only to remote cities not belonging to Canaan (see A. Biram, "*mas 'obed*", *Tarbiz* 23 (1944), pp. 137 ff.). Verse 15, which opens with the phrase, "thus you shall deal

In these two pericopes in Deuteronomy we find, for the first time, the use of the verb *hḥrym* concerning the Canaanites in the sense of annihilation.[23] We do not find this verb in the previous sources, neither in connection with God who dispossesses nor with the dispossessing by Israel. Nor do we hear in other sources commands such as: "you shall not let a soul remain alive (*l' tḥyh kl nšmh*)" in Deuteronomy 20:16 (cf. Deut. 2:34; 3:3),[24] and which the Deuteronomistic historiographer makes frequent use of (Josh. 10:28, 30, 33, 37, 39, 40; 11:11, 14). The book of Deuteronomy, which uses *hḥrym* concerning the Canaanites, consistently avoids using the verb *grš* for "expel", in order to indicate that the seven nations are not to be expelled, but exterminated. Alongside the verb *hḥrym* in Deuteronomy we find a series of other verbs which denote annihilation, such as *'kl* = 'devour' (Deut. 7:16, *klh* = 'put an end to' (Deut. 7:22), *hšmyd* = 'wipe out' (Deut. 7:24), and *h'byd* = 'cause to perish' (Deut. 7:24). When the author of Deuteronomy uses earlier sources which do use the verb *grš*, he intentionally changes this verb to another verb in order to establish his own point of view. Entire phrases are transformed by his hand for this purpose. For example, the passage in Exodus 23:27, which says that God will make the enemy panic so that he turns his neck to Israel (i.e. he flees) reads: "And I shall cause to panic (*whmty*) all the people among whom you shall go and they shall turn tail and run (*ntn 'rp*)", becomes in the hands of the author of Deuteronomy: "And YHWH, your God, shall give them unto you, and he shall throw them into a great panic

---

with all the towns that lie very far from you", has the force of the Rabbinic casuistic term: *bmh dbrym 'mwrym* 'in which case are these words said' = when does this apply, cf. A. Toeg, *Tarbiz* 39 (1970), p. 229.

23 The root *ḥrm* in the Semitic languages indicates both prohibition as well as sacrality; cf., e.g., Deut. 22:9: "You shall not sow your vineyards with another kind of seed, else the crop will become sacred (*tqdš*) (i.e. will be prohibited)", (compare Arabic *ḥrym*). *Ḥerem* in the context of war denotes dedication to God: if it is man or animal, it should be sacrificed to god, and if it is property, it should be devoted to him (Exod. 22:19; Lev. 27:29; Deut. 13:16; 1 Sam. 15:3, 33). The religious meaning of the root *ḥrm* is fully expressed in the Mesha inscription: "And I killed ... seven thousand men ... and women because I proclaimed them as *ḥerem* to Ištar—Kemoš (*ky l'štr kmš hḥrmth*), see Donner-Röllig, *KAI*, no. 181:17. In the second temple period and in later periods *ḥerem* acquired the meaning of expulsion and confiscation of property (Ezra 10:8). See W. Horbury, "Extirpation and Excommunication", *VT* 35 (1985), pp. 19-38.

24 Compare Num. 21:35: "until no remnant was left" (*'d blty hš'yr-lw śryd*) in a passage copied from Deut. 2:1-3. See the commentaries and my article: "The Extent of the Promised Land—The Status of Transjordan", in G. Strecker (ed.), *Das Land Israel in Biblischer Zeit* (Göttingen, 1983), p. 70, n. 4.

(*whmm mhmh gdwlh*) until they are wiped out (*'d hšmdm*)" (Deut. 7:23). Instead of "turning their back" meaning flight, the author of the book of Deuteronomy uses the term *hšmyd*. Moreover he adds the phrase: "Nobody will be able to stand against you until he causes you to destroy them" (Deut. 7:22; cf. 11:25; Josh. 1:5).[25]

Another example of intentional change by the author of the book of Deuteronomy on the subject of the removal of the pre-Israelite population is Exodus 23:28. There we read that the hornet (*ṣr'h*) is sent by God in order to drive out the Hivite, the Canaanite, and the Hittite from before the Israelites besides the angel, who is sent to bring Israel into his land (Ex. 13:20,23). The book of Deuteronomy completely drops the tradition of the angel as a matter of ideological taste (an objection to angelology),[26] but to the hornet he assigns a function different from that which appears in Exodus 23:28: God sends the hornet not—as was mentioned in Exodus 23:28—in order to drive out the Canaanites, but in order to annihilate the remnants and the hidden enemies (*hnš'rym whnstrym*) before the Israelites (7:20); the Israelites will destroy the non-concealed enemies themselves.

What is the reason for these differences in the book of Deuteronomy, and how do we account for the radical attitude concerning the pre-Israelite population precisely in this late book? *Ḥerem* in the sense of dedicating[27] and offering to God is known to us from ancient periods in Israel[28] and in other nations, as, e.g., in the the Mesha inscription.[29] Yet the ancient *ḥerem* was ostensibly a vow

---

25 For the military speech containing patriotic motives in the Deuteronomic work see my book (above, n. 18), pp. 45-51.

26 See my article "The Emergence of the Deuteronomic Movement. The Historical Antecedents", in H. Lohfink (ed.), *Das Deuteronomium. Entstehung, Gestalt und Botschaft* (Leuven, 1985), p. 84.

27 For the connection between *ḥrm* and *qdš* (compared to the akkadian *asakku*) see A. Malamat, "The *Herem* in Mari and in the "Bible", *Jubilee Volume Y. Kaufman* (Jerusalem, 1961), pp. 149-158, (Hebrew). See also my article "The Tithe in the Bible—its Royal and Cultic Background", *Beer Sheva* 1 (1973), p. 123, n. 6, (Hebrew), and also my article "Ḥilul, Kbisha Mirmas regel", *Meḥqerey Lašon*. *Festschrift Z. Ben-Hayyim* (Jerusalem, 1983), pp. 198-199, n. 20.

28 Exod. 22:19; Lev. 27:29; 1 Sam. 15:3, 18, 33; 1 Kgs. 20:42; and compare Micah 4:13. Cf. above, n. 23.

29 See the citation from the Mesha inscription, above, n. 23. For cultic extermination carried out by other nations see N. Lohfink, "*ḥāram*", *Theologisches Wörterbuch zum Alten Testament*, hrsg. G.J. Botterweck, H. Ringgren, Band III (Stuttgart, 1978), p. 204; S. Lowenstamm, "Herem", *Encycl. Miqra'it* III (Jerusalem, 1965), cols. 290-292, (Hebrew).

which the people vowed[30] at the time of the proclamation of outright war, as was the case with Jericho (Josh. 6:17-18) and Arad (Num. 21:1-3). Joshua proclaims in the siege of Jericho: "and the city shall be *ḥerem*, it and all which is in her, to the Lord" (Josh. 6:17). As a result of this everything which was in the city "from man to animal" (Josh. 6:21), the silver and gold, and the brass and iron are given to the temple treasury (Josh. 6:24). Were the *ḥerem* a custom which operated in accordance with the commands of the book of Deuteronomy—that all the population of the land of Canaan were subject to the law of the *ḥerem* (Deut. 7:2; 20:17)—there would be neither reason nor need to proclaim special status for the city of Jericho.[31] And the same goes for the case of the ḥerem of Arad in Num. 21:1-3: Israel vows (*ndr*) to the Lord that if God will give the Canaanite dwellings in the Negev into their hands, then the Israelites will devote (*yḥrmw*) the inhabitants of their cities, and they would turn the place into *ḥerem*. A parallel tradition of the ḥerem in the Negev district, which is accomplished by the hand of the tribe of Judah and Simeon, and of calling the place by the name *Ḥormah*, appears in Judges 1:18.[32] According to the *ḥerem* law in the book of Deuteronomy, the *ḥerem* applies to all seven pre-Israelite peoples anyway and the Israelites' vow to put to *ḥerem* the Canaanites of Jericho and Arad and its environs is thus superfluous.

It was the book of Deuteronomy which conceived the *ḥerem* as a commandment which automatically applied to all the inhabitants of the land, whether they fought or not. This *ḥerem* is not conditional on any vow or dedication; rather, it is from the beginning an a priori decree, which belongs more to the realm of utopian theory than to practice. Indeed, in practice, the inhabitants of the Canaanite cities were not destroyed but rather placed under corvée labor, as we learn from 1 Kings 9:20-21: "All the remaining people of the Amorites,

---

[30] Compare: Lev. 27:28-29, where *Ḥerem* executed against humans and beasts appears as part of a voluntary dedication, and as a result of a vow; cf. vss. 2 ("when a man shall clearly utter a vow", *ky ypl' ndr*), 14 ff. (and compare to v. 21: "As a field devoted", *kśdh hḥrm*), M. Greenberg, "Herem", *Encycl. Judaica* VIII (Jerusalem, 1972), cols. 344-350.

[31] Only by adopting the midrashic method could we claim that because Joshua had carried out in Jericho a more strict extermination than that which is found in Deuteronomy, a special kind of extermination had to be carried out (see BT, Sanhed. 44, a).

[32] Of the relation between the tradition in Num. 21:1-3 and Jud. 1:17 see discussion in commentaries.

the Hittites, the Perezzites, the Hivvites and the Jebusites which were not from the Israelites themselves, among those which were left ... which the Israelites could not destroy,[33] Solomon put them for corvée labor until this day." We also learn from old traditions (Judg. 1:21, 27-28, 29, 30, 31-33 and their parallels in Joshua 15:63; 16:10; 17:12-13, 14-18), that the remaining Canaanites dwelt in their cities until the days of David and Solomon, and these latter were placed under corvée labor (1 Kgs. 9:20-21; 2 Chr. 2:16). Furthermore, according to Judges 1:32-33, some of these Canaanites even placed the Israelites in the north (on the coast and in Galilee) under the corvée.

The imposition of corvée labor upon the pre-Israelite inhabitants of the land and not their dispossession—as we find in Judges 1—is represented as a sin. The angel of the Lord sent to bring the Israelites into the land (see above) reproves the Israelites on this and he represents this as a violation of the commandment not to make a covenant with the inhabitants of the land (Judg. 2:1-4). It ought to be admitted that in all the existing sources Israel is commanded to remove the Canaanites from the land, but in Deuteronomy the removal is interpreted as complete annihilation. In the other sources, both expulsion and dispossession are commanded. As we have already indicated, according to the historical works, the *ḥerem* on the Canaanites, as commanded in Deuteronomy 7:2; 20:16-17, was never carried out. The editor of the book of Joshua, who depends on the book of Deuteronomy, tried to draw a picture of the conquest according to commandment of the book of Deuteronomy, and therefore envisions total annihilation of all the inhabitants of the Canaanite cities of the land: "and Joshua smote all the land ... and all their kings did not leave behind a survivor, and every single soul were destroyed as YHWH, the God of Israel, commanded" (Josh. 10:40); "and all the cities of these kings and all their kings, Joshua seized and he smote them by the sword and annihilated them, as Moses the servant of the Lord commanded ... every man they smote by the sword until they destroyed them and they did not leave

---

33 It seems that 2 Chr. 8:7-8 deliberately changed the phrase: "whom the children of Israel could not destroy" to "whom the children of Israel consumed not" (*l' klwm*), and it views them as *gerim* (2 Chr. 2:16). See S. Japhet, *The Ideology of the Book of Chronicles and its Place in Biblical Thought* (Frankfurt a.M., 1989), p. 337.

any alive" (Josh. 11:12-14). According to this editor, all the territory "from the Mount of Halaq in the south to Baal Gad in the valley of Lebanon" was seized by the Israelites in the days of Joshua, and not a single Canaanite was left behind in this area (Josh. 11:14-15, 16-17, 20; 12:1-6). This picture stands in complete contradiction to the core accounts of the tribal conquest found in Judges 1 and the parallels in the book of Joshua, according to which the Canaanite inhabitants persisted in the coastal cities and in the lowlands until Davidic times. Indeed the survivors of the Canaanites which were left in the land are the strangers (*gerim*) which are mentioned in most of the law codes in the Pentateuch.[34]

The law of *ḥerem* in Deuteronomy is then a utopian law which was written in retrospect. Deuteronomy adopted for itself the commandments of the old *ḥerem*, which was practiced in encounters with the enemies and which was intertwined with a vow and with a dedication in proclaiming *ḥerem*, but Deuteronomy applied it in the manner of his theoretical *ḥerem* concerning all the pre-Israelite inhabitants. Furthermore, according to Deuteronomy not only the population which dwelled west of the Jordan were subject to the *ḥerem* but also the Transjordan population (Deut. 2:34; 3:10), which, according to the deuteronomic view, is a part of the promised land.[35]

The Rabbis could not accept this radical requirement of total *ḥerem* in Deuteronomy. They circumvented the plain meaning of the scripture, in their introduction to the accounts of Joshua's conquest as follows: "Joshua sent out three proclamations (*prostagmata*) to the Canaanites: 'Let him who would flee flee, let him who would make peace make peace, and let him who would make war do so.'"[36] Such an option given to the Canaanites stands in complete contradiction to the laws of *ḥerem* in Deuteronomy (7:2; 20:16-17), and it reflects the politics customary towards other nations during Hasmonean times. In those days there was no tendency to annihilate strangers according to the commandments of the *ḥerem*. The purpose was to cleanse the land from idols and convert the inhabitants to Judaism as far as possible, and anyone who opposed such measures

---

[34] See I.L. Seeligmann, "Ger", *Encycl. Miqra'it* II (Jerusalem, 1954), p. 547.

[35] See my article "The Extent of the Promised Land" (above, n. 24), p. 68.

[36] Lev. Rabah (ed. Margaliot, pp. 386-387); Yerushalmi, Shevi'it, 7:5, 36, d; Deut. Rabah, 5:14.

was invited to leave the area.[37] Thus, for example, as the men of Gezer requested that Simeon the Hasmonean make a covenant with them (''he will give them the right hand''),[38] he consented. Instead of annihilating them he expelled them from the city, he purified their houses of idols and settled men who observed the Torah (1 Macc. 13:43-44) there. He treated the inhabitants of the Haqra in Jerusalem similarly: ''he gave them the right hand'', he made them depart from the fortress and cleansed it of idols (1 Macc. 13:49-50).

Thus we have seen that the total *ḥerem* of the pre-Israelite population as described by the Deuteronomic writings, is unrealistic. What did in fact happen was the expulsion and clearing out of the pre-Israelite inhabitants, and even that was, taken as a whole, not a one-time event, but an on-going process (cf. Ex. 23:29-30).[39] The *ḥerem* of Deuteronomy, then, is a wish originating in the 8th-7th century B.C.E:, the time of crystallization of the book of Deuteronomy.

We have discussed the background of the *ḥerem* of Deuteronomy; now we need to establish the background of the commandments concerning expulsion and dispossession which precede the utopian ideology of Deuteronomy. The laws of expulsion and dispossession of the pre-Israelite population crystallized in a period of tension with the inhabitants of Canaan, and at a time when there was a feeling of unity between the tribes of Israel. The most suitable period is the period of King Saul, the period when there was a sense of tribal unification under one king. Furthermore, the most suitable place for the crystallization of these traditions is the shrine of Gilgal, which in the common opinion is the place of the formation of the stories

---

[37] We therefore cannot accept E. Meyer's opinion (E. Meyer, *Ursprung und Anfänge des Christentums*, 2: *Die Entwicklung des Judentums und Jesus von Nazaret* (Berlin, 1925), pp. 281-282), that the Hasmoneans followed the extermination law as found in Deuteronomy. On the contrary, in their time the law was taken out of its context, in order to be adjusted to a reality to which it did not apply.

[38] For this expression see M. Weinfeld, R. Meridor, ''Zedekiah's Punishment and Polymestor's Punishment'', in Y. Zakovitch and A. Rofé (eds.) *I.L. Seeligmann Volume. Studies in the Bible and the Ancient Near East*, I (Jerusalem, 1983), p. 229, n. 1. For *Qblt Ymyn* see: S. Liebermann, ''Zutot'', *Year book of the Schocken Inst.*, I (Jerusalem, 1967-68), pp. 98-101.

[39] The verse in Deut. 7:22 is dependent on Exod. 23:29-30 and contradicts Deut. 9:3: ''So shalt thou drive them out and make them to perish quickly'' *whwrštm wh'bdtm mhr* (compare Jos. 10:42: ''And all these kings and their land did Joshua take at one time'', *lkd Yehosua p'm 'ḥt*) with Jos. 11:18: ''Joshua made war a long time with all those kings'', *ymym rbym 'śh yhš' 't kl hmlkym h'lh mlḥmh*).

of conquest in Joshua 2-10.[40] The central place to which the stories of the conquest in Joshua 2-10 are linked is Gilgal. In Gilgal monumental stones are set to commemorate the crossing of the Jordan (Josh. 3-4); the Israelites were circumcised there (Josh. 5:2-8); there they celebrated the Passover (Josh. 5:9-12); there the captain of YHWH's Host (= an angel)[41] appeared to Joshua before the conquest began (Josh. 5:13-15); from Gilgal the Israelites went to war and thither they returned after the wars (Josh. 9:6; 10:6-7, 15, 43).

Gilgal was the cultic centre of the tribe of Benjamin, and in fact the events of the conquest according to Joshua 2-10 occur in the district of Benjamin. The events of the conquest begin in Jericho, they move to Ay, to Gibeon, and to Beth-Horon and conclude in the valley of Ayalon. All these cities belong to Benjamin's territory (Josh. 18:21-28),[42] and they delineate the main campaign of the conquest in Joshua 3:1-10:15. The origin of Saul, the first king of Israel, was in the tribe of Benjamin (1 Sam. 9:1), and the main sanctuary of this tribe was in Gilgal. Saul was bound to Gilgal by the following events: In Gilgal Saul was crowned (1 Sam. 11:14-15); it was there he came to sacrifice before the battle with the Philistines (1 Sam. 13:7-15); and he went there to celebrate the victory over Amalek (1 Sam. 15:12ff.). It seems reasonable that the main kernel of the laws of dispossession in Exodus 23:20-33 crystallized in Gilgal[43] in the times of Saul. The radical policy against the old inhabitants of the land characterizes the times of Saul. Saul is described as a man who plotted against the Gibeonites which were "a remnant of the

---

[40] See: A. Alt, "Josua", *Kleine Schriften* I (München, 1953), pp. 176 ff. and also: M. Noth, *Josua*, HAT I,7 (Tübingen, 1953), p. 12; J.A. Soggin, *Joshua*, OTL, (London, 1972), pp. 9-11.

[41] The 'Captain of the host of YHWH' is the angel sent by God to guide the children of Israel to the promised land (Exod. 23:20; 32:34; 33:2).

[42] Ayalon became part of the tribe of Benjamin after its expansion towards the west, as we learn from 1 Chr. 8:13: "And Beriah and Shema, who were heads of fathers' houses of the inhabitants of Ayalon, who put to flight the inhabitants of Gath", *hmh hbryḥw 't ywšby Gat*). The inhabitants of Gath who managed to kill the Ephramites (1 Chr. 7:21) were driven off by the people of Benjamin. See Z. Kallai, "The Settlement Traditions of Ephraim:—A Historiographical Study", *ZDPV* 102 (1986), pp. 68-74.

[43] N. Lohfink, *Das Hauptgebot. Eine Untersuchung literarischer Einleitungsfragen zu Dtn. 5-11* (Roma, 1963), pp. 176 ff; E. Otto, *Das Mazzotfest in Gilgal* (Stuttgart, 1975), pp. 204 ff.

Amorites'' and he sought to destroy them ''in his zeal for the Israelites and Judah'' (2 Sam. 21:2-3).

Against this background must be brought the story of the covenant with the Gibeonites in Joshua 9. This story revolves around the covenant which was made illegitimately with the Gibeonites (vv. 6-7, 14-15).[44] The expressions used to describe this covenant are the same as the law of dispossession in Exodus 23:20-33. The men of Israel say to the Hivite which is in Gibeon: ''Perhaps you dwell nearby (*yšb bqrb*) and how shall I make a covenant with you?'' (Josh. 9:7). In Exodus 23:32-33 similar words are spoken against the inhabitants of Canaan: ''You shall not make with them ... any covenant. They shall not dwell in your land (*yšb bqrb*) ...'' And indeed, as scholars have already shown,[45] the story of the Gibeonites in Joshua 9 can be understood only by assuming that the law had been set up in the light of the prohibition against giving the Canaanites the right to dwell among the Israelites. This is reflected in the desire of Saul not to allow the Gibeonites who dwelt in the land the right to settle in the mountains of the land of Israel.

Furthermore, even the institution of the *ḥerem* in its original form (see above) may be explained against the background of the time of Saul. The *ḥerem* of Jericho in Joshua 6:17-21 fits the hard line of Saul and seems to have originated at the sanctuary of Gilgal. The formulation of the *ḥerem* in Joshua 6:21: ''And they destroyed everything in the city, man and woman, young and old, ox, and sheep, and ass by the sword'' almost duplicates the formulation which appears in the *ḥerem* which Saul cast over Nob, the city of the priests: ''And Nob, the city of the priests he killed by the sword, man and woman, child and infant, and ox, and ass, and sheep by the sword'' (1 Sam. 22:19).[46] The same formulation appears in connection with the *ḥerem* on Amalek commanded by God to Saul: ''Go and smite

---

44 Special attention should be drawn to verse 14: ''...and they did not enquire of YHWH'' (*w't py JHWH l' š'lw*).

45 See M. Haran, ''The Gibeonites, the Nethinim and the Sons of Solomon's Servants'', *VT* 11 (1961), pp. 159-169; J. Halbe, ''Gibeon und Israel'', *VT* 25 (1975), pp. 613-641.

46 Of other Israelite cities which were to be exterminated in a total manner cf. what is said about the rebellious city (*'yr hnydḥt*) in Deut. 13:16: ''Thou shalt surely smite the inhabitants of that city with the edge of the sword, destroying it utterly and all there is therein and the cattle thereof with the edge of the sword'', and also the cities of Benjamin: ''... and smote them by the edge of the sword, both the entire city and the cattle and all that they found'' (Judg. 20:48).

Amalek and destroy all therein and you shall not have pity on them, but shall kill man and woman, child and infant, ox and sheep, camel and ass'' (1 Sam. 15:3).[47]

The period of Saul is then the most appropriate for the crystallization of anti-Canaanite ideology, in contrast to the period of David and Solomon, which did not practice the *ḥerem*[48] against the pre-Israelite inhabitants, whom they merely placed in corvée labor (1 Kgs. 9:20-21). Moreover, from 2 Samuel 24, the account of the census which David took of his kingdom, we learn that ''the cities of the Hivvites and the Canaanites'' are included in the census of the Israelite population (v. 7).[49] Indeed, to save their lives the Gibeonites turned to David to avenge them on the house of Saul, the king who had tried to annihilate them (2 Sam. 21:5, and see above), and David rescued them from annihilation. After the days of David and Solomon, there is no further mention of the destruction of Canaanite cities and their inhabitants. The author of the book of Deuteronomy therefore revived the *ḥerem* from the times of Saul.[50] But whereas the old *ḥerem* applied to concrete encounters—the Gibeonites, Nob, the city of the priests, and Amalek—the editor of the book of Deuteronomy depicted the *ḥerem* as originally applied to the seven peoples of the land of Canaan.

At the end of our discussion we should pose the question as to why the Philistines were not banned? The Philistines, bitter enemies of Israel, especially in the time of Saul, do not appear in the lists of the nations to be banned. Why not? The answer is this. The Philistines

---

[47] In the *Ḥerem* of Amalek we find, together with the donkey, the camel, which we have not found in other extermination formulae, because of the nomadic character of the enemy here. Like the Midianites and the Ismaelites, the Amalekites, who dwelled in the desert, used camels. See Jud. 6:3-5: ''The Midianites came up and the Amalekites and the children of the east . . . for they came up with their cattle . . . and their camels were without number''. Compare Jud. 7:12; 1 Sam. 30:17.

[48] On the change in the matter of *Ḥerem* in the time of David and Solomon see my article: ''Zion and Jerusalem as Religious and Political Capital: Ideology and Utopia'', in R.E. Friedman (ed.), *The Poet and the Historian. Essays in Literary and Historical Biblical Criticism*, Harvard Semitic Studies 26 (California, 1983), pp. 81-85.

[49] See: S. Abramsky, ''The Attitude Towards the Emorite and the Jebusite in the Book of Samuel. The Historical Foundation and the Ideological Significance'', *Zion* 50 (1985), pp. 27-58, (Hebrew).

[50] Cf. J. Milgrom, *HUCA* 47 (1976) (art. quoted note 13 above), pp . 6-8. However (pace Milgrom) the campaign against the Gibeonites is not to be equated with the total ban of all the Canaanites as Deuteronomy wants to have it.

were not natives in the Land of Canaan. They were, like the Israelites, intruders and appeared on the horizon in the middle of the 12th century after the Israelites had settled in the land. The native pre-Israelite nations were already defined at the beginning of the settlement, just as the delineation of the borders of Canaan was (cf. above) and this definition of the aborigines could not be altered.

This may explain the tradition about the covenant of the Patriarchs with the Philistines (Gen. 21:22-34; 26:26-31), which stands in contrast to the tradition about the attempt at covenant making with the Shechemites (Gen. 34), who belonged to the Hivvites (Gen. 34:2), and which failed.

In sum, in the biblical laws, the statutes relating to the pre-Israelite inhabitants show a development: In the first version, reflected in Exodus 23:20-33; 34:11-16, the commandment prescribes "expelling (*grš*)" the Canaanites and not to make any covenants with them, that is, not to allow them possessions in the land. "They shall not dwell in your land" (Ex. 23:33). In the second version, reflected in the priestly code in Numbers 33:50-56, the commandment prescribes the "dispossession (*hōrašah*)" of the inhabitants of the land, which was interpreted as either expulsion or destruction. In the third version, reflected in the Deuteronomy (7:2; 20:16-17), the commandment prescribes the "ban (*ḥerem*)", which is interpreted as annihilation: "you shall not let any soul live" (Deut. 20:16). The *ḥerem*, i.e. the toal destruction described in Deuteronomy, was never carried out (see 1 Kgs. 9:20-21), and this law must be seen as utopian.

The farther we move away from the historical situation the more rigid a picture appears, which shows that the laws gradually became idealized and unrealistic. The most extreme position crystallized during the period of the national revival during the days of Hezekiah[51] and Josiah. In former times, complete destruction was instituted as a vow and a dedication on the occasion of the proclamation of war on a specific city or on a hostile group, even within

---

[51] On the extermination of nomadic tribes in the time of Hezekiah see: 1 Chr. 4:39-43: "... and destroyed them utterly, unto this day", *wyḥrymwm ʿd hywm hzh*) (v. 411); "And they smote the remnant of the Amalekites", (*wykw ʾt šʾryt hplṭh lʿmlq*) (v. 43). These verses could explain the background of the inclusion of the obligation to wipe out the memory of Amalek in Deuteronomy (25:17-19). For the discussion of the tradition of 1 Chr. 4:39-41 see: N. Neeman, "Nomadic Shepherds in the South Western Border of the Judean Kingdom", *Zion* 52 (1987), pp. 264-267.

Israel.[52] In contrast, the Deuteronomic *ḥerem* was conceived in an *a priori* manner as applicable to all the inhabitants of the land of Canaan, whether they fought or not. Such a destruction must be seen as utopian, as indeed it originated in a theoretical manner a few centuries after the wars of Israel in Canaan.

---

[52] See above, n. 46.

EDUARD NIELSEN-BIBLIOGRAPHY

JAKOB H. GRØNBÆK
Lejre (Denmark)

1950 "Jeremia og Jojakim", *Dansk teologisk Tidsskrift* 13 (1950), pp. 129-145.

1952 "Mundtlig tradition I-III", *Dansk teologisk Tidsskrift* 15 (1952), pp. 19-37, 88-106, 129-146.
"The Righteous and the Wicked in Habaqquq", *Studia Theologica* 6 (1952), pp. 54-78.

1953 "Ass and Ox in the Old Testament", in *Studia Orientalia Ioanni Pedersen* (Copenhagen, 1953), pp. 263-274.

1954 *Oral Tradition. A Modern Problem in Old Testament Introduction*, Studies in Biblical Theology 11 (London, 1954), 108 pp.

1955 *Shechem. A Traditio-Historical Investigation* (Copenhagen, 1955), 384 pp. (Thesis presented for the Degree of Doctor of Theology at the University of Aarhus).
"The Burial of Foreign Gods", *Studia Theologica* 8 (1955), pp. 103-122.
Review: Bent Noack, Zur johanneischen Tradition, 1954, *Dansk teologisk Tidsskrift* 18 (1955), pp. 50-56.

1956 *Håndskriftfundene i Juda Ørken. Dødehavsteksterne* (Copenhagen, 1956), 181 pp.
"Det gamle testamente i ny belysning" (Gustav Tolderlund-Hansen, Det Gamle Testamente i historisk og evangelisk belysning, 1956), *Universitas* (1956), pp. 10-11, 13.
"Det Gamle Testamente, de nye fund og profetien om Messias", *Perspektiv* 3 (1956), pp. 33-34.

1957 "'Lemek-rullen' fra Det døde Hav", *Kristeligt Dagblad* (feature art., 27/2 1957).
"Abraham og Sara. (Lemek-rullen fra Det døde Hav, II)", *Kristeligt Dagblad* (feature art., 28/2 1957).
Review: Franz Hesse, Das Verstockungsproblem im Alten Testament, 1955, *Dansk teologisk Tidsskrift* 20 (1957), pp. 162-164.
E.W. Heaton, Hverdagsliv i Det gamle Testamente. Translated from "Everyday Life in Old Testament Times" by Grete Gersfelt in collaboration with Eduard Nielsen (Copenhagen, 1957). Introduction to the Danish edition by E.N., pp. 7f.
"Til kongres i Jerusalem", *Kristeligt Dagblad* (feature art., 22/8 1957).
"Skal vi stoppe ved næste hjørne?" *Kristeligt Dagblad* (feature art., 3/10 1957).
"Bibelhåndskrifterne fra Det døde Hav", *Samvirke* 20 (1957), pp. 12-14.
"Hvad står der i de ældgamle håndskrifter?", *Samvirke* 21 (1957), pp. 6-7.
"Er dødehavssekten en forløber for kristendommen?", *Samvirke* 22 (1957), pp. 20-21.

1959 *Grundrids af Israels historie* (Copenhagen, 1959), 196 pp. (2. edition Copenhagen 1960; later extended and revised editions).

Dødehavsteksterne. Skrifter fra den jødiske menighed i Qumran i oversættelse og med noter ved Eduard Nielsen og Benedikt Otzen (Copenhagen, 1959), 246 pp.
"Flemming Hvidberg død", *Berlingske Aftenavis* (obituary, 23/2 1959).

1960 "Det gamle Testamente", in *Teologien og dens fag*, red. Bent Noack (Copenhagen, 1960), pp. 13-42.
"Some Reflections on the History of the Ark", in *Congress Volume: Oxford 1959*, SVT 7 (Leiden, 1960), pp. 61-74.
Michel Join-Lambert, Jerusalem. Translated by H. Nyrop-Christensen in collaboration with Eduard Nielsen (Copenhagen, 1960). Introduction to the Danish edition by E.N., pp. 7-9.

1961 "Universitetslæreren" in *Frugtbar uro. En bog om Flemming Hvidberg*, red. Paul Honoré (Copenhagen, 1961), pp. 29-41.
"La Guerre considerée comme une religion et la Religion comme une guerre. Du chant de Debora au Rouleau de la Guerre de Qoumran", *Studia Theologica* 15 (1961), pp. 93-112.
"Det gamle Testamente i arkæologiens lys", *Kirkens Verden* 3 (1961), pp. 370–78.

1962 "Dødehavsteksterne og arkæologien", *Kirkens Verden* 4 (1962), pp. 105-115.
"Den gammeltestamentlige forskning i dag", *Præsteforeningens Blad* 52 (1962), pp. 281-291.
"Sidste nyt om Kong Salomon", *Kristeligt Dagblad* (feature art., 17/11 1962).

1964 "The Levites in Ancient Israel", *ASTI* 3 (1964), pp. 16-27.

1965 *De ti Bud. En traditionshistorisk skitse*. (Københavns Universitets festskrift i anledning af Hans Majestæt Kongens fødselsdag 11. marts 1965). (Copenhagen 1965), 138 pp. (= *Die zehn Gebote*, Acta Theologica 8 (Copenhagen, 1965); *The Ten Commandments in New Perspective*, Studies in Biblical Theology, Sec. Ser. 7 (London, 1968)).
Gads Danske Bibelleksikon, red. Eduard Nielsen og Bent Noack, vols. 1-2 (Copenhagen, 1965-1966; 2. edition 1981-82). Articles on Old Testament subjects.
"Om "det skjulte" og "det åbenbare" i Gammel Testamente", in *Festskrift til N.H. Søe, 29. November, 1965* (Copenhagen, 1965), pp. 113-129.

1966 "Politiske forhold og kulturelle strømninger i Israel under Manasse", *Dansk teologisk Tidsskrift* 29 (1966), pp. 1-10.
"Introduktion til det teologiske studium", *Kristeligt Dagblad* (feature art., 8/9 1966).

1967 "Political Conditions and Cultural Developments in Israel and Judah during the Reign of Manasseh", in *Fourth World Congress of Jewish Studies, Papers* 1 (Jerusalem, 1967), pp. 103-106.
"Konge og folk i Det gamle Testamente", *Kirkens Verden* 9 (1967), pp. 10-21.

1968 "Det gamle Israels Religion", in *Illustreret Religionshistorie*, red. J.P. Asmussen og J. Læssøe, vol. 2 (Copenhagen, 1968), pp. 57-130.
"Indledninger til 1.-5. Mosebog", in *Bibelen i kulturhistorisk lys*, red. Svend Holm-Nielsen, Bent Noack og Sven Tito Achen, vols. 1-9 (Copenhagen, 1968-1971), vol. 1, pp. 65-137, 247-270, 360-372; vol. 2, pp. 23-42.
"Profeti og politisk engagement", *Præsteforeningens Blad* 58 (1968), pp. 369-376.

1969 *Bibelen som helligskrift*, red. Eduard Nielsen og Hejne Simonsen (Copenhagen, 1969), 215 pp. Herein: "Religion og Bibel", pp. 7-17, and "Bibelen og den moderne historiske forskning", pp. 177-190.
"Johannes Pedersen's Contribution to the Research and Understanding of the Old Testament", *ASTI* 8 (1969), pp. 4-20.
"Døden i Det gamle Testamente" in *Den sidste fjende. En bog om Døden*, red. Bent A. Koch og N.J. Rald (Copenhagen, 1969), pp. 14-23.
Articles on The Old Testament in *Kristendomskundskab. Alfabetisk opslagsbog*, red. Per Christensen, Claus Harms og Bertil Wiberg (Copenhagen, 1969).

1970 *Deuterozakarja. Nye bidrag til belysning af Zak. 9-14* in Tekst & Tolkning 1, red. Niels Hyldahl, Eduard Nielsen og Børge Salomonsen (Copenhagen, 1970), 76 pp.
"Deuterojesaja. Erwägungen zur Formkritik, Traditions- und Redaktionsgeschichte", *VT* 20 (1970), pp. 190-205.
"Da Jerusalem faldt—for 1900 år siden", *Flensborg Avis* 1/7 1970.

1971 *Skal vi have en ny oversættelse af Det gamle Testamente?* (Copenhagen, 1971), 15 pp.
Det gamle Israels Religion (Copenhagen, 1971), 153 pp. Extended version of the article in *Illustreret Religionshistorie*, vol. 2 (1968).
"Literature and Structure", *Religion och Bibel* 30 (1971), pp. 23-28.
Det gamle Testamente. Forkortet udgave med indledninger til de enkelte skrifter ved Eduard Nielsen. Udg. af Det danske Bibelselskab (Copenhagen, 1971), 919 pp.
Member of The Editorial Board of *Vetus Testamentum* 1971-89.

1972 "Creation and the Fall of Man. A Cross-Disciplinary Investigation", *HUCA* 43 (1972), pp. 1-22.
"Om bibelsk eksegese som teologisk disciplin. Nogle bemærkninger til Noacks foredrag: Nytestamentlig exegese som teolgisk disciplin", *Dansk teologisk Tidsskrift* 35 (1972), pp. 96-105.
"Gensvar til Noack", *ibid.*, pp. 119-125.

1973 Review: R.P. Merendino, Das deuteronomische Gesetz, 1969, *Dansk teologisk Tidsskrift* 36 (1973), pp. 225-26.
Co-editor of *Acta Theologica Danica*, Copenhagen/Leiden 1973-.

1974 "1 QH, V, 20-27: An attempt at filling out some gaps", *VT* 24 (1974), pp. 240-243.
"Jesaja 27, 3-13", *Præsteforeningens Blad* 64 (1974), pp. 797-803.
"Bibeltro og bibelkritik", in *Haderslev Stiftsbog* 9 (1974), pp. 29-40.

1975 *Hilsen til Noack*, red. Niels Hyldahl og Eduard Nielsen (Copenhagen, 1975), 244 pp. Herein: "Du må ikke binde munden på en okse, når den tærsker", pp. 181-191.

1976 "Det gamle Testamentes plads i gudstjenesten", *Præsteforeningens Blad* 66 (1976), pp. 621-629.

1977 "Homo faber—sapientia dei", *SEÅ* 41-42 (1976-77), pp. 157-165.
"Det gamle Testamentes natursyn", *Fønix* 1 (1977), pp. 130-149.
"Weil Jahwe unser Gott ein Jahwe ist (Dtn VI 4f.)", in *Beiträge zur alttestamentlichen Theologie*, Festschrift für W. Zimmerli zum 70. Geburtstag (Göttingen, 1977), pp. 288-301.

1978 Review: S. Tengström, Die Hexateucherzählung, 1976, *SEÅ* 43 (1978), pp. 114-117.
"Historical Perspectives and Geographical Horizons. On the Question of North-Israelite Elements in Deuteronomy", *ASTI* 11, *Festschrift Gillis Gerleman* (1977/78), pp. 77-89.
"Af en endnu levendes papirer eller: Rapport fra en mandag med den theologiske forskningsmappe", *Kristeligt Dagblad* (feature art., 20/9 1978).

1979 "Le message primitif du livre de Jonas", *Revue d'Histoire et de Philosophie Religieuse* 59, *Mélanges Ed. Jacob* (1979), pp. 499-507.
"Prædikeren og Svend Holm-Nielsen", *Fønix* 3, *Tilegnet Svend Holm-Nielsen* (1979), pp. 90-100.

1980 "Øst for paradis—1. Mosebog kap. 4", *Præsteforeningens Blad* 70 (1980), pp. 789-797.

1981 "Om Det gamle Testamentes betydning for kristendommen", *Fønix* 5 (1981), pp. 352-359.
"Sur la théologie de l'auteur de Gn 2-4", in *De la Torah au Messie*. Mélanges Henri Cazelles (Paris, 1981), pp. 55-63.

1982 "Moses and the Law", *VT* 32 (1982), pp. 87-98.
"Fisk og profet", *Fønix* 6 (1982), pp. 42-44.

1983 *Law, History and Tradition. Selected essays*. Issued by friends and colleagues (Copenhagen, 1983), 179 pp.

1984 "The Traditio-historical Study of the Pentateuch since 1945, with special Emphasis on Scandinavia", in *The Productions of Time: Tradition History in Old Testament Scholarship*, ed. Knud Jeppesen & Benedikt Otzen (Sheffield, 1984), pp. 11-28.

1985 "Bibelen og historieforskningen. Den historisk-kritiske metode", in *Bibelsyn*, red. Niels Jørgen Cappelørn (Copenhagen, 1985), pp. 56-65, 70-71.

1986 "Udvælgelse og universalisme i Det gamle Testamente", in *Judendom och Kristendom under de första århundradene*. Nordisk patristikerprojekt 1982-85 (Oslo, Tromsø, 1986), pp. 52-67.

1987 *Første Mosebog fortolket* (Copenhagen, 1987), 368 pp.
"Israels oprindelse, kritisk belyst", *Dansk teologisk Tidsskrift* 50 (1987), pp. 1-19.

1988 "Mika-bogen—et trøsteskrift fra eksilet?", *Dansk teologisk Tidsskrift* 51 (1988), pp. 249-255.
"'Du må ikke have andre guder end mig'. Den gammeltestamentlige monoteisme", in *Kristendom og de andre religioner*, red. P. Nørgård-Højen (Århus, 1988), pp. 11-35.
"Hvorfor kan man ikke prædike over Gammel Testamente?", in *Teologi og Tradition*. Festskrift til Leif Grane 11. januar 1988 (Århus, 1988), pp. 49-61.
"Laurids Pedersen Thuras Højsangsparafrase 1640 og dens melodier", *Hymnologiske Meddelelser* 17 (1988), pp. 197-252. (In collaboration with H. Glahn and E. Dal).

1989 "Om oversættelse af ordspil fra hebraisk til dansk", in *Skriv synet tydeligt på tavler! Om problemerne ved en ny bibeloversættelse*. Udgivet i anledning af Svend Holm-Nielsens 70-års fødselsdag den 15. januar 1989, red. Knud Jeppesen og John Strange (Copenhagen, 1989), pp. 89-95.
"Om formkritik som hjælpemiddel i historisk-genetisk forskning, belyst ved eksempler fra Amos 1-2 og Mika 1", *Dansk teologisk Tidsskrift* 52 (1989), pp. 243-250.
"Der Fürbitter Israels", *Scandinavian Journal of the Old Testament* 2 (1989), pp. 94-99.
"Hvad syntes man om fisken?", *SEÅ* 54 (1989), pp. 146-150.

1990 *31 salmer fra Det gamle Testamente fortolket* (Copenhagen, 1990), 133 pp.
"Shadday in the Book of Job", in *Living Waters. Scandinavian Orientalistic Studies*, Presented to Professor Dr. Frede Løkkegaard on his Seventy-Fifth Birthday, January 27th, 1990 (Copenhagen, 1990), pp. 249-258.
"Et forsøg på at vurdere nogle gammeltestamentlige prædikener", *Kritisk forum for praktisk teologi* 10 (1990), pp. 5-15.
"Mødet ved brønden. Nogle betragtninger over Joh. Ev. Kap. 4", *Dansk teologisk Tidsskrift* 53 (1990), pp. 243-259.

1992 "Hvem skrev de for? Om bibelkommentatorerne", in *Fortolkning som formidling*, Forum for Bibelsk Eksegese 3 (Copenhagen, 1992), pp. 37-55.
Abrahams historie. En historisk-kritisk kommentar til Genesis (Copenhagen, 1992), 152 pp.
"'Lov og ret' i Det gamle Testamente". Afskedsforelæsning onsdag den 4. december, *Dansk teologisk Tidsskrift* 55 (1992), pp. 1-14.
"En hellenistisk bog?", *Dansk teologisk Tidsskrift* 55 (1992), pp. 161-74.

SUPPLEMENTS TO VETUS TESTAMENTUM

ISSN 0083-5889

2. POPE, M.H. *El in the Ugaritic texts.* 1955. ISBN 90 04 04000 5
3. *Wisdom in Israel and in the Ancient Near East.* Presented to Harold Henry Rowley by the Editorial Board of Vetus Testamentum in celebration of his 65th birthday, 24 March 1955. Edited by M. NOTH and D. WINTON THOMAS. 2nd reprint of the first (1955) ed. 1969. ISBN 90 04 02326 7
4. *Volume du Congrès* [International pour l'étude de l'Ancien Testament]. Strasbourg 1956. 1957. ISBN 90 04 02327 5
8. BERNHARDT, K.-H. *Das Problem der alt-orientalischen Königsideologie im Alten Testament.* Unter besonderer Berücksichtigung der Geschichte der Psalmenexegese dargestellt und kritisch gewürdigt. 1961. ISBN 90 04 02331 3
9. *Congress Volume*, Bonn 1962. 1963. ISBN 90 04 02332 1
11. DONNER, H. *Israel unter den Völkern.* Die Stellung der klassischen Propheten des 8. Jahrhunderts v. Chr. zur Aussenpolitik der Könige von Israel und Juda. 1964. ISBN 90 04 02334 8
12. REIDER, J. *An Index to Aquilla.* Completed and revised by N. Turner. 1966. ISBN 90 04 02335 6
13. ROTH, W.M.W. *Numerical sayings in the Old Testament.* A form-critical study. 1965. ISBN 90 04 02336 4
14. ORLINSKY, H.M. *Studies on the second part of the Book of Isaiah.*—The so-called 'Servant of the Lord' and 'Suffering Servant' in Second Isaiah.—Snaith, N.H. Isaiah 40-66. A study of the teaching of the Second Isaiah and its consequences. Repr. with additions and corrections. 1977. ISBN 90 04 05437 5
15. *Volume du Congrès* [International pour l'étude de l'Ancien Testament]. Genève 1965. 1966. ISBN 90 04 02337 2
17. *Congress Volume*, Rome 1968. 1969. ISBN 90 04 02339 9
19. THOMPSON, R.J. *Moses and the Law in a century of criticism since Graf.* 1970. ISBN 90 04 02341 0
20. REDFORD, D.B. *A study of the biblical story of Joseph.* 1970. ISBN 90 04 02342 9
21. AHLSTRÖM, G.W. *Joel and the temple cult of Jerusalem.* 1971. ISBN 90 04 02620 7
22. *Congress Volume*, Uppsala 1971. 1972. ISBN 90 04 03521 4
23. *Studies in the religion of ancient Israel.* 1972. ISBN 90 04 03525 7
24. SCHOORS, A. *I am God your Saviour.* A form-critical study of the main genres in Is. xl-lv. 1973. ISBN 90 04 03792 2
25. ALLEN, L.C. *The Greek Chronicles.* The relation of the Septuagint I and II Chronicles to the Massoretic text. Part 1. The translator's craft. 1974. ISBN 90 04 03913 9
26. *Studies on prophecy.* A collection of twelve papers. 1974. ISBN 90 04 03877 9
27. ALLEN, L.C. *The Greek Chronicles.* Part 2. Textual criticism. 1974. ISBN 90 04 03933 3
28. *Congress Volume*, Edinburgh 1974. 1975. ISBN 90 04 04321 7
29. *Congress Volume*, Göttingen 1977. 1978. ISBN 90 04 05835 4
30. EMERTON, J.A. (ed.). Studies in the historical books of the Old Testament. 1979. ISBN 90 04 06017 0

31. MEREDINO, R.P. *Der Erste und der Letzte.* Eine Untersuchung von Jes 40-48. 1981. ISBN 90 04 06199 1
32. EMERTON, J.A. (ed.). *Congress Vienna* 1980. 1981. ISBN 90 04 06514 8
33. KOENIG, J. *L'herméneutique analogique du Judaïsme antique d'après les témoins textuels d'Isaïe.* 1982. ISBN 90 04 06762 0
34. BARSTAD, H.M. *The religious polemics of Amos.* Studies in the preaching of Amos ii 7B-8, iv 1-13, v 1-27, vi 4-7, viii 14. 1984. ISBN 90 04 07017 6
35. KRAŠOVEC, J. *Antithetic structure in Biblical Hebrew poetry.* 1984. ISBN 90 04 07244 6
36. EMERTON, J.A. (ed.). *Congress Volume,* Salamanca 1983. 1985. ISBN 90 04 07281 0
37. LEMCHE, N.P. *Early Israel.* Anthropological and historical studies on the Israelite society before the monarchy. 1985. ISBN 90 04 07853 3
38. NIELSEN, K. *Incense in Ancient Israel.* 1986. ISBN 90 04 07702 2
39. PARDEE, D. *Ugaritic and Hebrew poetic parallelism.* A trial cut. 1988. ISBN 90 04 08368 5
40. EMERTON, J.A. (ed.). *Congress Volume,* Jerusalem 1986. 1988. ISBN 90 04 08499 1
41. EMERTON, J.A. (ed.). *Studies in the Pentateuch.* 1990. ISBN 90 04 09195 5
42. MCKENZIE, S.L. *The Trouble with Kings.* The composition of the Book of Kings in the Deuteronomistic History. 1991. ISBN 90 04 09402 4
43. EMERTON, J.A. (ed.). *Congress Volume,* Leuven 1989. 1991. ISBN 90 04 09398 2
44. HAAK, R.D. *Habakkuk.* 1992. ISBN 90 04 09506 3
45. BEYERLIN, W. *Im Licht der Traditionen.* Psalm LXVII und CXV. Ein Entwicklungszusammenhang. 1992. ISBN 90 04 09635 3
46. MEIER, S.A. *Speaking of Speaking.* Marking direct discourse in the Hebrew Bible. 1992. ISBN 90 04 09602 7
47. KESSLER, R. *Staat und Gesellschaft im vorexilischen Juda.* Vom 8. Jahrhundert bis zum Exil. 1992. ISBN 90 04 09646 9
48. AUFFRET, P. *Voyez de vos yeux.* Étude structurelle de vingt psaumes, dont le psaume 119. 1993. ISBN 90 04 09707 4
49. GARCÍA MARTÍNEZ, F., A. HILHORST AND C.J. LABUSCHAGNE (eds.). *The Scriptures and the Scrolls.* Studies in honour of A.S. van der Woude on the occasion of his 65th birthday. 1992. ISBN 90 04 09746 5
50. LEMAIRE, A. AND B. OTZEN (eds.). *History and Traditions of Early Israel.* Studies presented to Eduard Nielsen, May 8th, 1993. 1993. ISBN 90 04 09851 8